Why Not Better and Cheaper?

Why Not Better and Cheaper?

Healthcare and Innovation

JAMES B. REBITZER AND ROBERT S. REBITZER

OXFORD
UNIVERSITY PRESS

OXFORD
UNIVERSITY PRESS

Oxford University Press is a department of the University of Oxford. It furthers
the University's objective of excellence in research, scholarship, and education
by publishing worldwide. Oxford is a registered trade mark of Oxford University
Press in the UK and certain other countries.

Published in the United States of America by Oxford University Press
198 Madison Avenue, New York, NY 10016, United States of America.

Library of Congress Cataloging-in-Publication Data
Names: Rebitzer, James B., author. | Rebitzer, Robert S., author.
Title: Why not better and cheaper? : healthcare and innovation /
James B. Rebitzer, Robert S. Rebitzer.
Description: New York, NY : Oxford University Press, [2023] |
Includes bibliographical references and index.
Identifiers: LCCN 2023000204 (print) | LCCN 2023000205 (ebook) |
ISBN 9780197603109 (hardback) | ISBN 9780197603123 (epub) |
ISBN 9780197603130 (online)
Subjects: MESH: Health Care Sector—economics | Health Care Costs |
Diffusion of Innovation | Economic Competition | Social Norms | United States
Classification: LCC RA413.5.U5 (print) | LCC RA413.5.U5 (ebook) |
NLM W 74 AA1 | DDC 362.1/0425—dc23/eng/20230313
LC record available at https://lccn.loc.gov/2023000204
LC ebook record available at https://lccn.loc.gov/2023000205

DOI: 10.1093/oso/9780197603109.001.0001

Printed by Sheridan Books, Inc., United States of America

To our parents, wives, and daughters.

Contents

1

Introduction and Overview

Precis

Mass General Hospital (MGH) is one of the oldest and most prestigious hospitals in the United States. From 1821 until 1910, the average cost of treating a patient discharged from MGH was $997 in 2010 dollars. It wasn't until the early 1960s that costs surpassed $4,000 per patient. In 2002 the equivalent per patient cost exceeded $25,000, and in 2010 it was in the neighborhood of $35,000.[1] Put differently, the nearly nine-fold increase in the cost of treatment in the 50 years between 1960 and 2010 was far larger than the increase over the prior 150 years.

New, more valuable treatments have undoubtedly played a central role in the rising cost per patient of hospital care over the past 50 years. In 1950, for example, there were essentially no effective treatments for patients who survived heart attacks. Now we have effective therapies and medications (angioplasties and stents, thrombolytic drugs, and so on), and mortality in the month after a heart attack has declined by 75 percent.[2] As medical treatments become more effective, the demand for such therapies rises. Indeed, technological improvements that lengthen life spur demand for additional interventions. The patient who survives a heart attack in her 60s may need a knee replacement in her 80s.[3]

But why doesn't healthcare get better and cheaper? The evolution of the cell phones that we carry in our pockets demonstrates that quality can increase while prices fall. Why not in healthcare?

Our answer is that the health sector generates the wrong kinds of innovation. It is too easy to profit from low-value innovations and too difficult to profit from innovations that reduce care costs. The result is a healthcare economy that is profusely innovative yet remarkably ineffective in delivering increased value at a lower cost. The consequences of this skew in innovation accumulate over time and make society poorer and less healthy than it ought to be.

Why Not Better and Cheaper? James B. Rebitzer and Robert S. Rebitzer, Oxford University Press.
© Oxford University Press 2023. DOI: 10.1093/oso/9780197603109.003.0001

The root causes of the innovation problem in the health sector are the incentives, prevailing professional and social norms, and the competitive environment. We can point innovation in a better direction by improving incentives, mobilizing norms and narratives, and altering the regulatory and competitive environment.

Why Not Better and Cheaper?

In a famous essay, Nobel prize-winning economist William Nordhaus studied the evolution of lighting.[4] From medieval times until the beginning of the 19th Century, the most advanced lighting device was the wax candle. The 19th Century witnessed an era of rapid innovation: first oil lamps, then coal gas-powered lamps, then kerosene lamps, and finally Edison's electric filament bulbs. Innovation continued into the 20th Century with fluorescent bulbs (the 1930s) and compact fluorescent bulbs (the 1980s). Newer technologies such as light-emitting diodes (LEDs) continue the evolutionary process.

Over this period, residential lighting became much brighter and more reliable—and cheaper. Around 1800, lighting services we take for granted today imposed a high economic cost on even the wealthiest individuals. Thomas Jefferson's household consumed approximately 200 pounds of candles in a year, and his total lighting expenditures were roughly $250/year or 7 percent of his annual salary as secretary of state.[5] It took 5.4 hours of work at the average farm-laborer rate to produce 1,000 lumen-hours of light in 1800, while in 1992, this same amount of light could be paid for by just 0.43 seconds of work at the average hourly nonfarm rate. Put differently, the average cost of residential lighting in 1992 was 0.03 percent of what it was in 1800.[6]

Contrast the story of innovation in residential lighting to innovations in treating high cholesterol.

Among adults in rich countries, a large proportion of all deaths are due to blocked arteries. Over the past century, an impressive body of biochemical, biomedical, and epidemiological research established that lowering low-density lipoprotein cholesterol (LDL or "bad" cholesterol) through diet and medications reduces the incidence of coronary artery disease and coronary events and also prolongs life. In the late 1980s, a new class of drugs for lowering LDL in the blood, statins, was approved for human use. Subsequent clinical trials have established that statins decrease heart attacks and prolong life.[7]

A new class of LDL cholesterol-lowering drugs, PCSK9 inhibitors, were recently discovered that exploit a different physiological mechanism than statins. Two new drugs in this class, evolocumab and alirocumab, reduced LDL cholesterol in the blood. It is worth noting that these trials were of relatively short duration. Because coronary artery disease develops slowly over many years, the trials relied on biomarkers—indicators of a therapeutic response—rather than actual clinical outcomes such as strokes and heart attacks to assess efficacy. As a result, the trials offered only indirect evidence that these new drugs reduce disease and prolong life.

The initially approved uses for PCSK9 inhibitors were quite narrow and were focused on patients with a genetic disorder that makes it impossible for their bodies to remove LDL from the blood or on other patients who need to achieve a very low level of LDL. Later, the approved use of evolocumab expanded to include adults with cardiovascular disease at risk of heart attack or stroke. Further expansion of aliocrumab's approved uses is likely forthcoming.

The initial list prices for PCSK9 inhibitors exceeded $14,000 per patient per year. This is a high price considering that patients must take cholesterol-lowering drugs regularly throughout their lives. Much less expensive alternatives are available, some costing only a few hundred dollars annually. The high initial prices of PCSK9 inhibitors matter for patients: only half of the prescriptions for PCSK9 inhibitors were approved in the year these drugs became available, and one-third of the approved prescriptions were not filled due to high copayments.[8]

Residential lighting is the poster child for how innovation should work. Consumers buy innovations that lower the cost of illumination and cast better light. They can directly perceive the quality of light and bear the total cost of their purchasing decisions.

In contrast, patients can't directly perceive the quality of the cholesterol treatments available to them. They must rely on physicians who, in turn, evaluate scientific evidence. Moreover, this evidence has limitations. For PCSK9 inhibitors, these limitations include reliance on indirect measurements (biomarkers) rather than the outcomes that patients care about most: mortality and quality of life. So unlike consumers of lighting products, consumers must rely on agents—physicians—and imperfect information to make their purchasing decisions.

In addition, patients do not bear the total cost of their decisions. Instead, third-party payers such as Medicare, Medicaid, and private insurers pay most of the costs. Neither patients nor their physicians have to consider the cost-benefit tradeoffs that consumers of lighting products do. PCSK9 inhibitors may be a valuable treatment for a limited set of patients. However, the expanded use of PCSK9 for a broader group of patients—including some that may benefit from statins—illustrates that a high-cost innovation can find a market in healthcare even in the presence of lower-cost substitutes. PCSK9 inhibitors may be a treatment with low economic value for some of the patients for whom it is prescribed, meaning the benefits are low compared to costs.

The evolution of lighting illustrates the enormous economic value that innovations can produce, and the contrast with PCSK9 hints at a fundamental aspect of the U.S. healthcare system. The health sector is rife with innovation that fails to generate much economic value. Rather than delivering higher quality care at lower cost, healthcare innovation too often produces new treatments of uncertain value and fails to drive down costs.

Innovation in the health sector suffers from two interrelated problems: a value-creation problem and a related but distinct cost-reduction problem. Healthcare has a value-creation problem because new drugs, devices, and other interventions with low economic value can find a ready market, while inventions with high economic value may not. The prevalence of low-value treatment is such that nearly 80 clinical societies have combined with 70 consumer organizations to form Choosing Wisely, a national campaign to educate doctors and patients about low-value interventions. Choosing Wisely has identified more than 500 tests and treatments that may be of little or no value to patients. Indeed, recent estimates suggest that low-value or unnecessary treatments account for $75–100 billion in waste each year.[9]

The second innovation problem, the cost-reduction problem, results from a failure to adopt new drugs, treatments, devices, and processes that reduce the economic resources used to deliver a unit of health services. Finding new ways to deliver care more efficiently with less burdensome administration ought to be profitable, but for the reasons we detail later in this chapter, it is often hard for innovators to capture the value created by these innovations. As a result, innovators don't focus much on cost reduction, and when cost-reducing innovations do emerge, they struggle to move from pilot projects to widespread adoption.[10]

Taken together, the value-creation and cost-reduction problems mean that health sector innovation is not delivering the benefits to our society that it could. This book explores the reasons for this underperformance. Our analysis focuses on three issues:

- Incentives: Financial incentives for healthcare innovators align poorly with creating economic value. In addition, shared savings contracts—which payers can use to provide financial incentives for cost reduction—face severe challenges in the health sector. These incentive problems weaken the demand for value-enhancing and cost-reducing innovations.
- Norms: Professional and social norms often provide insufficient non-financial motivation for value-creating and cost-reducing innovation and, at times, actively inhibit the adoption of such innovations.
- Competition: The nature of competition in healthcare markets allows dominant incumbent firms to overlook potentially value-enhancing and cost-reducing innovations and inhibits disruption by more efficient new entrants.

We are not the first to observe that innovation responds to financial incentives.[11] Others have also discussed the roles that professional norms and competition play in the various dysfunctions of the U.S. healthcare system. However, prior work has not analyzed how these three factors lead to the value-creation and cost-reduction problems that plague innovation in healthcare.

The rest of this chapter gives an overview of our argument.

Financial Incentives

Rewarding Creation of Economic Value: Patents and Insurance

In the health sector, incentives for innovation provided by the patent and health insurance systems often fail to reward economically valuable innovations. These failures are the root cause of the value-creation problem in healthcare innovation.

Patents stimulate innovation by granting time-limited monopolies that enable inventors to earn profits from their discoveries. The incentives for innovation in patents contain a built-in market test—patent holders can only profit if there is demand for the patented discovery. Does this market test mean that the patent system steers innovators toward the most economically valuable discoveries? In many instances, it turns out that the answer is no.

Consider, for example, the development of new antibiotics. Saving lives by developing new antibiotics ought to be a profitable business, but this turns out not to be true. Typically, new antibiotics are more expensive than existing drugs and no more effective. Their value is most manifest when resistance to current antibiotics becomes widespread—a possibility that might arise at some unknown future date. In the meantime, wise stewardship mandates limiting the use of the new antibiotic and runs counter to the market test inherent in the patent system. As a result, inventing new antibiotics is a money-losing endeavor.[12]

Similarly, problematic incentives hinder the development of vaccines for communicable diseases. Anyone who gets vaccinated against an infectious disease benefits themselves as well as others. To the extent that the price of the vaccine reflects only the value to individuals and fails to account for the benefit to others, the market test inherent in the patent system understates the economic value of the vaccine. The market power granted to patent-holders can also distort innovation incentives by favoring the development of treatments over vaccines. As explained in chapter 2, drug makers with a monopoly treatment can charge more for the treatment than for an equally effective vaccine. Depending on the distribution of risk for the disease in the population, this exercise of market power can make it more profitable to focus development efforts on treatments rather than vaccines.[13]

The time-limited feature of patents can also loosen the ties of innovation to economic value. For example, the development of treatments for late-stage cancer is generally favored over treatments for early-stage cancer, even though earlier treatment generally delivers greater value. This is because—given the slow progression of many cancers—clinical trials for early-stage disease take longer to complete than trials for late-stage disease, which reduces the time from approval by the Food and Drug Administration (FDA) to patent expiration.[14] "Life-cycle management"—in which drugmakers use secondary patents and other methods to effectively extend the duration of monopoly protection—is another example of innovation in which economic value is an afterthought.[15]

The patent system interacts with the insurance system in ways that also influence incentives for innovation. For example, the owner of a patent for a new drug can sell the drug at a profit-maximizing price that far exceeds the marginal cost of the drug. Usually, high prices reduce unit sales. However, health insurance makes even high-priced drugs affordable to a larger market. Out-of-pocket costs to insured consumers tend to be quite close to the marginal cost of the drug. Health insurance should, on this basis, serve as a powerful incentive for pharmaceutical innovation. In practice, however, some of the additional revenues from the incremental drug sales are absorbed by pharmacy benefit managers and other market intermediaries.[16] These "middlemen" reduce the returns to innovation and thereby encourage the proliferation of "me-too" drugs that are less costly to develop but are also generally of lower value.[17]

Health insurance can also alter incentives for innovation by supporting the market for treatments with variable and uncertain benefits for patients. Under fee-for-service reimbursement, where prescribers also have great discretion in treatment decisions, physicians are more likely to prescribe interventions whose average outcomes are both small and highly variable.[18] If the provider believes their patient might benefit from a therapy even though the average patient may not, they may be willing to try it. The regulatory practices in the United States grant physicians great discretion in making this choice, and the drug approval process does not require that new treatments be more valuable than existing treatments. Medicare is also forbidden from using analyses of benefits and costs in its coverage decisions. These permissive regulatory practices in the United States end up supporting demand for low-value treatments. Such practices also enable "treatment creep," in which costly interventions that may be beneficial for one sub-population spread to other populations where the benefits are less certain.

Creating Demand for Cost-Reducing Innovations: Shared Savings Incentives

If innovators and implementers can't benefit from innovations that reduce costs, such innovations will be in short supply and, when they do appear, will fail to thrive and spread. This is the root cause of the cost-reduction problem in health sector innovation.

In healthcare, providers order (tests, procedures, drugs, etc.), and payers pay. With the notable exception of expenses directly billed to patients as copays, coinsurance, or out-of-pocket expenses, most costs are borne by third-party payers. Providers—who have the obligation and expertise to make decisions on behalf of their patients—may not know or give adequate weight to the costs their decisions impose on payers. Providers may also be less than eager to adopt cost-reducing new treatment modalities or management methods if the benefits of these cost reductions primarily accrue to payers.[19]

From this perspective, the demand for cost-reducing innovation hinges on a challenging principal-agent relationship. Payers are the principal in this relationship. They are responsible for the bulk of expenditures and need providers to work with them to lower the cost of delivering care. Providers are the agents who can further the payers' interests by devoting effort and attention to finding ways to reduce costs. The challenge in this relationship emerges from the fact that payers lack the knowledge and information to ensure that providers act as good agents. One way to resolve this information issue is through incentive contracts that reward agents for desirable outcomes.

The standard tool for analyzing a principal-agent relationship is the principal-agent model. This game-theoretic model focuses on the relationship between a single principal (the payer in this case) and the principal's representative, the agent (the provider). The canonical principal-agent model produces a powerful result. Even when the principal cannot directly observe the agent's actions—and even when the agent has information and knowledge that the principal lacks—a well-designed incentive contract can profitably and effectively motivate the agent to act in the principal's interests. Consistent with this theoretical conclusion, we find that incentive arrangements are used ubiquitously throughout the economy to manage principal-agent relationships.

In the context of healthcare, the appropriate incentive arrangement would be for payers to share some portion of cost savings with providers. According to the principal-agent model, we should see shared savings contracts used throughout the health sector. However, it turns out that powerful forces in the health sector make shared savings contracts far more challenging to implement than the standard principal-agent model predicts. The difficulty stems from three factors: common agency, capturing future cost savings, and free riding.

Common agency issues arise because of the multitude of payers in the U.S. healthcare system. In addition to government payers (Medicare, Medicaid, the Veteran's Administration, etc.), there are hundreds of private health insurers and a vast array of self-insured employers. Many different payers may cover a provider's panel of patients. This feature alters the principal-agent relationship. Rather than each physician responding to the incentives designed by a single payer, the physician responds to the totality of incentives implemented by the various payers with whom they have contracts.

When multiple principals try to influence a shared or common agent, the conclusions of the principal-agent model are overturned. In this situation, a payer may not bother writing a strong shared savings contract because the payer cannot be sure the benefits will accrue to them rather than to one of the other payers. Instead, they will settle for weak shared savings incentives or, sometimes, no incentives at all.[20] Under common agency, payers give providers little or no economic incentive to adopt cost-reducing innovations.

Different from the challenge of common agency is the challenge of capturing and sharing savings from investments to prevent or delay disease in the future. For example, investments in smoking cessation or diabetes prevention can take years to pay off in the form of lower medical expenditures. Capturing these future benefits requires long-term relationships between payers and their beneficiaries. The longer the relationship, the better.

But the structure of healthcare insurance markets works against the possibility of such long-term relationships. Most commercial health plans rely on one-year health insurance contracts. As people change jobs, they often change insurers. Also, smaller firms that typically don't self-insure frequently switch insurers when their contracts are up for renewal. Long-term relationships are unlikely under these conditions.[21] In addition, employer-based insurance contracts generally don't extend into retirement when Medicare covers Americans over age 65. Thus savings from controlling smoking, diabetes, or virtually any chronic disease in a 50-year-old may accrue to Medicare, rather than commercial insurance plans. The problem of capturing future savings may partly explain the remarkably slow uptake of behavioral approaches to preventing and treating chronic diseases.[22]

Free riding is the final challenge to creating incentives for cost reduction. Financial incentives to reduce costs also require measures that track the quality of patient care. Without quality measures, healthcare providers and the general public rapidly lose faith in the good intentions of payers. Such loss of confidence played a role in the backlash to and subsequent decline of health maintenance organizations in the 1990s.

However, quality metrics are quite noisy and must be aggregated over many patients and providers to be meaningful. Suppose, for example, that it takes 5,000 Medicare beneficiaries to reliably detect a 10 percent improvement in diabetes control. Given the average size of patient panels and the prevalence of diabetes in each panel, this implies that quality measures involving diabetes care might require pooling data across the patient panels of 20 physicians.[23] One can statistically determine which group of 20 physicians are doing better than other such groups. However, there is no way to be sure which of the providers within the group are doing a better job. Consequently, shared savings incentives would be shared by all the physicians in the group. But dividing shared savings incentives equally across 20 practices creates a significant free-riding problem that weakens the effect of the incentives. In a group of 20, performance incentives become so weak that the amount paid out in performance pay will exceed any possible savings the incentives might create.

We have seen that the challenges of common agency, capturing future value, and free riding undermine the use of shared savings contracts in healthcare. As a result, cost-reducing innovations often fail to take root and spread in healthcare. They "go missing." Missing innovations can take many forms. They can, for example, take the form of managerial or organizational innovations that fail to become widely used, such as alternatives to fee-for-service compensation of providers. Or they can take the form of clinical practice patterns and styles that remain oddly sequestered, such as the failure of the practice patterns in regions of the United States with lower healthcare costs to be adopted in higher-cost areas. Or they can take the form of categories of innovation that simply disappear from the mental maps of providers, payers, and patients altogether, such as "slightly worse but much cheaper" services that play an essential role in other economic sectors. It is not always easy to prove that an individual innovation has gone missing rather than failed for different reasons—but the accumulation of evidence suggests that this is a genuine concern in the health sector.

Beyond Financial Incentives

So far, we have argued that value-creating and cost-reducing innovations in the health sector are inhibited by distorted or weak financial incentives.

Can non-financial motivators fill the gap? We believe that the answer is yes under certain conditions. In chapter 5, we describe how Diane Meier and her colleagues developed and spread the palliative care model without the benefit of favorable economic incentives. Instead, they relied on the power of professional and social norms and narratives to mobilize what amounts to a movement for a new way of caring for the seriously ill. In the paragraphs that follow, we sketch some of the conditions in which norms and narratives can be a motive force for innovation.

Professional and Social Norms

The professional norms ingrained in healthcare providers are on display whenever one enters a hospital or a clinic. Social norms concerning individual and social responsibility for health are manifest whenever citizens and policymakers debate the nature of our healthcare system. These professional and social norms deeply influence almost every decision about healthcare and health policy.

Norms influence behaviors through channels that conventional economic models often overlook. The first such channel is the introduction of ethical duties and obligations into decision-making. If an action is proscribed as an ethical matter, then comparing costs and benefits is of little importance. Such moral reasoning can discourage entire classes of potentially valuable transactions or choices because they are morally repugnant.[24] Historically, life insurance contracts were once illegal because they were considered intolerable gambles against God. Currently, paying organ donors is unlawful because these payments allow for the morally dubious commercialization of the human body.[25]

The second channel through which the logic of norms departs from conventional economic models is by considering the meanings and intentions people assign to financial incentives. If people believe that a financial incentive furthers an ethical interest, the effects of the incentive are magnified. If financial incentives promote an unethical economic interest, the same incentive may generate resistance rather than cooperation.

Behavioral economists often restate this issue by asking whether financial incentives "crowd out" or "crowd in" norms-based motivations.[26] Concern about crowding out has a long history in healthcare. For example, it lies at the heart of an old debate about paying donors for blood donations. Some analysts have argued that paying donors leads to fewer blood donations be-cause financial incentives displace or weaken the prosocial norms that mo-tivate blood donors. Alternatively, financial rewards could signal the social importance of blood donations and so activate or crowd in social motives. A final possibility is that economic incentives and prosocial motivations do not affect each other; they are separable. Under separability paying for blood donations and appealing to prosocial motivation both increase blood donations, and neither alters the effectiveness of the other.

A new body of empirical and experimental studies suggest that all three possibilities occur in practice.[27] The context seems to matter significantly for both crowding in and crowding out. Donating a kidney, for example, is laud-atory if it is motivated by feelings of generosity, love, and altruism. Still, the same donation generates feelings of unease and disgust if it appears to be done for financial reasons. Similarly, providers carefully managing the costs of the care they deliver may be considered responsible if guided by a clear public purpose. The same actions may appear unethical if the aim is to de-liver financial gain for providers or payers.

A third way the logic of norms departs from conventional economic logic is that they bring the opinions of other parties into the decision process.[28] Consider an apparently frivolous example—norms against men wearing skirts. Like many gender norms, this norm is both descriptive (men don't wear skirts) and prescriptive (men ought not to wear skirts). The convic-tion that men ought not to wear a skirt can create discomfort for others who abide by gender dress norms, and these onlookers may respond negatively—perhaps with harsh derision or social exclusion. If social ridicule and exclu-sion are severe enough, even men who would on their own choose to wear skirts will not wear them.[29]

This prescriptive aspect of norms can alter the effect of financial incentives. Consider, for example, a setting where cost-reducing innovations require physicians to deviate from well-established professional attitudes and practices by using an artificial intelligence algorithm rather than relying on professional judgment. If this provokes an adverse reaction from professional peers—who may view the change as undermining the "art" of medicine—even a powerful financial incentive may not be sufficient for the innovation to be adopted.

The logic of norms suggests that they can stimulate cost-reducing innova-tion to the extent that cost reduction is:

- consistent with one's duties and obligations
- perceived as furthering an ethical rather than an economic interest
- aligned with social and professional standards of conduct

Narratives

Closely related to norms are narratives. In a provocative book, Nobel prize-winning economist Robert Shiller argues that economic fundamentals cannot fully explain the trajectory of an economy. He argues that economic narratives also matter. Narratives are stories that explain how the social world works and that persuade people to value some activities over others and some beliefs over others.[30] The conventional narrative in the health professions celebrates as heroes those who discover new cures for dread diseases, not those who invent new ways to more efficiently care for patients. As a result of this narrative, the story of Sidney Garfield—the visionary inventor of pre-paid group medical practice and one of the innovators who started and led Kaiser Permanente—is little known outside of that organization.

Narratives can shape the direction of innovation. The sustained, accelerating wave of technological innovation that made the Industrial Revolution a transformative event in world history began with a shift in the culture of innovation that took place in the period from 1500 to 1700 among a small elite of physicians, philosophers, engineers, and artisans. The new narrative was based on the then-novel belief that society could and should be enriched by closely studying natural phenomena and applying this knowledge in practical ways to economic transactions and production. This narrative was promoted by intellectual entrepreneurs such as Francis Bacon and reinforced by group norms and various institutions and incentives. Without a community of scholars operating within this shared set of cultural beliefs and motivations, the sustained innovations that characterize modern economies would not have been possible.[31]

In the technology sector, one can see the influence of narratives on the direction of innovation. Moore's Law—the notion that the number of transistors on an integrated circuit doubles roughly every two years—has enshrined the idea that cost and quality can progress rapidly, in tandem, and seemingly without end. Similarly, the narrative of entrenched firms displaced by innovative startups has fueled venture capital investment through many boom-and-bust cycles. Healthcare needs new narratives emphasizing the importance of innovations focused on value creation and cost reduction.

As powerful as norms and narratives can be, particularly in the health sector dominated as it is by professions with strong ethical commitments, they are not a substitute for financial incentives. As Meier points out, even the comparatively well-established palliative care model will not be on secure foundations as long as it must rely on philanthropic support. Moreover, the broader moral climate also shapes how norms and narratives function. As long as the United States remains ambivalent about whether healthcare is a shared social good to which all are entitled or a conventional private good, providers are left unsure of their obligations as stewards of scarce healthcare resources. Citizens are also left unclear about their responsibility to subsidize care for the sick and the poor. In this environment, the power of norms and narratives to spur value-enhancing and cost-reducing innovation diminishes, and such innovations may even be greeted with indifference and contempt.

Competition and Disruption

Hospitals and insurers enjoy significant market power and charge high prices. They would seem, on this basis, to be ripe for disruption. Why is it that no newcomers have arisen—like Amazon and Southwest Airlines in their respective industries—to sweep away the old incumbents in favor of cheaper and better ways of doing business? Similarly, why hasn't Kaiser Permanente risen from its regional stronghold in the western United States to become a dominant force nationally? There is something about healthcare that dampens the disruptive potential of new entrants and, in so doing, reduces the demand for the cost-reducing innovations that fuel disruption.

One possibility is that it is the market power of incumbents that suppresses disruptive innovation. However, there is no consensus on this question.[32] Joseph Schumpeter, one of the most influential economists of the 20th Century and coiner of the phrase "creative destruction," argued that monopoly and innovation are not opposed. Indeed monopoly can stimulate innovation if for no other reason than dominant incumbents have powerful incentives to adopt innovations that preserve their dominant position. In the 1960s, Nobel Prize-winner Kenneth Arrow took the contrary position that monopolists had weaker incentives to innovate than other firms.[33] Many current antitrust scholars support this conclusion.[34] Decades of empirical research have failed to resolve the question definitively. Some aggregate studies suggest that competition has an inverted-U relationship to innovation, so that very-low and very-high levels of competition depress innovation relative to intermediate levels.[35] Other focused case studies find that monopoly may indeed slow innovation.[36]

More recently, however, a new idea—switchover disruptions—has helped clarify how market power may influence the incentives for innovation in the health sector. The term switchover disruption refers to the phase-in period for new, cost-reducing or efficiency-enhancing technologies. During this phase-in period, firms struggle to make new products, processes, or services work and upend profitable operations. The cost of these disruptions increases with the market power of the firm. All else equal, a firm with a dominant market position will find it more costly to "move fast and break things" simply because their ongoing operations are very profitable.[37]

Switchover disruptions determine whether the dominant incumbents or their rivals are more motivated to adopt new technology. When switchover disruptions are unimportant, dominant incumbents have the more powerful incentives to adopt new technology to defend their profitable market position. However, when switchover disruptions become very significant, the losses from disruptions cause dominant firms to value the innovation less than their rivals. Indeed, they may conceivably ignore the innovation altogether.

Switchover disruptions are acute in healthcare. Changing a clinical pathway or guideline can put a patient's health at risk while providers learn the new methods. New treatments and interventions must pass high bars for scientific and professional acceptance, regulatory approval, and insurance reimbursement. Even administrative changes can involve high switchover disruptions because of the need to persuade physicians, patients, and other stakeholders that the change aligns with professional and social norms. Therefore, the theory of switchover disruptions suggests that in healthcare, incumbents may overlook valuable innovations and be content to use their market power to keep prices high and minimize disturbance to life as they know it.[38] In this case, switchover disruptions create opportunities for new, more efficient innovators to disrupt established business models.

However, would-be disrupters in healthcare face a host of obstacles that make entry into a healthcare market difficult, costly, and—at times—impossible. Sometimes these obstacles are the result of regulations or anti-competitive practices. Many observers also note that professional licensing laws can discourage potentially disruptive new entrants.[39] The lengthy development process for new pharmaceuticals also creates opportunities for incumbents to block new competitors. For example, in the early 2000s, Questor acquired the U.S. development rights for a potential competitor to its drug Acthar and shut down development before a marketable product was produced.[40] This is not an isolated case. A recent study examined more than 16,000 drug projects over the past 25 years and estimated that about 6 percent of the acquisitions fit this profile.[41]

Other times, entry barriers result from the same spillover problems that inhibit shared savings incentives. An interesting example of this latter type of obstacle concerns a potentially important process intervention—reducing the administrative cost of billing.

The U.S. health system has notoriously high administrative costs associated with billing and insurance. A likely contributor to these high costs is the near-universal reliance on a claims-based reimbursement system. Under this claims system, every billable activity is submitted to a payer as a claim for reimbursement, not an invoice for payment. The insurer evaluates each claim and rejects many of them rather than simply paying the provider's submission at the established price. The providers can then re-submit a modified claim or challenge the rejection. The payer can then accept the modified claim or respond to the challenge. Eventually, the claim is adjudicated (resolved) and paid.[42] The claims-based payment system is costly and slow, involving tens of billions in challenged revenues, resulting in payment delays, and requiring a small army of administrators at insurance companies and providers to manage the process.[43]

One can imagine an innovative insurer seeking a competitive advantage by moving to a more streamlined billing system in which providers simply submit bills and are reimbursed as in conventional businesses. Such a system would undoubtedly require the innovating insurer to make upfront investments in new billing protocols and teach new billing practices to providers. However, this investment can spill over to benefit the other insurers in the market who also interact with these providers. Such spillovers reduce any single insurer's incentives to invest in a more streamlined billing system.

The market power enjoyed by many incumbents in the health sector does more than keep U.S. healthcare prices high. When combined with high switchover disruptions and barriers to new market entrants, market power can stifle innovation. Under these conditions, established firms can ignore value-enhancing and cost-reducing innovations without fear of disruption.

Dilemmas and Opportunities

The U.S. health sector faces two cost dilemmas. The first is that the U.S. has much higher *levels* of health spending than any other rich country—without commensurate health outcomes. These expenditure levels are a uniquely U.S. problem and stem mainly from the ability of incumbent firms to set prices well above marginal costs.

The second dilemma concerns the *growth* of health expenditures as a fraction of Gross Domestic Product (GDP). All advanced economies share this dilemma. As we will explain in later chapters, this dilemma is a consequence of economic and psychological forces that cause the demand for health services to rise faster than national incomes. Since 1975, healthcare spending has grown on average about 2 percent more quickly than GDP. If these growth rates persist for another 75 years—the planning horizon of Medicare—the health sector will absorb 75 percent of GDP. Such trends point to a dystopian future in which health spending crowds out the consumption of other goods and services.

In policy circles and the popular press, observers treat these two dilemmas as different manifestations of the same problem—too much healthcare spending. In reality, they result from different economic forces and call for distinct responses. High levels of U.S. health expenditures reflect market power and other forms of excess returns. Consequently, high healthcare spending levels enrich some in the U.S. but make the nation poorer overall. Policies that reduce the market power of providers, insurers, pharmaceutical companies, and others in the health sector will ameliorate this dilemma.

The growth of health expenditures as a fraction of GDP is a different matter. The conventional policy response is to suppress the growth in healthcare spending by tying the increase in Medicare expenditures to the growth of GDP. This approach is a recipe for failure. Healthcare spending rises as a fraction of GDP because as societies get richer, they are happy to forgo growth in consumption in exchange for improved health outcomes. A better response to the growth of healthcare expenditures as a fraction of GDP is to make the healthcare system more efficient at converting foregone consumption into improved health outcomes. Linking incentives for innovation to value creation and cost reduction is essential for this purpose. Our analysis offers a guide for doing so.

Our recommendations fall into two categories. The first set of recommendations better aligns the patent system's incentives with the creation of economic value. The second set consists of ways to make it easier for innovators and implementers to make money from cost-reducing innovations. None of our proposals are individually sufficient to unweave the tangled web of incentives, norms, and competition that constrains value-enhancing and cost-reducing innovation in U.S. healthcare. Instead, we offer a bundle of overlapping strategies that together move innovation in a better direction.

The remainder of this book spells out the analysis in more detail. Chapter 2 explores the link between incentives for innovation and value creation, while chapter 3 discusses the phenomenon of missing cost-reducing innovations. Chapter 4 analyzes the strengths and limitations of financial incentives as an inducement to cost-reducing innovations. Chapter 5 outlines the interactions between professional and social norms and economic incentives. Chapter 6 explains why incumbent firms in healthcare markets are reluctant to adopt value-enhancing and cost-reducing innovations and why more innovative firms struggle to disrupt them. Finally, chapter 7 describes a set of reforms that, taken together, would strengthen the link between innovation and the creation of economic value in healthcare.

2

Economically Valuable Innovation

In 1982 the lab of the molecular biologist Robert Weinberg isolated a cancer gene from a rat tumor. The gene was called *Neu,* an abbreviation of the type of cancer to which it was linked. This gene produces a protein that sits on the cell's surface and could be attacked by a *Neu* antibody as part of a targeted anti-cancer therapy. The lab had also developed an antibody for *Neu*, however no one connected the two discoveries, and no anti-cancer treatment was developed.

In 1986, Axel Ullrich, a researcher at the biotech company Genentech, presented a seminar on his discovery of the Her-2 protein, a human analog of the *Neu* cancer gene. Dennis Slamon, a professor at UCLA, heard Ullrich's presentation and proposed a collaboration that led to the discovery that some unusually aggressive breast cancers had a mutation in the gene coding for the Her-2 protein. The two also worked to produce an antibody to bind to this protein and thereby serve as the basis of an anti-cancer drug. While this research was ongoing, Genentech decided to discontinue investment in cancer research. As a result, Ullrich left the company. Slamon, however, persisted and pressured Genentech so aggressively that the company reluctantly funded a small study, which demonstrated the effectiveness of the Her-2 antibody as an anti-cancer treatment. On this basis, Genentech reversed course and embarked on the full-scale development of Herceptin, which became one of the leading therapies for breast cancer with sales of billions of dollars annually.[1]

As the case of Herceptin illustrates, discoveries involve some combination of knowledge and chance. If Ullrich had not made his discovery about mutations in the HER-2 protein, if he had not encountered Slamon, if Slamon had not persisted in pressuring Genentech, if Genentech had not reversed its decision to exit the market for cancer drugs, the discovery of Herceptin may have been long delayed or not happened at all. If Weinberg had realized that he had both a promising oncogene and a promising therapeutic molecule, the development of a drug might have been accelerated by years.

Why Not Better and Cheaper? James B. Rebitzer and Robert S. Rebitzer, Oxford University Press.
© Oxford University Press 2023. DOI: 10.1093/oso/9780197603109.003.0002

Recognizing the critical role of serendipity in innovation seems contrary to the thesis of our book. Suppose each innovation is a lucky step beyond current knowledge that occurs by chance. In that case, the path of innovation will more closely resemble the random walk of stock prices than movement along a discernable path. How can we argue that healthcare innovation favors one direction or another? Our answer is that innovation tends in directions that maximize economic returns to innovators.[2] The economic value of innovation ultimately derives from some combination of quality improvements and lower costs. To encourage economically valuable discoveries, incentives for innovation ought to reward quality-enhancing or cost-reducing inventions while discouraging discoveries that do neither. In most economic settings, this is essentially what happens.

This chapter considers whether incentives for innovation in the health sector align with creating economic value. We focus on the incentives for discovery in the patent and health insurance systems. We discuss instances where incentives favor less economically valuable innovations over innovations of greater value or where they perversely reward innovations of dubious economic value.

Assessing Economic Value in HealthCare

How do we measure the creation of economic value? In most sectors, the answer is straightforward: if a consumer is willing to pay more for a good or service than its cost, the transaction has created value. However, things are not so simple in healthcare.

By virtue of their wealth, richer people are willing to pay more for treatments than poorer people. Consequently, a "willingness to pay" approach to assessing economic value in healthcare leads to the unpalatable conclusion that the wealthy value their health, and even their lives, more than the poor. An alternative to "willingness to pay" has become standard in the health sector, a quality-adjusted life-year or QALY. A treatment that adds one year to life in good health produces one QALY, and this QALY is assigned a standardized dollar value. The dollar value of a QALY is the same for any individual, regardless of their wealth or willingness to pay.

As a rough rule of thumb, health policy experts in the United States assign a value between $50,000 and $150,000 for an additional year of life in good health. For simplicity, we will value a QALY in the United States at $100,000.[3]

Using the QALY framework, we can compare the cost of any treatment to the QALYs it produces and arrive at a rough and ready measure of the economic value the treatment creates.

To illustrate, suppose that a new chemotherapy drug has a list price of $50,000 per patient for a course of treatment. Suppose further that the drug produces, on average, one additional QALY for each cancer patient. At a value of $100,000 per QALY, the drug has a ratio of benefits to costs of 2. The benefit of the drug ($100,000) exceeds its cost ($50,000). Now consider another chemotherapy drug. This drug adds only one-tenth of a QALY for each patient treated (1.2 months in good health). The drug has a benefit-cost ratio of 0.2, so its use does not create economic value because the $10,000 in benefits are less than the costs.[4]

When treatments have varying effects on individuals, the calculation of QALYs relies on population averages, and averages can be misleading. Suppose that a drug costing $10,000 has no beneficial effect on 90 percent of the treated population but produces benefits of one QALY for 10 percent of the population. The average benefit of the drug would still be 0.1 QALY, but the economic value it creates would be distributed unequally. A $10,000 price would yield a negative value for 90 percent of the population. But for the lucky 10 percent, the use of the drug creates $90,000 in value. It is often not possible to accurately predict who in the population will benefit from treatment. As we shall see below, variability of treatment effectiveness and uncertainty about who will benefit can alter incentives in the health sector.

Patents

Competitive markets are critical for well-functioning economies, but intense competition can drive prices so low that there is little left to reward innovators.[5] For this reason, even societies deeply committed to markets and competition have long granted innovators temporary monopolies over their inventions to create incentives for developing new ideas. Indeed Article 1 Section 8 of the U.S. Constitution gives Congress the power "to promote the progress of science and useful arts, by securing for limited times to authors and inventors the exclusive right to their respective writings and discoveries."

New drugs, medical tests, and devices gain a temporary monopoly when patented. A patent expires 20 years after the application is filed with the U.S. Patent Office in the United States. Because it takes about 2.5 years from filing to patent approval, the monopoly typically has a commercial life of 17.5 years. During this period, innovators can profit by selling their inventions at prices well above marginal cost.

The patent monopoly is a powerful incentive for innovation. Moreover, the value of the monopoly depends on a kind of market test. A monopoly on an invention nobody wants to buy is worth very little, but a monopoly on something in high demand can be valuable. Does this market test mean that the patent system steers innovative activity toward the most economically valuable innovations in the health sector? In many cases, the answer is no.

Vaccines versus Treatments

Anyone who gets vaccinated against an infectious disease benefits themselves as well as others. To the extent that the price of the vaccine reflects only the value to individual consumers and fails to account for the benefit to others, the price does not reflect the total value of the vaccine. One way to mitigate the problem of underpricing vaccines is for governments to become vaccine purchasers. Governments are responsible for public health and would be more willing to pay the total value of the vaccine than are individual consumers. Indeed, as we have seen in the case of the rapid development of COVID-19 vaccines, government purchases can create powerful incentives for vaccine development.[6] But the response to COVID-19 also reveals that governments do not always prioritize expenditures on public health. This reluctance to spend is particularly true if the disease in question affects primarily marginalized populations or groups who face discrimination or social stigma. Without sufficient government commitment to purchase, the incentives for developing vaccines against infectious diseases will not stimulate research activity commensurate with the economic value such vaccines create.[7]

An additional pricing issue also weakens incentives for the development of vaccines. This issue arises from choices patent-holders make on how to best profit from their monopoly. Consider a drug maker who can invest in either a vaccine that prevents a disease or a treatment that cures people once they become sick. A vaccine that completely prevents a disease is of great value to people at high risk for the illness. The same vaccine is worth less to those at low risk. In some circumstances, the best pricing strategy for the vaccine is to sell at low prices so that the entire population buys the vaccine. Alternatively, the best pricing strategy might be to sell the vaccine at a high price so that only those at increased risk of developing the disease buy. A treatment that cures the disease in question will command an even higher price than the high-priced vaccine. In many plausible situations, this additional pricing power makes treatments more profitable than vaccines.[8] In this case, the patent system favors the invention of new treatments over vaccines of equal (or even higher) clinical value.

We can illustrate this pricing issue with a numerical example for a hypothetical illness.[9] Suppose that out of 1,000 people, 10 percent get a disease. The disease manifests late in middle age, so a cure gives a patient another 10 years of good quality of life. If each additional year (QALY) is worth $100,000, then the value of the cure is $1 million per patient. Consequently, the drug company's maximum price cannot exceed $1 million per treatment. At this price, the company can earn a maximum of $100 million.

Alternatively, consider a vaccine that prevents the disease. The value of a vaccine is the value of a cure multiplied by the probability that an individual might develop the disease. If everyone has a 10 percent chance of getting the disease, the maximum value is $100,000 per person for the vaccine—because 10 percent of $1 million is $100,000. Under these conditions—when a disease risk is spread equally through the population—a vaccine generates the same revenues as an equivalent treatment.

Now consider a different example. Suppose that 95 percent of the population has only a 5 percent chance of developing the disease while the remaining 5 percent have a 95 percent chance of becoming ill. In this example, 95 people can be expected to get sick, and the maximum revenue for a treatment would be $95 million. Because the odds of illness are unequally distributed, a vaccine will not generate the same revenues as a treatment. Most people in the population are at low risk and, consequently, are not willing to pay as much for a vaccine.[10]

Let us now apply this thinking to an actual disease, the human immunodeficiency virus (HIV). It is possible to estimate the distribution of risk for HIV based on the distribution of the number of sexual partners in the United States.[11] People at low risk of HIV will gain few QALYs from a hypothetical HIV vaccine. For these people, the vaccine's benefits would be below the profit-maximizing price for people at higher risk. Given the estimated distribution of risk for HIV, a vaccine will be less profitable than a comparably effective treatment for people already infected.[12]

The differences between preventatives and treatments are starkly apparent when the same drug can be used for both purposes. Gilead Science's drug, Truvada, can be used to treat HIV-1 in conjunction with other medications. A lower dose daily pill regimen has been studied as a pre-exposure prophylaxis (PrEP) to prevent the spread of HIV-1. Used in this way, Truvada can be used as a kind of anti-HIV vaccine. Two clinical trials found the drug very effective, provided that users take the medication regularly. Gilead did not secure approval for Truvada as a preventative until eight years after the drug's approval as a treatment, and revenues for it have been far lower than for the treatment.[13] The Centers for Disease Control and Prevention (CDC) estimates that about 1.2 million Americans could benefit from PrEP because they are at high risk due to unprotected sex or needle-sharing. Still, as of 2019, only about 270,000 people were taking the drug.[14] The reasons for the slow uptake are complex, but part of the problem appears to be the high list price Gilead set for the treatment.[15] It seems plausible that Gilead has chosen to price Truvada above the profit-maximizing price for a vaccine to preserve revenues from treatment.

The same pricing considerations apply to screening tests that enable early interventions that prevent the development of expensive and hard-to-treat late-stage chronic diseases. Imagine that scientists discover a blood test that allows for the early detection of colorectal cancer. The blood test offers no clinical benefits on its own. Its value derives solely from the minimally invasive, early detection of tumors. Early detection, in turn, is clinically valuable only because it makes conventional anti-cancer treatments more effective. Suppose further that this new technology reduced death rates from colorectal cancer by 25 percent relative to no screening—an improvement roughly comparable to gains from a current detection method, flexible sigmoidoscopies.[16]

Suppose colorectal cancer risks were distributed equally throughout the population. In that case, the patent holder for this new test could capture the same value as a treatment with a similar effect on mortality.[17] The risk of colorectal cancer is, however, not distributed equally. It is greatest in sub-populations—notably patients with inflammatory bowel disease, a history of colorectal cancer, or who are obese and inactive. This unequal distribution of risk can reduce the revenues a test developer might capture relative to a treatment.

Treatments for Late-Stage Cancer

Late-stage cancer is far more challenging to treat than early-stage cancer, but patent-based economic incentives favor developing drugs for late-stage cancer.[18] This preference for developing drugs for late-stage cancer arises because early-stage cancers can take a long time to kill their victims. Therefore, trials for drugs to reduce mortality from early-stage disease are longer than trials for late-stage cancer treatments. These differences in duration can be substantial. For prostate cancer, for example, detecting survival improvements for late-stage disease may require monitoring patients for 12 months. For early-stage disease, equivalent monitoring may take nine years or more. Because pharmaceutical companies file patents at the time of drug discovery, successful drugs targeting late-stage cancers have considerably longer effective patent terms. All else equal, they are likely to be more profitable than drugs aimed at early-stage cancers. This disparate profitability encourages innovators to focus more on developing drugs for late-stage cancer than early-stage disease.

Consistent with this incentive, from 1973 to 2011, more than twice the number of clinical trials were conducted for harder-to-survive metastatic cancer than for localized cancer. However, the relationship between R&D activity and disease stage was not observed in trials for treatments of blood cancers that rely on biomarkers as proxies for survival. The incentive to focus on late-stage disease becomes moot for these cancers, so the skew in innovation disappears.[19]

The Development of New Antibiotics

Bacteria constantly evolve in response to antibiotics used in agriculture and medicine. Resistant bacteria kill 23,000 people yearly in the United States.[20] Such bacteria can also compromise common medical procedures. For example, more than 13,000 infections per year (more than 40 percent) resulting from prostate biopsies are estimated to result from resistance to fluoroquinolones, a large group of broad-spectrum antibiotics.[21]

Saving lives by developing new antibiotics ought to be a profitable business, and companies seeking these profits ought to create new classes of drugs aimed at resistant strains. Most commonly prescribed types of antibiotics were discovered before the 1960s, and only a few novel classes have been approved for clinical use in recent decades.[22] In 2021 only four major pharmaceutical companies still have an antibiotic research program.[23] Why has the drug development pipeline produced so few new antibiotics? The answer is that the anticipated profits from new antibiotics are less than one might guess based on their potential clinical value. As Isaac Stoner, the president and CEO of Octagon Therapeutics, put it when describing his experience pitching a new compound with the potential to be a novel antibiotic class. "Investor after investor turned us down. Antibiotics, they said, were practically guaranteed money losers."[24]

What is it about antibiotics that make them unprofitable? Typically, new antibiotics are more expensive than existing drugs and not any more effective at treating bacterial infections.[25] However, their value jumps when antibiotic resistance emerges—something that might happen at some unspecified time in the future. The value of pharmaceutical patents depends on generating sales during a fixed period of patent exclusivity. No guarantee exists that resistance to a specific bacteria will emerge during the exclusivity period. Moreover, the future value of a new antibiotic increases when it is *not* sold because withholding the use of the new drug today helps ensure its future potency against ever evolving pathogens. Commercial insurers typically do not consider these social benefits when deciding how much they are willing to pay for a novel antibiotic—although government payers might.[26]

Isaac Stoner's company, Octagon Therapeutics, moved from their potential antibiotic to another product after failing to garner interest from investors. "I've seen firsthand that there are plenty of talented researchers eager to work on the challenge of fighting antimicrobial resistance. But without a marketplace that rewards innovation, brilliant scientific minds, and well-run drug discovery companies will focus on disease areas where the market is operating efficiently."[27]

Life Cycle Management of Patents

Vaccines, cancer treatments, and antibiotics are cases in which incentives can work against the development of economically valuable interventions. Conversely, the patent system also creates incentives to develop interventions of little or no economic value. "Life cycle" management is an example of this phenomenon.[28]

A patent on a pharmaceutical's active ingredient is the "primary patent." Pharmaceutical makers may also win "secondary" patents covering diverse formulations of the drug, different ways to use the drug to treat a particular disease, manufacturing methods, or other chemicals related to the active ingredient. Successful secondary patents (like primary patents) must be deemed new, useful, and non-obvious—but these innovations do not need to show clinical improvements or create additional economic value to be patentable.

The opportunity for secondary patents creates incentives for research into new applications of existing drugs. Such research can produce valuable results. For example, Evista was initially patented in 1983 as a treatment for breast cancer, and in 1997 the Food and Drug Administration (FDA) approved a secondary patent for the prevention of osteoporosis. However, pharmaceutical makers can also use secondary patents and follow-on patents to extend the period over which they have exclusive control over a pharmaceutical. While profitable, this use of secondary patents creates no value for patients. The term of art for this practice is evergreening. With evergreening, one would expect to observe multiple patents attached disproportionately to the most profitable drugs because extended exclusivity would be most valuable for these products. Consistent with evergreening, there are, on average, 2.7 patents per drug listed in the Orange Book, a comprehensive list of approved small molecule drugs in the United States, but the top 12 drugs by revenue had an average of 71 patents per drug.[29]

A related method for extending the effective life of a patent is "product hopping." Product hopping occurs when a drugmaker with a dominant market position tries to switch consumers to a newer version of the same (or similar) drug with later expiring patents. If the new formulation is widely adopted, this can delay generic competition and allow the drugmaker to extend the period of high monopoly prices for their drug. Recent litigation, for example, alleges that Abbott pursued such a strategy with its anti-cholesterol drug, TriCor.[30] Press reports suggest that Gilead is following a similar strategy to replace its HIV prevention drug—which is going off-patent—with a newer on-patent version, Descovy, that reportedly has fewer side effects.[31]

A third strategy for extending pharmaceutical patent protection is creating "patent thickets." By acquiring a densely connected set of patents for a drug or its manufacture, a drugmaker can make it more costly or risky for competitors to enter the market. Patent thickets are an effective way of managing the life cycle of biologic drugs. Biologics are distinct from more traditional small molecule drugs. They involve large, complex molecules often produced by manipulating microorganisms, plant cells, or animal cells. The complex process of manufacturing biologics from living cells offers more secondary patent opportunities than conventional chemical synthesis. For example, more than 130 patents protect the blockbuster biologic, Humira. This thicket of secondary patents can prevent the entry of "biosimilar" drugs that aim to compete with Humira the way that generics compete with other small molecule drugs. AbbVie, the maker of Humira, filed a lawsuit against biosimilar manufacturers, and its patent thicket enabled a settlement that delayed biosimilar market entry until seven years after the primary patent on Humira had expired.[32] Compare this outcome to the situation in Europe where Humira biosimilars entered in 2018 and have already captured substantial market share.[33] Such tactics extend the period of market exclusivity to the benefit of the drug manufacturer while generating little value for patients.

Evergreening, product hopping, and patent thickets are responses to the incentives inherent in the patent system. They exemplify how incentives can direct innovation away from creating economic value. We find a similar problem with the incentives for innovation inherent in the health insurance system.

Third-Party Payers and Incentives to Innovate

Where the Money Goes

It seems self-evident that insurance increases the incentives for developing economically valuable drugs. For example, the pharmaceutical company, Gilead, would never have attempted to charge $84,000 for its breakthrough cure for hepatitis C, Sovaldi, if third-party payers did not essentially cover the cost.[34] The reality, however, is more complicated. Insurance enables more people to afford expensive patented drugs, but the money must get back to the innovators to stimulate innovation. The way things stand today, this may not happen.

Figure 2.1 provides a simplified depiction of the cash flows for the sale of drugs in the United States.

Imagine that an individual health insurance policyholder (the consumer in figure 2.1) is prescribed a patented drug purchased from an online pharmacy run by a pharmacy benefit manager (PBM). If the PBM adds a drug to its formulary, the drug is assigned to a tier. Drugs assigned to the lowest tiers require a relatively small out-of-pocket payment from the consumer. Drugs assigned to higher tiers require larger copays.

Drugmakers compete for placement in a lower tier by offering the PBM a per-unit rebate off the list price. This rebate allows the PBM to purchase the

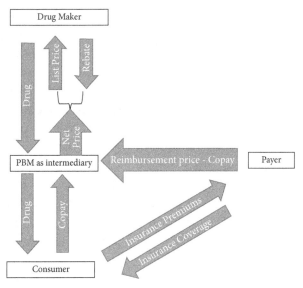

Figure 2.1 Simplified Cash Flow for the Sale of Patented Drugs in the
United States

drug for a net price that is often far below the list price. When the consumer
buys the drug from the PBM's pharmacy, the PBM charges the insurer a "reimbursement" price. The markup of the reimbursement price over the net
price is an essential source of profits for the PBM.

The difference between the reimbursement price insurers pay for a drug
and the copay paid by the consumer is a drug subsidy built into health insurance. Insurers recoup the cost of the subsidy through what economists call a
two-part tariff. Under this pricing strategy, consumers pay a small per-unit
charge (the drug copay) and a fixed access fee (an insurance premium). This
strategy is familiar to anyone who has gone to a bar with a high cover charge
but relatively low prices for drinks or to a health club with a membership fee
and a small additional charge per session.

We can now see that the cash flows in the pharmaceutical supply chain
are the result of numerous pricing decisions made by several different
participants: the list price of the drug, the net price to PBMs, the reimbursement price that PBMs charge insurers, the size of insurance copays,
and the premiums insurers charge policyholders. With so many players
scrambling to capture revenues generated by pharmaceutical sales, it would
be surprising if all the value created by insurance coverage returns to the

drugmakers. Indeed, a recent theoretical analysis argues that if PBMs have sufficient market power, drugmakers receive *none* of the added value created by insurance subsidies for drug purchases.[35] In this way, intermediaries such as PBMs can dampen the incentives for drug companies to innovate. One result of this dampening may be the rise of "me too" drugs that deliver less economic value than scientifically novel treatments but are less costly to develop.[36] We see indirect evidence for such an effect after the introduction of Medicare's pharmacy benefit, Medicare Part D.

Medicare Part D was enacted into law in 2003 as part of the Medicare Modernization Act. By 2011, Part D covered 30 million enrollees. However, because many of these enrollees already had some form of drug coverage, the number of new individuals with drug coverage was much smaller, approximately 5 million individuals. Nonetheless, Medicare Part D stimulated an increase in pharmaceutical use by the elderly and induced additional pharmaceutical innovation. However, an analysis of the target-based action (TBA)—or biological approach—used in these clinical trials found that trials aimed at conditions with a high Medicare market share were less likely to use a novel TBA than those directed toward conditions with a low Medicare market share.[37] One explanation for this result is that the expansion of Medicare Part D is relatively modest compared to the worldwide market for drugs. Under a modest incentive to innovate, drugs with previously explored TBAs may be favored over potentially more novel and economically valuable drugs because they are less expensive to develop. We may expect a similar result when PBMs weaken incentives for drugmakers.

Treatments of Dubious Value

Conceptually, one may divide medical technologies into three categories.[38] Category One includes "home run" technologies that are cost-effective and useful for nearly everyone in the relevant population. An example of a Category One technology is antiretroviral drugs for the treatment of HIV. Category Two includes technologies that are cost-effective but also have variable benefits on average. Examples include angioplasty, antidepressants, and imaging technologies. Category Three contains technologies whose effects are even more modest and uncertain than Category Two technologies. Examples include arthroscopic knee surgery for knee osteoarthritis and ICU beds for terminally ill patients.

Category Two and Category Three technologies are important contributors to the growth of costs and are more widely used in the United States than elsewhere. For example, Category Three treatments likely explain the relatively rapid growth of spending on coronary disease in the United States and the dramatic rise in the average cost of saving an additional life year. The United States leads in using Category Three innovations such as "robotic" surgery tools, proton beam therapy for prostate cancer, and the use of ICU beds at the end of life. The United States also experiences relatively widespread use of Category Three pharmaceuticals.

Where payers compensate providers on a fee-for-service basis—with no capitation or value-based component to their reimbursement—and where providers face few restrictions in their choice of treatments, many providers will be willing to prescribe Category Two and Category Three interventions if they believe their patient might have a chance, however small, to benefit from a therapy. In this way, fee-for-service payments and deference to provider decision-making shifts demand in favor of Category Two and Category Three technologies relative to an alternative arrangement that limits access to technologies with poor cost-effectiveness ratios. Of course, this shift in demand will increase the expected profitability of new Category Two and Category Three technologies. The U.S. regulatory structure, which minimizes cost-effectiveness considerations in approving new drugs and devices, amplifies these incentives.[39]

In the United States, the FDA authorizes the use of pharmaceuticals, biologics, implantable devices, lab tests, imaging, and radiation therapy. To approve a drug, the FDA requires proof of safety and efficacy. Drug developers can only market their products to physicians for FDA-approved indications, but physicians have significant discretion and can prescribe an approved product for indications outside of the authorized uses if they believe it will benefit their patients. The FDA does not review evidence on the economic impact of the pharmaceuticals it studies and also does not require that new drugs be more valuable than existing therapies.[40]

Similar regulatory practices are at work for medical devices. Devices that are life-sustaining or pose significant risks go through a pre-market approval process comparable to pharmaceuticals. Between 2003 and 2007, only 1 percent of the 15,000 new medical devices went through pre-market approval.[41] In addition, incremental changes to existing devices can be approved without *any* clinical data. Intermediate risk devices can also be approved with limited additional evaluation if they are substantially equivalent to already approved devices.

FDA approval is a necessary but not sufficient condition for an innovation to find a market. It is also essential that Medicare or private insurers include the innovation in their covered benefits. Since its creation in 1965, Medicare has generally covered tests and treatments if the services are "reasonable and necessary." A consequence of this standard is that Medicare does not deny coverage simply because a new product is less cost-effective than an alternative. Typically, Medicare covers treatments that receive FDA approval, even when prescribed for indications different from those initially authorized by the FDA. Private insurers generally follow Medicare's lead in this regard.

One consequence of the permissive regulatory practices in the United States is "treatment creep." Consider the case of implantable cardiac defibrillators (ICDs). ICDs are devices intended to prevent sudden cardiac death (SCD) by shocking patients' hearts when the implanted device senses a life-threatening arrhythmia. ICDs were initially found beneficial for patients with a prior history of cardiac events and were approved for so-called secondary prevention of cardiac death. Subsequent randomized trials examined whether ICDs could also benefit the much larger pool of patients who had not had a first event. A series of studies found that the benefits were not as clear-cut for this larger population of patients and that effectiveness varied more than in the original patient population.[42]

Nonetheless, based on these studies, the Center for Medicare and Medicaid Services (CMS), which administers the Medicare program, expanded its coverage, and providers began implanting more of these devices. More than 400,000 ICDs were implanted between 1990 and 2002, and more than half a million were registered in the National Cardiovascular Data Registry between 2006 and 2010. Annual expenditures for ICDs are estimated to exceed $4.5 billion per year. The 30–40 percent reduction in relative mortality resulting from the widespread use of ICDs comes at a high price: roughly $34,000–$72,000 per QALY. The age distribution of patients receiving ICDs is older than the population included in the original studies—more than 40 percent are over 70 and 10 percent are in their 80s.[43] Subsequent research showed that older patients benefit from ICD therapy, but the cost-effectiveness of the treatment is reduced due to the higher chance that the elderly experience death from other causes.[44]

Treatment creep is also a feature in the use of pharmaceuticals. Avastin is a case in point.[45] Avastin is a drug that prevents the development of new blood vessels. Since blood vessel growth is essential for cancer growth, Avastin is a valuable anti-cancer drug. It has been used to treat breast, lung, colon, and other cancers.

After positive early trials, the FDA initially gave Avastin accelerated approval for the treatment of metastatic breast cancer—provided that the manufacturer, Genentech, conducted additional trials. These trials found that Avastin does not reduce mortality for metastatic breast cancer, and the FDA eventually revoked its approval for this indication. In the meantime, however, Avastin was added to the Compendium of Drugs and Biologics. Under CMS rules and federal law, inclusion in the compendium means that Medicare must pay for Avastin as an "off-label" treatment for metastatic breast cancer. The cost per course of treatment with Avastin at the time exceeded $100,000, but it yielded only 0.135 QALYs for metastatic breast cancer patients. In other words, Medicare had to spend an extraordinary $745,000 to gain an additional QALY, more than seven times the $100,000 consensus value of an additional life-year in the United States. The moral of this story is that a potentially valuable drug can be approved for use, even when its incremental value relative to price is quite low.[46]

The problem of demand for new treatments of low value goes beyond the example of Avastin. It is a systemic issue. Comparisons of the utilization and diffusion of a large sample of new drugs in the United States, Australia, Canada, Switzerland, and the UK found that drugs with a low value relative to existing treatments diffuse more rapidly in the United States.[47] Such demand creates incentives for drug developers that are not aligned with considerations of economic value.

This chapter illustrates how the patent system, the health insurance system, and regulatory practices reward new treatments of dubious economic value and fail to reward some new treatments with high potential value. The predictable effect is that innovation creates less value than it could. In chapter 3, we turn to a distinct but related issue: the difficulty of introducing innovations that reduce costs.

3

Missing Innovations

Chapter 2 showed that incentives in the patent and insurance systems lead to a value-creation problem; interventions of low economic value can find a ready market, while innovations of high economic value may not. These incentives shift innovation away from the creation of economic value.

This chapter introduces a distinct but related cost-reduction problem: innovations that reduce costs often "go missing." New processes, business models, or managerial practices that reduce the resources needed to provide care fail to take root and spread across the health sector. We discuss seven areas suggestive of missing innovations: pervasive fee-for-service payment contracts; regions that persistently deliver more expensive care than other regions; the long, slow decline of small, single-specialty medical practices; lagging adoption of information technologies; failures to develop alternatives to slow and cumbersome insurance claims payments; a dearth of slightly worse but much cheaper interventions; and limited investment in research into the relative benefits and costs of treatments. This list is by no means exhaustive, but it illustrates a pattern: time and again, the healthcare sector overlooks cost-reducing opportunities lying in plain sight. The failure to exploit such opportunities influences the overall direction of innovation in the health sector. Innovators will work on other problems if there is no ready market for cost reduction.[1]

Writing about missing innovations is tricky, not least because it risks self-delusion. Perhaps the cost-reducing innovations we highlight are not missing at all. Maybe they are simply not as good as the status quo they seek to replace. To make a case for the missing innovations' unrealized potential, we must make use of theoretical counterfactuals, evidence gleaned from demonstration projects, or studies of selected regions or atypical organizations. For this reason, we cannot definitively establish the relative benefits of any specific innovation that we claim is missing. Despite these limitations, we believe that the cumulative weight of these examples is sufficient to make the point that failure to exploit opportunities for cost reduction is a real and

Why Not Better and Cheaper? James B. Rebitzer and Robert S. Rebitzer, Oxford University Press.
© Oxford University Press 2023. DOI: 10.1093/oso/9780197603109.003.0003

pervasive phenomenon in the health sector. Having made the case that this phenomenon exists, we devote subsequent chapters to examining its causes.

Alternatives to Fee-for-Service Physician Payments

Under fee-for-service reimbursement, payers pay for each service that providers deliver. It is the payment system for traditional Medicare and most other reimbursement schemes in use today. Fee-for-service rewards providers who generate volume—in the form of doctor visits, procedures, hospital admissions, etc.—even if the volume of services is costly for payers or of limited value to patients. For this reason, the National Commission on Physician Payment Reform, sponsored by the Society of General Internal Medicine, recommended a rapid transition away from fee-for-service payment because of its "inherent inefficiencies and problematic financial incentives."[2] As discussed in chapters 1 and 2, fee-for-service supports the demand for high-cost drugs and devices even when their value is low or uncertain.[3] In addition, fee-for-service is a piece-rate payment scheme for providers. Like all piece-rate schemes, it discourages experimentation and innovation because time spent improving processes is time lost for revenue-generating activities.[4] Empirical studies have shown that moving physician compensation away from fee-for-service can generate significant cost savings for payers.[5]

Given the much-discussed deficiencies of fee-for-service and the empirical evidence that alternative systems might do better, it is noteworthy that physician compensation in the United States is still overwhelmingly fee-for-service.[6] This prevalence is remarkable in light of evidence that capitation and other alternative payment systems are eminently scalable. For example, in California, Kaiser Permanente—a system based on per-member fees and not fee-for-service compensation—commanded 30 percent of the California market for health insurance in 2017.[7]

Remaining with fee-for-service payment rather than introducing more cost-efficient alternatives seems like a straightforward example of a missing innovation. But fee-for-service also has significant practical benefits. It is transparent, relatively simple to understand and administer, and assures fair compensation for treating even the sickest patients. When considering these factors, fee-for-service payment may persist because, despite its limitations, it is better than the alternatives.

However, this explanation for the persistence of fee-for-service is hard to square with Medicare's successful move away from fee-for-service payments for hospital visits. At its inception, Medicare paid hospitals fee-for-service by applying a daily rate to the number of days a patient stayed in the hospital. However, in 1983 Medicare adopted a new type of system. Under this system, hospitals receive a fixed payment for each Medicare patient with a given diagnosis (known as a "diagnosis-related group" or DRG).[8] After Medicare's switch to DRGs, other public and private payers implemented similar payment schemes. This change has reduced both hospital admissions and the length of time people stay in the hospital.[9] While the DRG system is imperfect, it offers reasonable transparency, administrative simplicity, and fair compensation for even the sickest patients.

The fact that Medicare's implementation of its DRG system jump-started similar changes in the private sector is noteworthy. If the move away from fee-for-service for hospital stays were inefficient, why did private payers follow Medicare's example? If the move was efficient, why didn't the private payers move first? Why did they wait for the slower moving, more bureaucratically encumbered public payment program to introduce changes? We return to the role of Medicare as a jump-starter of innovation in chapters 4 and 7.

Persistent High-Cost Regions

In traditional fee-for-service Medicare, spending per enrollee varies by as much as 200 percent across the country.[10] This variation is not the result of price differences or differences in covered benefits. Instead, the difference lies in the quantity of services utilized in different regions.

Are some regions simply more efficient and, therefore, able to deliver similar outcomes with fewer services? Or are patients in the areas with higher spending different in some way that causes greater utilization? If the former, then the persistence of the high-cost regions may be evidence of significant missing innovation.

One way to answer these questions is to track Medicare enrollees who move from a low-cost to a high-cost region.[11] If the enrollees exhibit the same utilization after the move, then the characteristics of that enrollee are an important driver of cost variations. On the other hand, if the costs of Medicare movers shift markedly upon relocating to a new region, this suggests it is the regional effect that matters. Applying this insight across a large population of Medicare movers, studies estimate that 50–60 percent of the geographic variation in Medicare utilization is attributable to region-specific factors. These differences in utilization do not appear to be associated with marked differences in the quality of care. But limitations in the available quality measures mean that we cannot rule out variation in the quality of care.

Does it follow that regional variations in utilization are entirely due to missed opportunities for cost reductions? Many prominent accounts of waste in the healthcare system adopt this interpretation.[12] However, there are other possible explanations. For example, if some regions acquire more expertise in expensive, high-tech treatments than others, regional differences in cost may not represent wasted resources but rather regional differences in specialization. People in these high-intensity regions may be getting more expensive care, but that care is appropriate given the type of specialization prevalent in the area. Indeed, studies of regional variation in the treatment of heart attacks find evidence of precisely this sort of specialization.[13]

In addition to specialization, some studies find that regional cost differences are associated with regional variation in physician beliefs and practice styles. In one such study, physicians were classified as "cowboys" or "comforters" according to their responses to hypothetical treatment scenarios.[14] Cowboys generally favored aggressive treatments even if evidence-based clinical guidelines did not support these treatments. Comforters were physicians who favored less aggressive treatment options such as palliative care. Regions with more cowboys were associated with more Medicare spending on end-of-life care. A one standard deviation increase in the percentage of cowboys in an area was associated with a 12 percent increase in spending in the final two years of life. More comforters in a region had the opposite effect. One standard deviation increase in the percentage of comforters was associated with a nearly 6 percent reduction in the same measure of costs. Similar associations appeared when focusing on the medical expenses of patients who have suffered heart attacks (acute myocardial infarction or AMI). Neither care quality measures nor the one-year mortality rates of heart attack patients seem to vary with the regional concentration of cowboys or comforters.

In sum, there is persuasive evidence of differences in care costs across regions. These regional differences are not the result of cross-area variation in patient characteristics and suggest that providers in some areas fail to adopt more cost-effective care styles. Strategies for addressing these missing innovations depend on the reasons for the failure to adopt them. To the extent that regional differences result from regional specialization patterns, it may not be sensible to persuade individual practitioners to change their practice styles. Change strategies would be different if provider attitudes, beliefs, and norms primarily drive regional differences. We return to the role of professional and social norms in adopting innovations in chapters 5 and 7.

Larger, Multi-specialty Practices

Historically, sole practitioners operating out of their private practices delivered the bulk of medical care in the United States. This arrangement granted physicians a great deal of professional autonomy that they were un-willing to surrender to larger, potentially more efficient organizations. To prevent absorption into larger entities, physicians mobilized politically and economically. As a result of these efforts, healthcare delivery remained in the hands of small, single-specialty physician practices for decades.[15]

The historical dominance of small medical groups continues into the present day despite evidence of change in recent years. One study estimated that in 1998, nearly 30 percent of physicians worked in solo practices and 55 percent in practices of nine or fewer physicians. In con-trast, less than 20 percent of physicians were employed in practices having 50 or more physicians. Since the beginning of this century, physicians have slowly migrated toward larger practices. By 2010, nearly 20 percent were solo practitioners, and 40 percent worked in practices of nine or fewer physicians.[16] Despite this transition, small practices still deliver a great deal of care. According to the 2010 National Ambulatory Care Survey, more than 30 percent of office visits were to solo practices and more than two-thirds were to practices with five or fewer physicians. Only about one-fifth of office visits were to multi-specialty groups.[17]

There is a long-standing and highly influential belief in health policy circles that large, multi-specialty groups and organized clinics offer the pros-pect of improved care quality at a lower cost, particularly if these entities provide closer integration with hospitals.[18] If this claim is correct, then the persistence of small and solo practices is an example of a missing innovation.

The claim for efficiency gains in large, multi-specialty group practices is not without controversy.[19] Opponents of this claim argue that physi-cian practices offer limited opportunities to improve efficiency by growing larger (economies of scale) or expanding their activities' range (economies of scope). They claim that the evidence that large multi-specialty groups operate more efficiently is thin. They bolster this claim by appealing to Nobel prize-winning economist George Stigler's "survivorship principle," the idea that market forces lead firms to adopt the most efficient scale of operation.

However, scale and scope are not the only economies relevant to the organization of medical practice. The ability to better coordinate care and to make joint decisions among multiple providers and specialties is also critical, and larger, multi-specialty groups have an advantage in this regard.

A case study comparing technology assessment and procurement for cardiac and orthopedic implantable devices by five hospital systems in Orange County illustrates some of the benefits of greater coordination.[20]

Efficient procurement requires a technology assessment committee that includes practicing physicians and senior management. The committee assesses alternative technologies, decides from whom to purchase the devices, and persuades physicians to use what was purchased. The goal is to concentrate purchases with a small number of manufacturers and thereby negotiate volume discounts and simplify hospital operations.

In two of the systems, the medical staff came from multiple small practices. In the other three systems, the medical staff was part of large multi-specialty groups closely affiliated with the hospital. In one of the closely affiliated systems, Hoag, the surgeons owned the specialty orthopedic hospital. In another system, Kaiser Permanente, the physicians were employees in an integrated delivery system that included a health insurance plan, a multi-specialty medical group, and hospitals.

Medical staff from small groups had a more challenging time coordinating technology purchases. The systems that relied on large, closely integrated groups had an easier time persuading physicians to abide by their purchasing guidelines. They were, therefore, able to negotiate better prices with device manufacturers. They also developed more standardized processes for the use of the devices, which made their clinical operations more efficient.[21]

Coordination is also vital in the delivery of care. The Institute of Medicine's literature review on care quality concluded that care delivery is often poorly coordinated. Poor coordination, in turn, leads to wasted resources, gaps in coverage, loss of clinically relevant information, and care delivery that is slower and less safe.[22] In-depth case studies have supported this view.[23]

A classic example of the challenges of care coordination is physician referrals.[24] Sometimes the referring primary care doctor does not convey critical clinical information to the specialist. Sometimes the feedback loops fail, and the primary care provider does not learn what the specialist recommended or even if the visit took place at all. Role ambiguity further complicates referrals. Sometimes, a specialist acts as a consultant to assist primary care physicians in diagnosing patients or referring them for procedures. Sometimes a specialist becomes a co-manager of care with the primary care physician—as often occurs in treating congestive heart failure. Other times, as with end-stage renal disease, the specialist becomes the principal care manager. Each of these roles requires a different kind of involvement by the specialist. Ambiguity about who is playing what role is typical. Successful coordination requires physicians to understand what to expect of each other. Poor coordination can lead to undesirable and costly outcomes such as missed or delayed diagnoses, duplicative or unnecessary tests, and referrals to inappropriate specialists. Inappropriate specialist referrals can also spark an expensive cascade of testing, follow-up visits, and even unnecessary hospitalizations.

Physicians do a better job coordinating care if they regularly work together. If a primary care physician refers all her cardiac patients to the same cardiologist, the repeated interactions encourage dialogue, information flows, and a shared understanding of roles and responsibilities. In contrast, if a primary care physician refers patients to many different cardiologists, there is less opportunity for mutual understanding to develop. Consistent with this reasoning, studies find that when primary care physicians repeatedly refer to the same small set of specialists, the costs of treating a patient are lower than when they scatter referrals across many different specialists.[25] This finding holds in both commercial and Medicare populations—even after controlling for fixed patient and physician characteristics.

To the extent that referrals within larger multi-specialty groups facilitate better coordination between primary care physicians and specialists, these groups would have a cost advantage over smaller, single-specialty groups. Working against this conclusion, however, is the limited direct statistical evidence to support this claim.[26] Another consideration is that large multi-specialty groups can accrue considerable market power and increase prices, particularly when aligned with hospital systems. High prices can eclipse efficiency gains from better coordination.[27] Finally, experience with Accountable Care Organizations (ACOs)—a policy to stimulate the formation of multi-specialty entities—has produced only modest cost reductions.[28]

Notwithstanding controversies and debates, the transition from small group practice is proceeding at a glacial pace measured in decades.

Incentives, competitive market dynamics, and the challenges of building a physician group culture all play a role in this slow rate of change. We discuss these factors at greater length in subsequent chapters. At this juncture in our story, the main point is that a change so slow to occur is an opportunity lost. The persistence of small group practice signals an innovation effectively gone missing.

Rapid Adoption of Health Information Technologies

A good illustration of the potential of Health Information Technology (HIT) to reduce costs comes from a randomized trial of a decision support system conducted between 2000 and 2001.[29] Electronic health records (EHRs) were scarce at that time, and even where they were in place, relevant information did not flow easily across organizations or between inpatient and outpatient settings. In response, a health IT startup, ActiveHealth Management, developed a then-novel software system designed to overcome these problems. Rather than build an electronic medical record, ActiveHealth assembled information from insurer billing records, patient lab results, and pharmacy records to construct a virtual electronic health record. Once collected, this information was passed through a set of decision rules culled from the medical literature. When the software uncovered an issue with a particular patient, it sent a message to the primary care physician that included the patient's name, the problem discovered, a suggested course of corrective action, and a citation to the relevant medical literature. The issues identified varied in severity and ranged from potentially life-threatening (e.g., a patient's blood potassium level was off); to moderately important (the patient was a good candidate for an ACE inhibitor); to less severe issues—primarily preventative care interventions such as reminders that a diabetic patient hadn't had an eye exam.

The randomized trial assigned commercial patients in a single health management organization (HMO) to treatment or control groups. The key findings from this trial were that HIT lowered average charges by 6 percent relative to the control group. This reduction in resource utilization primarily resulted from reduced inpatient and associated professional charges for the most costly patients. Issues were resolved at a higher rate in the study group as well, suggesting the system improved quality even as costs per patient fell.

Despite studies like the ActiveHealth Management trial that showed cost savings and quality improvements, it was clear that the adoption of IT in the health sector in the early part of the 21st century lagged behind other sectors of the economy. U.S. investments in HIT also lagged behind other industrialized nations' healthcare systems, including the UK, the Netherlands, Scandinavia, Australia, and New Zealand.[30]

An indicator of the state of HIT in this period was the rate at which physicians and hospitals adopted EHRs. A nationally representative survey of physicians conducted in late 2007 and early 2008 found that the use of EHRs in ambulatory care settings was quite rare. Only 4 percent of physicians reported having a fully functional electronic-records system, and 13 percent reported having a more basic system.[31] A survey of hospitals conducted in 2008 found that 1.5 percent of U.S. hospitals had a comprehensive electronic-records system implemented across all major clinical units. Nearly 8 percent had a basic system in at least one clinical unit.[32]

To encourage the adoption of EHRs, the Obama administration introduced the Health Information Technology for Economic and Clinical Health (HITECH) Act as part of its stimulus plan during the great recession of 2009. Starting in 2011, physicians received extra Medicare payments for meaningful use of a certified electronic health record. Physicians who demonstrated meaningful use in 2011 received incentive payments totaling $44,000 over five years. Meaningful use of EHRs in 2011 earned hospitals money too: a one-time bonus payment of $2 million plus an add-on to the Medicare DRG payment.[33] Overall, HITECH authorized $19 billion in Medicare and Medicaid payments over 10 years to eligible providers[34] and combined these incentives with penalties that grew over time. Physicians who did not use EHRs by 2015 received 1 percent less for equivalent services than physicians who adopted them. The penalty grew to 3 percent by 2017. Hospitals faced similar penalties for not adopting EHRs.[35]

The HITECH act immediately accelerated the adoption of EHRs.[36] By 2013 adoption in outpatient settings reached nearly 50 percent, almost double the percentage in 2009. All told, about 65 percent of eligible professionals received incentive payments totaling approximately $22 billion under the program as of February 2014.[37]

However, despite the impact of the HITECH Act, the issue of slow adoption of HIT continues. For instance, much of the value of EHRs for improving care coordination comes from digitally exchanging patient data with different physician practices and hospitals. This feature is called interoperability.

Evidence suggests that providers are lagging in adopting interoperable systems—just as they did with EHRs. The fax machine, a technology that has all but disappeared elsewhere, remains a feature in the healthcare back office as a silent witness to the failure to achieve interoperability.[38]

The HITECH Act did not require systems to be interoperable, which undoubtedly contributed to the slow spread of interoperability. But this explanation begs the question of why government incentives are needed to spur HIT adoption in an age of transformative IT.[39] After all, in other dynamic sectors of the economy, investments in IT produced transformative business models that delivered new and valuable services at reduced costs.[40] There was no need to implement a multi-billion-dollar federal program of incentives and sanctions to introduce a modern, IT-based infrastructure in these sectors.

The general thrust of the academic literature is that HIT lowers costs and improves quality, notwithstanding some careful, large-scale studies that point in the other direction.[41,42] However, other sectors did not wait for scholarly analysis to make massive investments in computer systems in the 1980s and 1990s.[43] Firms made these investments based on their expectations that such investments would eventually pay off. In healthcare, even very substantial government incentives have not induced comparable investments in HIT. Later chapters will argue that slow adoption of HIT and other cost-reducing innovations has deep roots in the fragmented structure of healthcare markets, professional and social norms, and competitive dynamics. For instance, the resistance to seamless electronic exchange of health information may stem from a desire by some hospitals to make it harder for patients to switch to competing hospitals. For now, it is sufficient to point out that in the case of fast-moving IT, an adoption process measured in decades indicates that valuable innovations have gone missing.

Alternatives to Insurance Claims

The costs of administering the U.S. healthcare system are famously high, reaching nearly $500 billion in 2019. These estimates are conservative because they do not include the value of the time and energy patients put into deciphering and paying incomprehensible bills.[44]

Two questions complicate the analysis of the causes of high administrative costs. First, to what extent can we clearly distinguish administrative costs from the costs of delivering care? After all, providers may complain about the administrative burden of entering data into EHRs, but some of the data recorded is also used to manage patient care. The second question is more difficult. Which costly administrative tasks are appropriate, and which are wasteful and unnecessary? Operating at the lowest administrative costs may, for example, eliminate checks and balances in the payment system and open the door to fraud and abuse.

Analysts have typically relied on international comparisons to assess whether high administrative costs are wasteful. One study found that administrative costs of care (relating to planning, regulating, and managing health systems and services) accounted for 8 percent in the United States versus 1–3 percent in the other 10 highest-income countries.[45] Two factors complicate these sorts of comparisons. First, the opportunity cost of physician time differs dramatically between different countries; ideally, international comparisons must take these differences into account. Second, international comparisons necessarily rely on untested counterfactuals. We do not know that administrative costs would fall if the Canadian, Japanese, or German systems were transplanted into the United States—nobody has tried that experiment. In the absence of such evidence, it is helpful to develop a more detailed understanding of what is driving administrative expenditures in the United States. We focus on an important subset of administrative expenditures, billing and insurance-related (BIR) costs, to develop such an understanding.

Administrative costs associated with billing and insurance are the largest and best-studied component of administrative expenditures in the United States. On the payer side, BIR costs include insurance company profits and overhead. For providers, BIR costs include such tasks as record keeping for claims submissions and billing.[46] A likely contributor to high BIR costs in the United States is the near-universal reliance on a claims-based system for reimbursing providers. Under a claims system, a payer submits a claim for reimbursement, not an invoice for payment. The insurer must evaluate (and often rejects) each claim. The providers can respond by re-submitting a modified claim or challenging the rejection. The payer can then accept the modified claim or respond to the challenge. Eventually, the claim is adjudicated (resolved) and paid.[47] With an invoice, in contrast, the payer simply pays the provider's submission at the established price.

The claims-based payment system is costly and slow, involving tens of billions of dollars in challenged revenues, payment delays, and a small army of administrators at insurance companies and providers to manage the process. A detailed study of just five specialty categories—cardiology, internal and family medicine, obstetrics and gynecology, orthopedics, and pediatrics—estimated that the total amount contested by payers was $11 billion annually but could be as high as $54 billion.[48]

Both insurers and providers would benefit from a more streamlined and rational billing system in which providers simply submit invoices and receive payment. Instead, both parties spend heavily on consultants and costly technologies to win skirmishes in the war over what is euphemistically called the "revenue cycle."

Adjudicating a health insurance claim requires answers to several questions. First, is the treatment covered under the patient's benefit plan? Second, is the patient a member of the covered group? Establishing group membership is particularly challenging for employer-based groups because employees often change employers. Third, is the provider within the insurer's network of providers? And finally, what is the reimbursement rate? In the fragmented U.S. healthcare system—with hundreds of insurance companies and thousands of employers, benefit plans, and independent providers with individually negotiated provider contracts—correctly answering these questions can be staggeringly complex.

There are many ways to reduce this complexity and thereby reduce costs. Benefits could be standardized and simplified as they are for Medicare and the insurance products sold on the Affordable Care Act's healthcare exchanges. The payment formula could be simplified by adopting capitated or bundled payment schemes. Reducing the number of insurance companies with which providers do business can simplify matters (as with Kaiser Permanente, Geisinger Health, and other vertically integrated insurers). Trusted third parties could manage and attest to the validity of payments, as with credit card payments. None of these solutions is pain-free or straightforward. Putting these solutions into practice involves overcoming legal, political, and other barriers. However, providers and insurance companies continue to struggle over the revenue cycle rather than make such changes. It is hard to imagine a clearer signal of missing innovation.

Slightly Worse but Much Cheaper Interventions

Tesla versus Toyota. Whole Foods versus Walmart. Most goods and services offer choices that permit trade-offs between cost and quality. The availability of options that are slightly worse but much cheaper enables these trade-offs. It helps consumers match what they buy to their individual preferences and their economic means. In addition, slightly worse but much cheaper products are an important channel for economic dynamism. New entrants offering slightly worse but much cheaper products and services can displace entrenched incumbent firms.[49]

However, Victor Fuchs, a trenchant observer of the U.S. healthcare system, has noted that the mix of products and services in healthcare appears skewed toward high-cost, high-quality offerings.[50] He cites as examples overbuilt hospitals, a high proportion of specialist physicians, and an abundance of imaging technology geared to convenient access rather than cost-efficient operation. It's as if one could only buy groceries at Whole Foods. Everyone might enjoy the high-quality groceries on offer, but surely many would benefit from purchasing lower-cost food at Walmart and putting the money they save to other uses.

The example of rapid home tests for COVID-19 illustrates the challenges faced by slightly worse but much cheaper interventions in the health sector. Nucleic acid amplification tests—such as polymerase chain reaction (PCR) tests—are the most sensitive test for the SARS-CoV-2 virus. They are considered the gold standard for testing for COVID-19. However, they are costly—as much as $150 per test—and the result is often unavailable for days. In contrast, home antigen tests cost about $10 and deliver results in about 15 minutes, but they are a less sensitive test for COVID-19. Home tests were difficult for consumers to obtain in the United States in the first phase of the pandemic even though the tests were widely used in Europe and elsewhere. The delay was due to many factors, including slow regulatory approval, confusion in the medical community about how to use a cheaper, faster, but less sensitive test, insurance coverage issues, and consumer hesitation. The result was slow diffusion of a cost-effective—and much-needed—test during a public health emergency.[51]

One way to track the health sector's reluctance to introduce more cost-effective alternatives is to examine the cost-effectiveness of new treatments relative to existing treatments. A study examining new treatments entering the healthcare market found that only about 2 percent were slightly worse but much cheaper. Sixty-eight percent of the new technologies in the study had a lower ratio of benefits to cost than the pre-existing technologies. The average new treatment cost nearly 140 percent over the prevailing standard of care, while the average quality increase was less than 30 percent.[52]

Another study reviewed all the cost-benefit analyses cited in MEDLINE—a database of biomedical literature maintained by the National Institutes of Health—from 2002 to 2007, in search of medical innovations that were slightly worse but much cheaper (or, as the authors put it, much cheaper but almost as good).[53] Innovations qualified for this category only if they saved $100,000 for each reduction in a quality-adjusted life-year (QALY) compared to alternatives. Of the 2128 cost-effectiveness ratios from 887 publications, only eight—0.3 percent—were slightly worse but much cheaper. Examples included watchful waiting versus surgical repair of inguinal hernias and percutaneous coronary intervention versus coronary assisted bypass surgery (CABG) in treating coronary artery disease.[54]

Thanks partly to the remarkable progress of medical science, the ideal in modern medicine is treatment and cure. Interventions that fall short of a cure, for example, better management of a chronic condition, are perceived as less than ideal. Worse yet, are treatments that do not rely on the conventional biomedical armamentarium, such as behavioral interventions to prevent or slow the onset of chronic diseases. These behavioral interventions suffer from the perception of inferior quality and consequently have struggled to achieve widespread use.

Chronic diseases such as diabetes are an important driver of healthcare costs. Exercise, diet, weight control, smoking cessation, and other behavioral interventions are widely believed to postpone or prevent the onset of chronic diseases and slow their progression. Evidence from randomized trials supports this belief. In one such trial, lifestyle interventions reduced the incidence of diabetes by nearly 60 percent relative to a placebo.[55] In another trial, monetary incentives proved an effective intervention to help people quit smoking.[56] Type 2 diabetes affects approximately 8 percent of adults in the United States, and smoking is the leading preventable cause of premature death in the United States.[57] Such findings suggest that behavioral interventions have the potential to be an essential tool for lowering healthcare costs.

Despite the potential, some analysts have observed that the healthcare system has been remarkably slow in pursuing behavioral approaches to preventing and treating chronic disease.[58] Historically, healthcare has emphasized treating disease rather than altering behaviors. Payers who willingly reimburse for expensive biomedical therapies with poor cost-effectiveness ratios are reluctant to cover preventative behavioral interventions. Instead, they hold these therapies to a higher standard of effectiveness than biomedical interventions. Federal agencies seem similarly unwilling to invest in new behavioral research. Only 2.5 percent of the National Institutes of Health's research expenditures are devoted to investigating behavioral interventions and their underlying social science.[59]

Research on the Relative Costs and Benefits of Treatments

Any system of health insurance must decide which treatments it will cover. In the absence of data about an intervention's relative costs and benefits, payers will make these decisions arbitrarily or rely on the discretion of providers. We saw in chapter 2 that provider discretion can, under the current institutional arrangements, result in the selection of treatments with low economic value.

Research into treatments' relative costs and benefits is essential for rational decision-making about coverage and reimbursement. The UK recognized this necessity when it established the National Institute for Health and Clinical Excellence (NICE) to conduct cost-benefit research to inform coverage decisions for the National Health Service.

However, in the United States, Medicare is expressly forbidden from using cost-effectiveness in deciding what treatments to cover.[60] Research that compares the benefits of various treatments, such as that supported by the Patient-Centered Outcomes Research Institute (PCORI), suffers no such restriction. However, comparative effectiveness research only compares treatments according to their relative benefits as measured in QALYs. It says little about the cost-effectiveness of treatments.

In contrast to Medicare, commercial insurers in the United States can incorporate evidence of cost-effectiveness in their coverage decision. Given the importance of such data for payers, we might expect to see industrial-scale private sector investments in cost-effectiveness research. However, this sort of private data collection effort has not happened.

Thinking through the incentives of private sector actors can help explain why they devote so little effort and resources to cost-effectiveness studies. Drug or device manufacturers want to finance cost-effectiveness research to the extent that it makes their products more attractive. But sometimes such studies would find their product is less cost-effective than alternatives. While this information creates value for society, it destroys value for the individual manufacturer. Thus the private return of cost-effectiveness research is less than the social value of this knowledge. For this reason, drug manufacturers will not fund cost-effectiveness research at anything close to optimal levels.

Private insurers and other payers care about covering treatment/drugs that patients demand. Unlike drug manufacturers, they don't have a direct financial interest in one or another product. For this reason, the payer's interest in cost-effectiveness research more closely corresponds to society's interests than a drug manufacturer's. Indeed, if there were only one monopoly insurer, payers would have the right incentives to invest in cost-effectiveness research at optimal levels.[61] However, if there are numerous competing payers, the incentives to invest in such research erode, and in perfectly competitive markets, payers' incentives to conduct these studies disappears almost entirely.[62] This conclusion follows because price competition drives premiums down toward marginal cost, and payers would not have the revenues to fund the substantial costs of comparative effectiveness research. In addition, comparative effectiveness studies produce knowledge that benefits payers who do not invest in the research. This leakage of benefits further depresses investment in comparative effectiveness.

In the United States, payers rarely manage their prescription drug programs. Instead, they typically source this function to the pharmacy benefit managers (PBMs) discussed in chapter 2. PBMs have the expertise to conduct or utilize comparative effectiveness research because their core competence is developing and managing lists of covered drugs, called formularies, for their clients. They also have the requisite scale and market share to capture a large portion of the returns to such research. The PBM industry serves more than 266 million Americans and is heavily concentrated, with the top three firms, Express Scripts, OptumRx, and CVS, dominating the industry.[63]

PBMs would seem to have the expertise and scale to profit from comparative effectiveness research, but, as yet, they have so far demonstrated little interest in making such investments. Things may, however, be changing. In August 2018, CVS Caremark announced that it would use estimates of cost-effective pricing set by the independent Institute for Clinical and Economic Review (ICER) to determine whether its formulary will include a particular drug.[64] This announcement is a step in the right direction, but a far cry from the level of investment one would expect based on the need.

Cost-effectiveness research is not, in itself, a cost-reducing innovation. However, it is an indispensable component of the information infrastructure that payers, innovators, and implementers need to create economic value and reduce the cost of care. The low level of investment in such critical infrastructure is a missed opportunity to reduce costs. In chapter 7, we address the need for a more robust information infrastructure to support cost-reducing innovation.

4

Shared Savings

In healthcare, third-party payers pay most of the costs. However, providers, in conjunction with their patients, choose the tests, drugs, and procedures that determine the utilization of resources. Providers and patients do not give much consideration to the costs their decisions impose on payers. They may be less than eager to adopt cost-reducing, new treatment modalities or management methods if the benefits of these changes accrue primarily to payers.[1]

Cost reduction, therefore, hinges on a challenging principal-agent relationship. Payers are the principal in this relationship. They need providers to work with them to lower the cost of delivering care. Providers are the agents who can further the payers' interests by devoting effort and attention to finding ways to reduce costs. However, payers lack the knowledge and information to ensure that providers act as good agents. Agreements that reward providers for reducing costs align the interests of both parties. Economists refer to such agreements as shared savings contracts.

Shared savings contracts in healthcare suffer from three limitations that reduce their prevalence and power: common-agency, capturing future returns, and free riding. These limitations decrease the demand for cost reduction and, consequently, for innovations that lower costs. They are at the heart of the story of missing innovations described in chapter 3.

Common-agency

The eponymous tool for analyzing principal-agent relationships is the principal-agent model.[2] This game-theoretic model produces a powerful result. Even when the principal cannot directly observe the agent's actions—and even when the agent has information and knowledge that the principal lacks—the principal can still rely on incentives to motivate the agent to act in the principal's interests. In other words, these contracts allow people who may not trust or fully understand each other to work together productively.

Why Not Better and Cheaper? James B. Rebitzer and Robert S. Rebitzer, Oxford University Press.
© Oxford University Press 2023. DOI: 10.1093/oso/9780197603109.003.0004

Principal-agent relationships and the accompanying incentive agreements are everywhere in the economy: in one's relationship with one's employer, in relationships between CEOs and shareholders, in the relationships between franchisors and franchisees, and in relationships between sales representatives and their parent companies. As a testament to its significance, the principal-agent model is one of only a handful of formal economic models regularly taught in business management programs.

A familiar example of the principal-agent model arises when selling a home. A typical homeowner may not know much about the market value of their home, may not understand the regulations governing these sales, and may not have effective means of reaching out to potential buyers. Real estate agents offer expertise in these areas. Engaging an agent is a convenient solution for the seller. But how can the homeowner be sure that the realtor will work hard to get them the best price? The answer is to share a fraction of the sales price with the agent. This sales commission provides the incentive that motivates the real estate agent.

One way to give the realtor powerful incentives would be to set the sales commission to 100 percent. Under such an arrangement, the realtor gets all the revenue from selling the house. A rational agent will then work hard enough that the marginal benefit from extra effort equals that effort's marginal cost. Economists call this type of incentive arrangement first-best, because it realizes all the possible economic value in the relationship between the seller and the realtor. The realtor will give the seller a fixed up-front payment in exchange for the right to sell the house at such a generous commission. The distribution of value between buyer and seller will ultimately depend on the fixed up-front payment.

One hundred percent real estate commissions are uncommon. The standard principal-agent model predicts that most principal-agent relationships in real estate and elsewhere involve "second-best" incentives. These second-best incentives give agents only a fraction of the value produced by their additional effort, and so elicit less effort from the agent than first-best arrangements.[3] To understand why a principal might prefer a second-best to a first-best incentive, consider that a 100 percent sales commission creates a considerable risk for the realtor. An unexpectedly good market would be a bonanza, but a lousy market could be a disaster. A risk averse realtor may demand additional payments to mitigate their risk. Lowering sales commissions reduces the realtor's incentives to get the highest possible price for the home. However, it also saves the homeowner money by reducing the realtor's demand for a risk premium. The tradeoff between incentives and risk is a common explanation for the prevalence of second-best incentives in principal-agent relationships.[4]

The principal-agent model predicts that healthcare should be full of second-best incentive contracts in which physicians would share in the cost savings they produce for payers. But this is not what we see when we scan the healthcare landscape. Instead, we often find no shared savings incentives at all.

The most promising explanation for the scarcity of shared savings contracts is the fragmented payment system in the United States. The U.S. healthcare system contains numerous payers, including Medicare and Medicaid, hundreds of private health insurers, and a vast array of self-insured employers. This fragmentation means that an individual physician may have contracts with many different payers. Rather than each physician reacting to the incentives of a single insurer, the physician responds to the totality of incentives implemented by all the payers with whom they have contracts.

A "common-agency" model is appropriate for understanding pay-for-performance in a fragmented healthcare system. In common-agency, multiple principals are trying to influence the behavior of a shared or common agent.[5] Common-agency models have only recently been applied to healthcare, although they have a prior history in other areas of economics. Common-agency models produce a different result than principal-agent models. Introducing multiple payers makes even second-best incentives infeasible. It can, in many cases, lead to no incentive contracts at all.

A thought experiment illuminates the logic of common-agency and illustrates why it changes incentive contracts so dramatically. Consider a physician deciding whether to improve their EHR system by making it interoperable. Improving the system in this way places a burden on the provider. New systems are costly and often require changing workflows, training staff, and other inconveniences. Nonetheless, the physician will invest in such a system if the benefits to them exceed the costs. The complication is that some of the benefits of interoperable electronic health records accrue to others in the healthcare system—often to payers. An interoperable electronic health record system could, for example, make it easier for insurers to track and discourage duplicative testing and low-value treatments and to detect inappropriate referrals to specialists or avoidable emergency room visits. In other words, some of the new system's benefits accrue to the insurer, even though the physician incurs the costs. Sometimes, the benefits to the physician alone are insufficient to warrant the investment, even if the combined benefits to the physician and insurer would make the investment worthwhile. In these circumstances, the physician may forgo the investment.

The principal-agent model suggests a solution: the payer shares a portion of the benefits they receive from the electronic health record system with the physician. If shared savings and direct benefits to the physician exceed the implementation costs, the physician will invest. These incentives will likely be second-best, good enough to cause the physician to invest, and optimal given the incentive costs.

Now imagine that the physician's patient population is equally divided between two payers. When Payer 1 subsidizes the costs of improving the system through shared savings incentives, some of the benefits of the inter-operable system will spill over to Payer 2. Payer 1 is effectively subsidizing benefits that accrue to Payer 2.[6] The best strategy for each payer under these circumstances is to adopt incentives that are even weaker than second-best incentives. Because spillover effects worsen as the payers become more numerous, these "third-best" incentives become more ineffective as the number of payers increases.[7]

In addition, even third-best incentives may become unworkable when the investment requires high fixed costs. In this circumstance, it may not be possible to write any incentive contract at all. We call this unhappy equilibrium a sticking point. The likelihood of sticking points grows as the payer system becomes more fragmented and the fixed costs of responding to incentives rise.[8] This result is significant because most management and system changes involve substantial up-front fixed costs.[9]

Common-agency explains many of the missing innovations discussed in chapter 3. Alternatives to fee-for-service reimbursement, the creation of large integrated practices, adoption of health information technology, moving away from the insurance claims system, and investment in cost-benefit re-search all have spillover effects among multiple payers and significant up-front, fixed-cost investments. Under these conditions, sticking points arise, and payers will fail to create incentives for cost-reducing innovations that they otherwise wish to occur.

Common-agency analysis applies when physicians contract with multiple payers. Patients, however, usually have only one payer at a time. Perhaps so-called consumer-driven health plans—in which patients have powerful incentives to reduce spending—can circumvent common-agency problems.

After all, consumers drive demand for lower-cost goods and services in most sectors of the economy.

Consumer-directed health plans encourage patients to make healthcare decisions like consumers do when they purchase other goods and services. These plans generally share three features: high out-of-pocket expenditures, a tax-advantaged personal spending account, and digital tools to help shop for medical services.[10] Enrollees in consumer-directed health plans tend to have higher income and education levels than enrollees in other types of plans. They also exhibit better self-reported health status and more health-promoting behaviors. The number of consumer-directed health plans is increasing rapidly, from 4 percent of employees in 2006 to 20 percent in 2014.

Spending falls 5–15 percent in the first year of enrollment in consumer-directed health plans, and these reductions may persist into subsequent years. Reductions in spending are largest for enrollees with low or medium health risks.[11] Evidence on the effects of these plans on low-income populations is scarce, as is evidence of their impact on the individual and small-group insurance markets.

Although consumer-directed plans reduce health expenditures in some market segments, various studies raise doubts that the plans turn patients into savvy healthcare consumers. Enrollees don't do much shopping for care or exhibit a keen understanding of the incentives that the plans offer.[12] Evidence from studies of Medicare suggests that the high cost-sharing payments characteristic of consumer-directed plans cause patients to forgo valuable, even life-saving treatments.[13] In addition, providers influence their patients' choices even when patients have incentives to shop and have sophisticated decision tools to help them make choices.[14]

Providers thus remain indispensable partners for payers in reducing the cost of healthcare. Consumer-driven health plans will not substitute for workable shared savings arrangements with providers. Therefore, overcoming the obstacles that stem from common-agency is essential for stimulating cost-reducing innovation. Chapter 7 suggests ways to accomplish this aim.

Capturing Future Returns from Improvements in Health

If a person stops smoking today, her health will likely be better in the future. Among other things, her risk of cancer, cardiovascular disease, and many other ailments will go down. As her risk of illness goes down, so do her expected future expenditures on medical care. The smoking example illustrates a more general point; a rational payer might be willing to spend resources today to save on future medical expenditures. Sometimes these investments may take the form of primary prevention, like smoking cessation and childhood vaccines, which forestalls disease onset. Cost savings can also occur in cases of so-called secondary prevention when early diagnosis and timely treatment can slow the progression of a disease process like diabetes or high blood pressure (hypertension).

A study of the effects of Medicare availability at age 65 on the relative health of the previously uninsured illustrates the importance of spending today to improve health in the future.[15] The study relied on various self-reported health outcomes and events (heart attacks, severe angina, heart failure hospitalizations) as well as measures of hemoglobin A1C, a key indicator of diabetes control.

The study followed a nationally representative sample of adults and compared health outcomes for those continuously insured between ages 55 and 64 to those who were intermittently uninsured during these same ages. The intermittently insured were less healthy than the continuously insured if they had a prior diagnosis of hypertension, heart disease, stroke, or diabetes. Their health declined with age relatively rapidly until they reached age 64. At age 65, something unusual happened. The previously insured and the previously uninsured became eligible for Medicare, and their average health status began to converge. As a result, the health differentials between the previously insured and uninsured under Medicare were much less than if the pre-Medicare trends had continued unchanged. The convergence after age 65, however, was incomplete. Even at age 72, the continuously insured had better outcomes than the intermittently uninsured. This suggests that the benefits of prior insurance persisted for years for chronic diseases like hypertension, heart disease, stroke, and diabetes.

If current spending can improve future health outcomes for people with chronic illness, do payers have sufficient incentives to make these investments? The answer depends partly on the length of the relationship between beneficiaries and their insurer, because it takes time for today's investment to translate into better health. The longer the relationship, the greater the payer's incentives to make such investments.

There is some direct evidence that longer relationships increase the incentives for payers to make investments in health and that these investments result in lower future healthcare costs. In the United States, most commercial insurance is through employers. So one might expect to find longer insurer relationships—and more investments in future health—in jobs with low turnover. If this turnover hypothesis is correct, we should find that workers in jobs with low turnover will have higher medical expenditures while working because their employers are financing investments in future health. We should also find that these workers have lower medical expenditures and better health in retirement as the prior investments in future health pay off.

The study found evidence for both of these propositions.[16] Using Medical Expenditure Survey Data, they observed that workers with longer current job tenure are associated with higher medical expenditures, more doctor visits, and an increased likelihood of employer-sponsored health insurance. Using different data from the Health and Retirement Survey, they also found that retirees who had been in their jobs longer had reduced expenditures on healthcare in retirement.[17]

However, the structure of healthcare insurance markets works against the possibility of long-term relationships. First, employer-based plans through which most Americans receive coverage don't, as a rule, extend into retirement. Private insurers that invest in future health are achieving savings for Medicare, not necessarily for themselves. Second, most employer-based health plans rely on one-year contracts. As people change jobs, they often change insurers. And firms often switch out insurance companies when their contracts are up for renewal.

Why don't insurers implement long-term contracts to make investments in future health more feasible? The challenges of correctly pricing risk over extended periods make such long-term contracts unlikely.

The health risks of an individual, or a group of individuals, can change over time. An obese smoker can lose weight and stop smoking. Or a seemingly healthy person can develop cancer that requires years of costly treatment. Pricing such risks is more straightforward in one-year insurance contracts because annual price negotiations incorporate changes in patient health status. Economists have invented dynamic agreements that can, in theory, mitigate some of these problems for long-term health insurance contracts, but these agreements are complicated financial arrangements that require data that is often not available and so have not caught on in the marketplace.[18]

As with health risks, so with technology risks. New treatments are constantly arising to treat patients. Many of these treatments come with hefty price tags. For example, CAR-T, an immunotherapy that alters a patient's immune cells to attack malignancies, can practically eliminate some forms of treatment-resistant leukemia. It was first used experimentally in a patient in 2010 and was approved by the FDA in 2017. A version was brought to market by the pharmaceutical firm Novartis under the brand name Kymriah at $475,000 per dose. The total cost of treatment with Kymriah may exceed $1 million per case.[19] A long-term health insurance contract will need to incorporate the cost of such unanticipated new technologies into its price. A short-term contract doesn't need to forecast the future in this way.

In most circumstances, a series of short-term agreements with employer-based health plans cannot match the incentives for investment in future health that long-term contracts offer. The cancelation rate of health insurance policies for employer-based insurance is estimated to exceed 20 percent per year. This churn is due to normal employee turnover and to imperfections in the commercial health insurance market that causes employers to regularly switch their insurance plans in search of a better deal.[20] In such a dynamic environment, payers generally are not investing much in long-term health.

Free Riding

Incentives for cost reduction need to be linked to measures of the quality of care delivered.[21] Otherwise, financial incentives might harm patients by rewarding providers for withholding necessary care.

However, quality in healthcare is notoriously hard to measure. Clinical quality measures reflect some combination of actions and luck. Bad luck will cancel out good luck with a large enough sample. However, with a small sample, quality measures cannot reliably distinguish between variations in quality that arise from better care and those that arise from chance.[22]

Individual physicians generally do not have enough patients in their panel to create statistically reliable quality measures. In Medicare, for example, primary care providers have annual median caseloads of 260 Medicare patients. The average primary care physician has a Medicare panel of 25 eligible for mammography screening for breast cancer and 30 with diabetes. With such small numbers of patients, quality measures cannot cancel out the noise. Indeed, the metrics will not reliably detect even a 10 percent improvement in care quality.[23] For Medicare populations, a minimum of 5,000 beneficiaries are required to measure quality meaningfully.[24] An average of 260 Medicare patients per primary care physician implies pooling together performance data from a minimum of 20 physicians.

Pooling individual physicians into groups solves a statistical problem for quality measurement but creates an incentive problem. To see the incentive problem, consider an incentive contract that states that the physicians in the group only get shared savings incentives if they also achieve average group quality targets. In a group of two physicians, the quality measure will be determined by the actions of both physicians. If one physician underperforms, the average quality of the group will likely suffer. In a group of 20 physicians, any individual physician can underperform on quality and not much affect the aggregate measure. The underperforming physician can, in effect, free ride on the efforts of the other 19 group members. Free-riding problems inherent in group-based incentives become more intractable as the number of physicians in the group grows.

One might expect some optimal organizational size to balance the marginal costs from free riding against the marginal benefits of more precise performance measures. It turns out that this intuition is wrong.[25] Increasing the number of providers in a group always makes the organization's incentive problem more severe. The benefits of improved precision in group performance measures are never enough to offset the reduced power of the group incentives.

This result has managerial implications. The principal-agent relationship relies on financial incentives to motivate individual agents. But in healthcare, a payer wanting to share savings with physicians will need to create incentives for groups of doctors rather than individuals. A shared savings program that might be efficient and self-financing for an individual physician may be neither of these things when applied to a group of the requisite size. Financial incentives aimed at groups may influence the priorities of the group's leader whose bonus may be linked to quality targets, but they are not sufficient on their own to motivate individual providers whose actions determine the quality of care.

These management challenges can be seen clearly in accountable care organizations (ACOs), established under the Affordable Care Act to move traditional Medicare away from fee-for-service payments and stimulate similar changes in the private sector. There are currently about 600 ACOs in the United States. The vast majority of these make shared savings payments to a group of providers, and these payments are contingent on the group meeting quality standards. For the statistical reasons we discussed earlier, ACOs may involve hundreds of physicians. On average, they include 179 primary care physicians and 241 specialists. These large numbers mean that the free-riding problem created by group incentives in ACOs is quite severe.[26]

The case of Baystate Health and Pioneer Valley Accountable Care is illustrative.[27] Baystate Health is a large integrated healthcare delivery system in Western Massachusetts. It includes an academic medical center, three community hospitals, and emergency and outpatient facilities. It also owns a health insurer, Health New England, and is part owner of a physician-hospital organization, Baycare Health Partners. Baycare Health Partners employs about 200 physicians and coordinates outpatient medical management activities on behalf of nearly 1,400 participating physicians. It has had considerable previous experience with shared savings incentive contracts by virtue of participation in previous pay-for-performance programs such as Blue Cross of Massachusetts' Alternative Quality Contract. If any health system were primed for success in the operation of ACOs, Baystate Health would seem to be one.

In January 2013, a subsidiary of Baystate Care, Pioneer Valley Accountable Care, formed an ACO and joined Medicare's shared savings program. Under their shared savings contract, Pioneer Valley could share any savings below 2 percent of benchmark costs. Despite Baystate Health's leadership and their own prior experience, Pioneer Valley could not achieve the savings targets and withdrew from the program. In 2016, CMS introduced an alternative accountable care payment model with more risk but easier to achieve savings targets. This time Pioneer Valley Accountable Care was able to generate revenue from shared savings of $4.5 million—a modest success.

It would seem that Pioneer Valley Accountable Care had all the tools to succeed. They had experienced and supportive leadership from Baystate Health, a good data and quality measurement infrastructure, and experience with pay-for-performance contracts and quality measurement. The primary care providers included in the Pioneer Valley Accountable Care were selected because they were open to the concept. Yet, despite these advantages, the transition to an ACO proved very challenging.

The many challenges of shared savings contracts described in this chapter suggest that the motivation to take costs into account when practicing medicine will not come from financial incentives alone. Non-financial motivation is also needed. The next chapter asks if professional and social norms can provide the necessary motivation.

5

Beyond Financial Incentives

In 1995 Diane Meier—a mid-career geriatrician—and a small group of colleagues began working on palliative care at Mount Sinai hospital in New York. Meier and her friends were dissatisfied with conventional medical approaches for the seriously ill, often people suffering from multiple chronic diseases. They saw the need for a new approach that would aim to improve the quality of life for these patients through anticipating, preventing, and treating their suffering. The palliative care model they developed involves a specialized team of doctors, nurses, and other providers who work closely with the patient's other physicians. The palliative care team are experts in managing physical and emotional symptoms, including complex pain, depression, anxiety, fatigue, shortness of breath, constipation, nausea, loss of appetite, and difficulty sleeping. They also help patients and families articulate their goals and priorities, align their treatment plans with these goals, and coordinate plans among all the providers caring for the patient. In contrast to hospice care, which is reserved for the last few months of life and requires patients to forego curative treatment, palliative care is appropriate at any age and any stage in a serious illness and can be offered alongside curative treatment.[1]

Private sector philanthropic organizations funded Meier's initial work on palliative care. In 1999, the Robert Wood Johnson Foundation provided money to Meier and her colleagues to start the Center to Advance Palliative Care (CPAP), devoted to taking the palliative care model from the fringes of clinical practice to the medical mainstream.[2]

Today, palliative care is regarded as a success story—even as a model—for how innovation in clinical practice can take root and flourish. Starting from near zero in the 1990s, more than 70 percent of hospitals with 50 beds or more now have a palliative care program, rising to more than 90 percent for hospitals larger than 300 beds. More than 80 percent of hospitalized patients in the United States are in hospitals with a palliative care team. In 2008, palliative care was recognized as a medical subspecialty, and thousands of physicians, nurses, other health professionals have been certified in the

Why Not Better and Cheaper? James B. Rebitzer and Robert S. Rebitzer, Oxford University Press.
© Oxford University Press 2023. DOI: 10.1093/oso/9780197603109.003.0005

field.[3] In recognition of her contributions to the advancement of palliative care in the United States, Diane Meier was awarded a MacArthur Foundation Fellowship, a "genius award," in 2008.

Advocates for palliative care claim that in addition to improving the quality of life for patients and families, palliative care also reduces the cost of care.[4] But palliative care is not on the list of missing innovations mentioned in chapter 3, despite facing the same headwinds as those innovations. In Meier's words, "That palliative care has grown and thrived squarely in the context of the current fragmented and irrationally financed health care marketplace is instructive. The palliative care movement has proven that change is possible, even now, amid a broken health care system."[5]

Meier likens her approach to advancing palliative care to a political campaign.[6] She assembled a multi-disciplinary team with expertise in fields such as social marketing, public policy, and business analysis. She paid careful attention to messaging for each of the main groups with a stake in palliative care: patients, providers, hospitals, and philanthropies. For patients, this meant framing palliative care as "relief without giving up." For physicians who refer patients to the palliative care team, a palliative care consultation was positioned as a way to help doctors manage their most time-consuming patients more efficiently while also providing optimal care. For hospital executives, palliative care was justified as a way to avoid unnecessary costs and improve quality. For philanthropists, palliative care was described as a logical response to the healthcare financing crisis brought on by an aging population suffering from high levels of chronic disease. Coalitions were built with academic medicine and representatives of "organized medicine," such as the Joint Commission, the National Quality Forum, the American Hospital Association, and the American Cancer Society. Allies introduced palliative care into nursing and medical training and eventually achieved formal recognition of palliative care as a medical subspecialty.[7]

Meier believes that the palliative care model illustrates many of the general features of a successful innovation: it is better than the status quo, compatible with existing systems and processes, easy to understand, can be tested and refined in small pilots, produces measurable results, and can be expanded on a broad scale. The palliative care movement has also benefited from other factors, such as enlightened leadership, robust technical support, and substantial philanthropic contributions.

Palliative care is an example of the power of non-financial incentives to spur innovation in healthcare. As Meier puts it, "Despite poor reimbursement and physically and emotionally arduous workdays, palliative care has attracted growing numbers of young and mid-career health professionals because the work restores the fundamental impulses of health care professionals to pride of place."[8]

Nonfinancial incentives influence behavior in several ways. First, they introduce ethical duties and obligations into decision-making. The palliative care movement, as Meier suggests, draws inspiration and energy from the ethical commitment of the healthcare professions to healing.

Second, non-financial incentives can alter the meaning that people assign to financial incentives and thereby change the response to these incentives. Meier and her colleagues were careful to distinguish palliative care from hospice care partly because hospice care is a defined benefit that is reimbursable under Medicare. They wanted to ensure that palliative care was perceived as a way to improve patient care and not as a "grab" for additional fee-for-service revenue. A financial motivation, they reasoned, might work against acceptance of the palliative care model.

Third, non-financial incentives bring the opinions of others into the decision-making process—often through social and professional standards of behavior. The recognition of palliative care as a medical subspecialty and its integration into the training programs of physicians, nurses, and other health professionals legitimizes the establishment of palliative care teams in hospitals and the choice to refer patients to those teams.

Fourth, non-financial incentives rely less on market forces than on narratives, compelling stories that people tell each other about how the world works or ought to work. Meier and her colleagues artfully reinterpreted the modern medical narrative to emphasize both curing disease and the relief of suffering. Reframing the narrative in this way created an opening for the palliative care model.

In the remainder of this chapter, we illustrate how non-financial incentives influence behavior in healthcare, how they interact with financial incentives, and what conditions are needed for non-financial incentives to stimulate innovations.

Ethics and Incentives

In 2017 there were approximately 750,000 end-stage renal disease (ESRD) cases in the United States.[9] ESRD is a serious and often deadly illness for which the only definitive treatment is kidney transplantation. Mortality statistics give a rough sense of the advantages of transplants. Adjusted all-cause mortality for ESRD patients on dialysis in 2017 was 165 per 1,000 patient-years, more than five times higher than the mortality rate for ESRD patients who received a transplant.[10]

In the United States in 2017, approximately 21,000 kidney transplants were performed. On December 21, 2017, the active transplant waiting list had nearly 50,000 candidates. The number needing transplants far exceeded the available supply of kidneys. The supply of donor kidneys comes from both deceased and living donors, but in 2017, living donors accounted for only about 30 percent of kidneys transplanted.[11]

For an economist, the suffering caused by the shortage of kidneys has an obvious solution: set up a well-regulated market that compensates living donors for providing a kidney. Since donors can live healthy lives with only one kidney, market-based compensation could stimulate an additional supply of organs for transplantation at an equilibrium price that (in the absence of gross market failures) maximizes social value.

What seems self-evident to economists is not nearly so obvious to policymakers. The United States does not currently have a market for kidneys, and U.S. law forbids selling organs for transplantation.[12] The United States is not alone in this policy decision. Indeed, no country in the world, except for Iran, has implemented a market-based solution to the problem of kidney donation.

A remarkable study investigates why markets for kidneys do not enjoy widespread public support.[13] The authors conducted a structured survey of more than 2,600 adult residents of the United States about their opinions about a paid-donor system for kidney transplants. The sample roughly matched the adult U.S. population's age, gender, education, and ethnicity. Survey participants were randomly assigned to give their assessment of alternative kidney procurement and allocation systems.

The alternatives presented in the study varied along several dimensions (including the amount of compensation, whether recipients or a public agency paid donors, and the rules governing compensation). Respondents saw five different scenarios. Each scenario differed in its supposed effect on the supply of kidneys, from almost no impact to meeting 100 percent of organ demand. Respondents indicated their support for the paid-donor system in each scenario compared to the current system.

The study found that average support for legalizing kidney markets increased markedly with the number of additional transplants the system enabled, but this average masked a notable finding. Only about one-fifth of the respondents' attitudes shifted in response to the impact of the paid-donor system on kidney supply.

The survey also asked respondents to assess the paid-donor system ethically. Specifically, did the system raise concerns about exploitation, free choice, undue influence, fairness (for donors or patients), or human dignity? On average, respondents did have ethical concerns, but these moderated if the system yielded more transplants. However, some respondents—those with the most strongly held views in favor or against the proposal—did not vary their ethical assessments as the number of transplants increased.[14]

These results help explain why the economist's self-evident solution to kidney shortages has gained so little traction. Some people simply do not assess the prospect of a market for organs based on the number of additional kidneys that would be made available for transplant. For these people, opposition to a kidney market is not a matter of costs and benefits. It is a matter of ethical commitment. Increasing the incentive in the scenarios—the number of kidneys available for needy recipients—does not change their opposition to the proposed market. The example of markets for kidneys illustrates a general feature of the interaction between ethical commitments and incentives. When an incentive conflicts with a moral commitment, people who firmly hold that commitment are less likely to respond to the incentive, regardless of its magnitude.

Physicians and other healthcare providers operate under compelling ethical obligations to care for their patients. As is true in kidney markets, these obligations alter the usual economic calculus of comparing the costs and benefits of actions. Ethical reasoning may cause providers to ignore financial incentives to reduce costs if the actions they reward conflict with their moral obligations to patients. Cost-reducing innovations may similarly be unwelcome in this context—unless the innovations align with the caring mission in other ways.

Ethics and Corporate Governance

In his classic study *The Social Transformation of American Medicine*, Paul Starr details a long battle by physicians to retain control over the organizations that employ them and to resist subordination to corporations.[15] Others have documented related conflicts over governance.[16]

Physician opposition to corporate control over the organizations that employ them is puzzling—at least from the perspective of the conventional economic approach to corporate governance. According to the standard theory of corporate governance, taught to countless aspiring managers in MBA programs, the managers of corporations work for shareholders. They are obliged to make decisions that are in the interest of shareholders. Shareholders, in turn, want to maximize the value of their firm. Individual shareholders may have ethical concerns, they may donate to charity or care about the environment, but these values can and should be distinct from the task of maximizing shareholder value.[17] The conventional governance theory predicts that it should make no difference to physicians whether they work for corporate entities owned by shareholders or for organizations owned and controlled by physicians. In both cases, managers will take the same actions—the actions that maximize shareholder value.

But what if shareholder value and ethical concerns cannot be separated? Does acting in the interests of shareholders require managers to discard the shareholder's ethical concerns? Imagine an energy company choosing between investments in highly profitable but environmentally damaging oil production or less profitable solar power. Will environmentally concerned shareholders instruct managers to maximize shareholder value by investing in oil? Or will they sacrifice some shareholder value for their environmental concerns?

These questions are the subject of a theoretical study of corporate decision-making that turns the standard doctrine on its head.[18] In most cases, shareholders will not set aside their ethical commitments when choosing between oil and solar power, for example. Sufficiently motivated owners would instruct managers to invest in environmentally friendly solar power because the extra profits from oil do not fully compensate them for their aversion to the social harm from pollution. Less environmentally attuned owners, in contrast, might instruct managers to maximize shareholder value by investing in oil production.

A second point about ethics and governance also emerges from this analysis. Individuals care about the social harms resulting from their actions to the extent that they feel responsible for the activity that caused the damage. Thus, people opposed to littering may not feel compelled to pick up trash they find on the sidewalk. Littering is a sin of commission for which the litterer is directly responsible. Failing to pick up the garbage left by others is a sin of omission. Sins of commission carry the greater moral weight.

This issue of personal responsibility explains why corporations may disregard the ethical concerns of shareholders. Environmentally aware shareholders may favor their company adopting lower profit solar energy over higher profit oil production. However, because the individual investors are not directly responsible for the action causing the environmental harm, they may not feel the same aversion to the resulting environmental damage. This feature of moral judgment can impart an "amoral drift" to the decision-making of corporations such that value maximization wins out over ethical concerns.

This analysis implies that the medical profession's long resistance to corporate control matters for reasons that the standard doctrine overlooks. Anonymous corporate shareholders who feel little personal responsibility for the care of patients may introduce amoral drift into the strategic choices of healthcare systems. By virtue of their training and professional ethics, physicians likely feel a more personal responsibility for healthcare decisions—even for patients who are not their own—than do standard-issue shareholders. For this reason, an organization governed by physician leaders may be less likely to maximize profits at the expense of patient welfare. Physicians may be more receptive to cost-reducing innovations in such organizations than in other organizational settings.[19]

However, physicians' ethical commitments are not limited to concerns about patient welfare. Physicians also place great moral value on preserving their professional autonomy. Physician-led organizations may be willing to pass up value-creating and cost-reducing innovations if these threaten their professional independence. We return to this issue in a discussion of retail clinics in chapter 6.

Money and Markets

Conventional economics assumes that money and markets are neutral instruments for facilitating the exchange of goods and services. But non-economists don't always see things that way. Exchanges that are otherwise unobjectionable can become noxious when cash changes hands.

Organ donation again provides a helpful illustration. The U.S. system makes it illegal to exchange money for organs, but it does not prohibit other forms of organ exchange. For example, a barter exchange in which a patient with an incompatible donor exchanges a kidney with another mismatched patient-donor pair is commonplace and acceptable.[20] However, bartering in this way is less efficient than a purely monetary transaction because it requires a "double coincidence of wants." In this case, patient A's willing donor B must match patient C, while patient C's ready donor D must be a match for A. Why are these cumbersome barter exchanges morally and legally acceptable, but more efficient monetary transactions are not?

Philosophers suggest that four ethical criteria are central for assessing the morality of markets and monetary transactions.[21] The first criterion is "weak agency." Weak agency occurs when participants in the transaction have inadequate information and so are either uninformed or must rely on others to act as their agents. Weak agency might affect kidney exchanges to the extent that donors are poorly equipped to spot unfair or deceptive practices by their counterparties.

The second criterion is "vulnerability." Vulnerability arises when the thing in question is desperately needed or when the parties to an exchange have highly unequal needs for the goods/services being exchanged. Incorporating money into kidney donation raises questions of vulnerability—effectively coercing the poor into mutilating their bodies for the benefit of the rich. The possibilities for such coercion increase if organ donations could be used to repay outstanding debts or tax obligations.

The third and fourth criteria relate to when the transaction could result in "extreme harms for individuals" or "extreme harms for society." Harm for individuals refers to transactions that could result in destitution or other severe degradation of human welfare. In the context of kidney donation, concerns about individual harm may arise to the degree that the donation presents risks to the donor's health.

Harm to society refers to transactions that promote servility and dependence or undermine democratic governance and the values on which democracy depends. Permitting financial gain in exchanging organs or body parts risks turning a person into an object, violating their dignity as human beings. The widespread sale of body parts could contribute to a humiliating subordination of the poor to the privileged and undermine the possibility of a society of equals.

Weak agency, vulnerability, and the risks of extreme harm to individuals and society are pervasive in healthcare. One can see these issues in disparate and contentious matters such as abortion, birth control, euthanasia, ownership and use of genetic data, health insurance reform, and healthcare information privacy. Indeed, healthcare is a minefield of potentially repugnant markets and monetary exchanges. In such an ethically fraught environment, cost-reducing innovations that rely on financial incentives and market forces may be regarded as unacceptable, like markets for body parts. Consumers and voters can and do oppose cost-reducing innovations they consider morally repugnant. Such opposition played a significant role in the reaction against managed care organizations in the 1990s. To illustrate the state of public opinion, surveys conducted during this period reported that more than two-thirds of Americans believed that managed care organizations would hold back on a child's cancer treatment. Majorities saw the money saved by managed care as helping insurance companies earn more profits and allowing employers to pay less for health insurance. Just under half believed that cost savings would make healthcare more affordable for people like themselves.[22]

Monetary Rewards and Social Motives

Vaccine development is a costly and lengthy three-phase process. The most expensive and time-consuming part of the process is Phase 3, during which researchers give the vaccine to volunteers and compare outcomes between those who receive the vaccine and those who receive a placebo. This phase requires the participation of many thousands of people who have been exposed to the pathogen.

In the first year of the COVID-19 epidemic, speeding up Phase 3 trials by even a few months was a matter of life and death. One way to accelerate the process was through challenge trials. These are trials in which study participants volunteer to be infected with the virus under tightly controlled conditions. The website 1Day Sooner recruited tens of thousands of willing volunteers to participate in a challenge study.[23]

These volunteers were prepared to risk their health to accelerate vaccine development. Their motives were altruistic; no payment was involved. In the language of social scientists, these volunteers exhibited "prosocial" preferences. Prosocial motives are easy to find in our society. They inspire people to donate kidneys, make charitable contributions, and engage in such public service as joining the military or the Peace Corps. A long-standing debate in the social sciences asks whether monetary compensation and market exchanges strengthen or weaken prosocial motives.[24]

Conventional economic theory offers a clear answer to this question. People with strong social motives would continue to participate because they would be made no worse off by getting some money in their pockets. People with weaker social motives might also volunteer because the compensation makes it worth their while. From this perspective, prosocial and financial motives are separable. Both are ways of motivating participation, and neither approach alters the efficacy of the other.

But what if prosocial and financial motives are not separable? Suppose the original group of volunteers for challenge trials wanted to signal to themselves and others that their motives were altruistic and not self-serving. Monetary compensation can obscure such a signal and thus reduce motivation to participate. In this case, financial incentives would "crowd out" social motives, and the supply of altruistic volunteers would be lower than it would have been without the incentives. Alternatively, monetary incentives can reinforce public perception of the urgency and importance of a challenge trial and, in this way, lead to greater altruism. Financial incentives are said to "crowd in" prosocial motives when this happens.

Anyone who has spent time as a patient knows that healthcare depends on providers' intrinsic, prosocial motivations to care for their patients. If monetary incentives crowd out these intrinsic motivations, well-intended efforts to reward providers for higher-value care may have unintended consequences for the quality and cost of care. Alternatively, if financial incentives can enhance the intrinsic motivations of providers, then they are a tool to be embraced.

The empirical evidence for crowding in versus crowding out is mixed. For example, some advocates argue that paying for blood donors discourages altruistic motivations and reduces the quantity and quality of the blood supply. Indeed, many analysts use the case of blood donation as the primary real-world example of crowding out.[25] The positions of the World Health Organization and other blood collection agencies are that economic incentives to donors are detrimental to the quantity and quality of blood supplied. Surveys and lab experiments find that respondents are generally opposed to receiving money for donating blood. However, field experiments find that economic rewards have significant and positive effects on blood donation with no observed adverse safety effects.[26] For example, a $10 gift card increased blood donations to blood drives in the United States by 7 percentage points over a baseline donation rate of 13 percent.[27]

These field experiments offer valuable empirical insights into the practicality of financial incentives to elicit blood donations, but they do not settle the issue of separability. Evaluating separability empirically requires a carefully controlled lab environment in which one can measure the degree to which the introduction of prosocial motives changes the expected response to financial incentives. One study reviewed the results of over 100 such experiments involving over 26,000 subjects from 36 countries.[28] All the experiments took place in stylized environments where game-theoretic models could predict the experimental subjects' choices without social motives.[29] The review found evidence of crowding in or crowding out in all of the experiments they reviewed—soundly rejecting the separability assumption. The sheer number of independent experiments in the study increases confidence in this finding. The authors speculate that the relationship between financial incentives and prosocial motives is determined by three considerations: the purpose of the incentive, the social acceptability of the incentive, and the degree to which the incentive undermines the intrinsic pleasure people derive from doing things of their own volition.

Chapter 4 argued that the statistical limitations of quality measurement in healthcare require financial incentives for cost reduction to be directed to groups of physicians rather than to individual physicians. We saw how this measurement issue raises a management challenge: motivating individual physicians to respond to group incentives. We can now see that the answer to this challenge is to activate the prosocial motives of individual physicians. Given that financial incentives and prosocial motives are not separable, the group's financial incentives must align with the deeply held cultural precepts of the practice of medicine. In addition, the organizational culture must clarify how these group incentives translate into the actions of individual physicians so that the intrinsic value of the work is honored. Only a handful of healthcare organizations, including exemplars such as the Permanente Medical Groups and Intermountain Healthcare, have successfully met these requirements. Such success is years in the making and requires exceptional leaders, particularly physician leaders. We return to these topics at greater length in chapter 7.

This line of thinking suggests that the questions typically asked about incentives—"how much" and "for what"—may not be sufficient for understanding how incentives work. These questions focus on what people get for undertaking actions. But the research on crowding in and crowding out of prosocial motives suggests that people want to do more than get things in exchange for their efforts. People also want to be someone—both in their own eyes and in the eyes of their peers. These motivations are particularly salient in healthcare, shaped as it is by powerful professional identities. We take up the role of professional identities in the next section.

Social Norms and Social Comparisons

A famous New Yorker cartoon from 2011 depicts two businessmen relaxing over drinks in a corporate jet. One says to the other, "I would happily pay more in taxes if somebody made me." This caption neatly captures how social comparisons and social identity alter conventional economic decision-making. If the businessman was happy to pay more taxes, why didn't he do so? If the government forced him to pay more taxes, why be happy about it? The answer, of course, is that the businessman is so wealthy that he doesn't care much about the taxes per se. Instead, he wants to be seen as savvy in the eyes of his peers. Canny operators don't pay any more in taxes than they must. As a candidate for president of the United States, Donald Trump affirmed this attitude when he responded to accusations that he had evaded taxes by proclaiming, "that makes me smart."

The traditional economic view of motivation emphasizes individual preferences as the basis for decision-making. But, in situations where group identity matters, group comparisons and norms enter into the calculation along with personal preferences.[30]

Consider an apparently frivolous example—norms against men wearing skirts. Like many gender norms, this norm is descriptive (men don't wear skirts) and prescriptive (men ought not to wear skirts). The conviction that men ought not to wear a skirt can create discomfort for others who abide by gender dress norms, and these onlookers may respond negatively—perhaps with harsh derision or social exclusion. If social ridicule and exclusion are severe enough, even men who would choose on their own to wear skirts will not wear them.[31]

The prescriptive aspect of norms can matter for healthcare decisions just as it can for dress style. For example, Ozarks Healthcare in Missouri is reported to have created a "private setting" for COVID-19 vaccinations to protect vaccine recipients from ridicule and exclusion by their vaccine-hesitant neighbors.[32] Like patients, physicians are not immune from the prescriptive aspect of norms. Consider, for example, a setting where physicians can save valuable time, improve quality, and reduce costs by handing over some parts of clinical decision-making to an artificial intelligence algorithm. Traditionally physicians place great store on the autonomous practice of the "art" of medicine. Ceding decision-making to an algorithm might benefit the physician, but group norms and social comparisons also impose costs on first-movers. Physicians, like other people, feel better about their identity and gain the approbation of others when their actions match prescriptive group norms. Deviations from such norms, on the other hand, can expose them to unfavorable social comparisons. Early algorithm adoption might cause others to believe that the physician views her judgment as insufficient or flawed. For this reason, a physician seeking the respect of her peers might avoid the algorithm even if the net benefits of the new technology were positive. Leaders of leading healthcare delivery organizations have noted this sort of peer-based resistance to change.[33]

The logic of social norms and social comparison also suggests that it will be easier for physicians to adopt a new technology or treatment if they know that other professionals they respect endorse the innovation. The extensive use of "key opinion leaders," or KOLs, by drug and device makers to promote the adoption of their products is evidence of the power of social comparisons and norms to encourage adoption. KOLs are well-respected and well-established physicians whose endorsement signals that the drug or device is well within the mainstream of professional practice.

Social norms and comparisons have also been used to encourage clinical practices that improve the value of care. These efforts provide physicians with data that compares their practice patterns with those of their peers. Unfortunately, the reported results of these interventions are mixed.[34] Many factors play a role in determining the efficacy of social norms and comparisons, including the choice of a reference group, the degree of medical uncertainty associated with the point of comparison, and how the comparison itself is constructed and reported.[35]

As motivators, social identity and comparisons are double-edged swords. They can serve to either augment or reduce support for innovation. Which way they work depends in part on understandings that are shaped early in clinical training, a topic to which we return in chapter 7.

Narratives

In a provocative book, Nobel prize-winning economist Robert Shiller argues that the trajectory of an economy is driven by more than economic fundamentals.[36] Economic narratives, by which he means compelling stories about how the world works, also matter.

Narratives can build upon popular beliefs, but they can also refer to stories shared among communities of professionals. These professional narratives may have a grounding in evidence, but their influence also derives from their emotional resonance. The skill and charisma of intellectual entrepreneurs who promote one narrative or another help determine which narratives become dominant. As they spread, professional narratives shape the profession's sense of what is known and knowable. Narratives make some issues and problems appear highly salient and make other questions appear less compelling, less legitimate, and less worthy of exploration. Narratives can also influence which behaviors, activities, and attitudes become group norms.

The dominant narratives in healthcare celebrate the curing of disease through biomedical intervention. In these narratives, the heroes discover new treatments for dread diseases, but they give short shrift to innovators that find ways to deliver care more efficiently. Best-selling books detail the life stories of leaders in the fight against cancer and heart disease.[37] In contrast, the story of Sidney Garfield—the inventor of prepaid group medical practice and one of the innovators who founded Kaiser Permanente—is little known outside of that organization.

Narratives can shape the direction of innovation. The sustained, accelerating wave of technological innovation that made the Industrial Revolution a transformative event in world history began with a shift in the narrative surrounding science and innovation that took place from 1500 to 1700 among a small elite of physicians, philosophers, engineers, and artisans.[38] The new narrative built on the then-novel idea that society could and should be enriched by carefully studying natural phenomena and applying this knowledge in practical ways to economic transactions and production. Cultural entrepreneurs such as Francis Bacon refined and promoted this narrative. It proved to be contagious, inspiring a transnational "republic of letters" that emanated from Bacon's belief in gathering, collating, and disseminating knowledge through planned and cooperative scientific research. Within this network of scientists and scholars, norms and new incentives developed. Scientific knowledge was contestable. It was subject to challenge. The idea was to use evidence, experiment, logic, and persuasion to resolve disputes without appealing to political or religious authority. Members of the republic of letters were obliged to truthfully place new knowledge and information in the public domain. They measured success by original contributions to new knowledge as acknowledged by peers.

One can see today the influence of narratives on the direction of innovation. "Moore's Law"—the notion that the number of transistors on integrated circuits doubles roughly every two years—has enshrined the idea that cost and quality can progress rapidly, in tandem, and seemingly without end. Similarly, the narrative of established firms displaced by innovative startups has sustained the venture capital industry through many boom-and-bust cycles.

There are signs that the narratives in healthcare may be shifting. Brent James, the visionary practitioner of measuring and standardizing clinical processes to improve their value to patients, has been the subject of a celebrity profile in the New York Times.[39] Atul Gawande, a respected surgeon, public health researcher, government official and best-selling author, writes popular books and articles promoting cost reduction and celebrating efficient delivery of healthcare.

The Right Conditions

Diane Meier and the palliative care movement have shown that non-financial motivations can promote valuable innovations under the right conditions. This chapter suggests some of these conditions. Innovations are more readily accepted when aligned with ethical commitments and professional obligations. Such innovations are more easily implemented by organizations that providers and patients trust to prioritize healing over financial interests. Nonfinancial motivators are particularly important when market transactions and financial payouts are perceived as morally repugnant. In settings where financial incentives are in regular use, assessing whether they crowd prosocial motives in or out is essential. Finally, social comparisons, norms, and narratives can be powerful motivators—but depending on circumstances, they can promote either change or resistance to change.

As crucial as non-financial incentives can be in healthcare, they are not substitutes for financial incentives. As Meier has noted, palliative care will not be on a secure foundation as long as it relies on philanthropic financing.[40] Our current fee-for-service payment system—skewed toward higher reimbursement for procedure-based specialties—is unlikely to provide that foundation.

Moreover, norms and narratives do not operate in a vacuum. They play out in a broader moral context shaped by our cultural, social, and political institutions. In the United States, this context includes a fundamental and unresolved question about healthcare. Is healthcare a shared social good to which all are entitled, like education, or is it a conventional private good like the other goods and services we purchase daily?[41] Without agreement on this question, the ethical duty of healthcare professionals to wisely manage healthcare resources is unclear. The responsibility of citizens to subsidize care for the sick and the poor is likewise unclear. The absence of moral clarity undermines non-financial motives to create value and to control costs. Under these circumstances, innovations may be greeted with indifference or contempt by providers, patients, and the general public.

6

Competition, Innovation, and Disruption

Heart attacks (myocardial infarctions or MIs) are common and life-threatening medical events. Three treatments are highly effective—and highly cost effective—following heart attacks: aspirin, beta-blockers, and reperfusion therapy to restore blood flow. However, not all hospitals have put these innovations into practice to the same degree. Hospitals with the greatest propensity to use these innovations experience survival rates nearly 3 percentage points higher than hospitals in the bottom 20 percent of adopters, a very significant difference statistically and one that matters greatly to patients.[1]

Why have some hospitals been slow in adopting these lifesaving and cost-reducing treatments? And why didn't competition from more nimble hospitals force the laggards to change their practices more quickly or go out of business altogether?

The conventional answer to this question emphasizes information. Quality of healthcare is difficult to measure—even for experts. Third-party payers bear most of the costs of care, so these costs are hard for physicians and patients to track directly. If valuable information about quality and cost is hard to obtain, competition will not do a good job allocating market share to the best providers.

However, these information challenges do not necessarily stop the market from rewarding superior performers. For example, a study examined hospital performance in treating Medicare patients for heart attacks, congestive heart failure, pneumonia, and a common set of surgical procedures—hip and knee replacements.[2] For these conditions, which together account for nearly one-fifth of Medicare hospital spending, higher-performing hospitals tended to have a larger and more rapidly growing market share. So it appears that enough of the information needed to reward superior hospitals can flow through healthcare markets—notwithstanding the difficulties in acquiring that information.

In this chapter, we argue for an alternative explanation for the failure of healthcare markets to spur valuable innovations. Our explanation

Why Not Better and Cheaper? James B. Rebitzer and Robert S. Rebitzer, Oxford University Press.
© Oxford University Press 2023. DOI: 10.1093/oso/9780197603109.003.0006

emphasizes the effect of market competition on the incentives to innovate. Implementing new processes and business models entails costly disruptions to otherwise profitable operations. These disruptions, known as switchover disruptions, dampen the incentives to innovate because during the transition to the new way of doing business profits from the old way are reduced or disappear altogether. All else equal, switchover disruptions are especially costly for dominant incumbent firms because their market power allows them to run highly profitable operations. The net result is that dominant firms experience a kind of stagnation. Innovations are welcome only if they fit nicely with how these profitable incumbents already operate.[3] In contrast, for competitors trying to enter a new market, switchover disruptions do not upend profitable ongoing operations. The returns to innovation for new entrants are, all else equal, higher, which gives these firms a greater incentive to innovate than incumbents. However, if hungry new entrants are blocked from entering the market, stagnant incumbents will feel free to disregard disruptive innovations.

We illustrate the relationship between market power, switchover costs, and innovation with examples from industries far removed from healthcare. We then show that dominant firms with market power and high switchover disruptions are widespread in the health sector, as are a variety of barriers to the entry of new firms. Our analysis suggests that we can increase demand for value-enhancing and cost-reducing innovations by making healthcare markets more open to new firms and less protective of incumbents.[4] We discuss the policy implications of this conclusion in chapter 7.

Market Power, Switchover Disruptions, and Innovation

Northern Minnesota's Mesabi Range supplied iron ore to the great steel-producing centers in Pittsburgh, Cleveland, Chicago, and Gary for generations. The easy transport of this ore down Lake Michigan and Lake Erie gave the mines of the Mesabi a dominant position in the U.S. market for iron ore from the late 1800s through the 1970s.

In the early 1980s, things changed dramatically. The mines faced unexpected competition from Brazilian producers who could deliver iron ore at much lower prices. The Mesabi mines responded to these competitive pressures by altering their production processes to sharply increase productivity and reduce the unit cost of Mesabi iron ore.[5] A big part of this change involved investments in new work practices that increased labor productivity and kept machines working for a larger fraction of each day.

The dramatic fall in unit costs precipitated by the threat of competition from Brazil did not result from some new scientific discovery or technological breakthrough. The innovations had been available to the Mesabi mines long before they were adopted. The Mesabi mines chose to adopt these innovations—and incur the costs of angering their unions, who had insisted on processes and work rules to protect the interests of their members—because their dominant market position came under threat from the Brazilian mines.[6]

The story of the Mesabi iron mines raises the question of the relationship between market power and innovation. Does market power make a firm more likely or less likely to innovate? This question has been the subject of a long-running economic debate, sometimes called the Arrow-Schumpeter debate, after its two most famous contributors.[7]

Joseph Schumpeter, coiner of the phrase "creative destruction," argued that monopoly could stimulate innovation.[8] Looking around, one can find examples to support Schumpeter's view—cutting-edge new products and processes often seem to emerge from large firms with considerable market power. Bell Labs, the famous research department of the old AT&T telephone monopoly—which pioneered such breakthrough innovations as the transistor—is the paradigm for this side of the debate.[9]

However, in the early 1960s, Nobel prize-winning economist Kenneth Arrow argued that firms with market power are a drag on innovation. To see Arrow's argument, consider that the incentive to innovate is the difference between the profits earned with an innovation and profits made without it. An incumbent firm with market power starts with high profits, so incentives for innovation must clear a higher bar to entice investment. Put differently, the innovation only becomes attractive to the incumbent firm once it has replaced the original high profits.[10] Due to this "replacement effect," monopoly power weakens incentives to adopt innovations.

Arrow's replacement effect can explain the Mesabi mine's long period of indifference to innovation. However, it cannot explain their sudden and rapid embrace of new production methods under threat from the Brazilians. To account for this change, one must consider the incentives to innovate when failure to do so threatens the incumbent firm's dominant position. Under such a threat, firms with market power have more powerful incentives to adopt innovations than potential new rivals. The higher the incumbent's profits, the greater incentive it has to preempt competitors by adopting the new technology before they can. This argument overturns Arrow's "replacement" effect. Firms with market power facing a threat to their dominant position ought to be a wellspring of innovation.[11]

But this reasoning does not settle the matter. History is full of instances where incumbents fail to respond effectively to threats to their market dominance. Why are such firms sometimes sluggish but at other times highly aggressive innovators? What was it about the nature of competition from the Brazilian mines, for example, that stimulated successful innovation by the Mesabi mines after years of stasis?

The answer rests in part with switchover disruptions. This term refers to the transitory disturbances to otherwise profitable operations when firms phase in innovations. Such disruptions are significant in many economic sectors, and, as we shall see, they play a prominent role in the health sector.

Firms with market power fear losing their high profits and spend heavily on innovations that preserve their dominant position. The same economic logic gives such firms powerful incentives to avoid new technologies that bring temporary disruptions to profitable operations. These disruptions become more costly with the degree of market power the firm has.[12]

You can see the influence of switchover disruptions in the case of the Mesabi iron mines. The miners' unions could have disrupted production in many ways if the company tried to adopt new production methods and work rules perceived as anti-union. Anticipating the costs of these switchover disruptions, the mining companies did not press the issue. However, the existential threat posed by Brazilian mines significantly reduced the odds that the union would slow production and thereby lose well-paid jobs to foreign competition. Suddenly, the expected cost of switchover disruptions decreased, and the iron mines' incentives to adopt cost-reducing innovations increased.

Switchover disruptions are not limited to union work actions. They occur whenever innovations require new production processes or novel organizational capacities. There is inevitably a phase-in period when firms struggle to make new products, processes, or services work. These struggles can lead to sharply higher production costs or dramatic drops in productivity, which can upend profitable operations for some time. The higher the markups large dominant firms enjoy, the more they will lose from the phase-in period.

The introduction of the iPhone in January 2007 illustrates the switchover disruptions accompanying innovative new products. At the time of Apple's introduction of the iPhone, the dominant incumbents in the mobile phone market were Nokia, Sony-Ericsson, Motorola, and Blackberry. These firms became dominant because they could refine and perfect a mobile phone that combined voice, text communication, and email. The iPhone used similar components to those found in other mobile phones but combined them in different ways to achieve a new purpose—a handheld computer capable of running various apps using a touch screen. Scholars of innovation refer to this as an architectural innovation because it focuses less on improving the capabilities of individual components and more on changing how the components interact with each other. In the case of the iPhone, this architectural innovation required a greater emphasis on software. For the dominant mobile phone manufacturers, the effort needed to go "all in" on the novel smartphones would naturally draw significant amounts of effort, attention, and talent away from the job of continuing to refine profitable mobile phones. Architectural innovations of this sort seem to impose severe switchover disruptions on organizations. As a result of the switchover disruptions, outsiders—notably Apple's iOS and Google's Android operating system—took over the smartphone market rather than incumbent mobile phone manufacturers.[13]

When switchover disruptions are unimportant, dominant incumbents have powerful incentives to adopt new technology to defend their profitable market position. However, when switchover disruptions are high, the incumbent's incentive to adopt the new technology falls because of the profits lost during the switchover. So long as the costs of switchover disruptions are not too great, dominant incumbent firms will have more powerful incentives to adopt innovations than their rivals. However, when switchover disruptions become significant, the situation reverses, and dominant firms value innovation less than their rivals. This switch creates an opportunity for new firms to sweep in with valuable innovations that incumbents ignore.[14]

Like the U.S. market for iron ore before the 1970s and the mobile phone market before the iPhone, healthcare markets in the United States have incumbent firms with substantial market power who are reluctant to pursue innovations with significant switchover disruptions. One might expect that, in this setting, new entrants would introduce new methods and business models. However, healthcare is also rife with barriers that make it difficult for new firms to enter. The net result is a circumstance in which market power, switchover costs, and barriers to entry act together to slow the pace of innovation in the health sector. As innovation stagnates, opportunities to improve the healthcare system are lost.

Market Power, Switchover Disruptions, and Innovation in Healthcare

Market Power: Evidence from International Comparisons

Some have argued that market power in the U.S. health sector is the root cause of the high levels of spending in that sector compared to other wealthy countries.[15] In 2016, for example, healthcare spending accounted for nearly 18 percent of U.S. gross domestic product (GDP). Comparable numbers for Switzerland are 12 percent, for Germany and France 11 percent, and for Canada, the UK, and Australia, 10 percent.[16]

Total healthcare expenditures are the product of the quantity of goods and services consumed and the prices paid for these goods and services. It is unlikely that the quantity of goods and services consumed in the United States health sector accounts for our exceptional level of expenditures on health. As a nation, we simply don't use that much more healthcare than other wealthy countries.[17] Differences in the number of providers, hospitals, and the type of medical technology we employ in our delivery system are also insufficient to explain the high relative level of expenditures in the United States, notwithstanding our outlier status in some categories, such as imaging technology.[18]

If the quantity of goods and services does not explain the relatively high levels of expenditures in the U.S. health sector, then high prices—an indicator of market power—become a prime suspect.[19] The limited available international pricing data supports this idea. Pharmaceutical prices, for example, are higher in the United States than in other wealthy countries.[20] The same is true for the prices of healthcare services and provider salaries.[21] These international differences in prices, salaries, and fees may indicate a high degree of market power in the U.S. health sector, but the case is not closed. Other factors might also be at work.[22]

In the next section, we review more direct evidence of market power in the health sector by focusing on pricing patterns within the United States.

Market Power: Evidence from U.S. Prices

Drug companies in the United States use patents, marketing, and branding to charge prices far exceeding the unit cost of producing a drug. High markups are possible partly because Medicare cannot bargain over drug prices, and the Federal government has adopted policies that insulate the U.S. drug market from cheaper imports from other countries. Whether these policies are good or bad is debatable and depends greatly on how pharmaceutical firms use the additional profits. But good or bad, the exercise of market power through high markups is a feature of pharmaceutical markets in the United States.

However, branded prescription drug spending accounts for only about 10 percent of U.S. healthcare expenditures.[23] Care delivery accounts for a much higher share of costs. But, determining markups in care delivery is complicated by the administered prices in the traditional Medicare program and by the secrecy surrounding the market prices charged to commercial insurers.

Medicare spending, which accounts for about 20 percent of total national health expenditures, goes through two programs, Traditional Medicare and Medicare Advantage. As we write, traditional Medicare covers the largest portion of the Medicare population. (However, Medicare Advantage is growing rapidly and may soon overtake Traditional Medicare in market share.) It pays providers on a fee-for-service basis and pegs its rates to the average costs of the service. Provider market power does not directly influence these prices.

Providers can, however, exercise market power in the Medicare Advantage and commercial insurance markets. Investigating these markups is challenging because the prices providers negotiate with commercial insurers have, until recently, been a closely guarded secret. Providers typically operate with two sets of prices: a charge or list price and a transaction price. List prices are posted and so are available for study. Unfortunately, these prices are notional and unrelated to the prices used in actual transactions. Only individuals who self-fund their care pay these charges. The critical prices are transaction prices, and providers conceal these prices behind a cloak of secrecy.

The Health Care Cost Institute (HCCI) has made available for study insurance claims from some of the very largest commercial insurance companies in the United States. A study using HCCI data offers the most comprehensive view to date of transaction prices.[24] In their sample, authors found that Medicare pays substantially less than commercial insurers: Medicare payments were 45 percent lower than commercial rates for inpatient care. They found similar patterns for specific procedures. Medicare paid 55 percent of commercial rates for hip and knee replacement, 62 percent for cesarean and vaginal delivery, 51 percent for angioplasty, 37 percent for colonoscopy, and 25 percent for MRIs. These price differences are significant. Holding the quantity of services fixed, the authors estimate "that if private prices were set at 120 percent of Medicare rates rather than at their current levels, inpatient spending on the privately insured would drop by 19.7 percent."[25]

High markups in the prices that providers charge commercial insurers indicate that providers have market power.[26] Other signals of market power come from an examination of market structure. The market for most hospitals is local, so one would expect that hospitals in geographic areas with fewer competing hospitals will charge higher prices than hospitals with more competitors. This pattern is apparent in the data. Hospitals with a monopoly have prices that are more than 12 percent higher than hospitals in markets with four or more hospitals and nearly 8 percent higher than in areas with only two competing hospitals. As one would expect based on these findings, hospital mergers that reduce the number of competitors increase prices throughout the market.[27]

There is also evidence that lack of competition raises prices for commercial health insurance.[28] One study found that health insurance premiums increased as employer profits rose—a form of price discrimination that we do not expect in a competitive market—and that this effect was most pronounced in local markets with six or fewer competing health plans.[29] Another study found that a reduction in competition from mergers of insurance companies was associated with increased insurance premiums paid by large employers.[30]

Market structure is not the only source of market power in health insurance. Informational challenges can also give rise to market power. Insurance is a complex and multi-dimensional service, so it is difficult for even the most sophisticated buyers to compare the various offerings effectively. When comparison shopping is hard, consumers will do less of it and will be more likely to stay with their existing insurance arrangements. Savvy insurers can exploit this consumer inertia by offering low-priced plans to attract new enrollees and then raise prices upon renewal of the insurance contract. Evidence for this "bargains then rip-offs" pricing strategy has been found in Medicare Part D plans—commercial insurance plans that provide pharmaceutical coverage for Medicare beneficiaries.[31] Another study of the small group commercial insurance market estimated that the challenges in comparison shopping could cause prices to rise to nearly 30 percent above costs.[32]

Switchover Disruptions in Healthcare

We have seen that many incumbent firms in the health sector have considerable market power and may therefore face significant switchover disruptions. To see the importance of switchover disruptions in healthcare, consider the case of telemedicine, which incorporates communication and information technologies into the practice of medicine. The rise of the internet and the explosion of computing power and bandwidth create unprecedented opportunities to move the delivery of medical services from a "bricks and mortar" enterprise to a seamless blend of online and in-person experiences similar to contemporary retail or financial services.

Before the COVID-19 crisis, the health sector failed to realize the transformative potential of telemedicine. For example, in 2014, less than 2 percent of Medicare beneficiaries used telemedicine services.[33] Kaiser Permanente, however, was a notable exception to this pattern. In 2017 virtual visits at Kaiser Permanente outnumbered in-person visits with providers.[34] Switchover disruptions help explain why.

To implement what has become one of the nation's leading telemedicine platforms, Kaiser Permanente invested in new assets and capabilities, the most important of which was an electronic health record (EHR) system. An EHR is the backbone of a telemedicine platform. It makes medical information about a patient available to any provider at any time or location. Kaiser Permanente began work on EHRs in the mid-1990s and, after several failed attempts, completed the implementation of its HealthConnect system in 2010, at an estimated cost of more than $4 billion.[35]

A telemedicine platform needs to link its EHR to an effective care access system. In the 1990s, Kaiser Permanente had a well-deserved reputation for poor access to care. Individual physician offices fielded patient calls just as they would in small physician groups. Members couldn't get through to providers via the telephone, and appointments were difficult to schedule. Other industries, such as airlines, have solved the problem of delivering telephone access, advice, and scheduling through centralized call, advice, and appointment centers. Adopting these solutions in Kaiser Permanente involved wholesale changes in care delivery for millions of members and thousands of physicians.

The effort to design and implement centralized call, advice, and appointment centers was comparable to the level of effort needed to implement the EHR. These centers required, for example, a standardized scheduling system and a standard nomenclature of appointment types and durations instead of the many local and departmental systems then in use. In addition, assigning a primary care physician to each member was necessary to facilitate interaction between the physician responsible for patient care and the call centers. The call centers also had to develop and adopt detailed protocols to guide the work of customer service representatives and ensure the appropriate handling of clinically significant interactions. Since no set of protocols can anticipate all contingencies, Kaiser Permanente also needed to find ways to embed clinicians into the customer service process so that medical advice could be integrated, when required, into the encounter. Communications between providers and members also needed a new secure email system. To keep demands on the call and appointment system manageable—and to satisfy the rising expectations of their members—Kaiser Permanente also integrated hundreds of web-based resources and phone-based apps into the platform so members could obtain some of the information they needed.

The most significant switchover disruption that Kaiser Permanente faced in adopting these innovations was physician resistance to the new way of doing business. Permanente physicians, like physicians everywhere, want to care for their patients without bureaucratic interference. Like all physicians, they also want to control how they use their time during the day. A system of centralized centers to schedule appointments and provide advice threatens these professional prerogatives. The fear was that in this new system, faceless bureaucrats might determine patient care and the physician's schedule without directly knowing the patient or the physician's practice style or preferences.

As with the Mesabi miner's unions, physician resistance to losing control presented Kaiser Permanente with a potentially insurmountable obstacle to change. To address physician concerns, Kaiser Permanente executives and physician leaders positioned telemedicine as a means to improve patient care quality. They also changed their organization to make the new system more palatable. These changes included revised compensation practices so that physicians were credited for their time delivering care over the phone, via email, or through video. Change on such a large scale took years to get right.

Why did Kaiser Permanente undertake this costly effort when nearly all other health systems engaged only in small-scale pilots and experiments? The answer is that the organization saw itself as facing an existential crisis that threatened its dominant market position in its primary California markets.

During the mid-1990s, preferred provider organizations (PPOs) could negotiate fee-for-service contracts with providers at discounted rates that nearly matched Kaiser Permanente's cost of care. Moreover, PPOs offered their members something that Kaiser Permanente could not: the ability to choose any provider. Kaiser Permanente members are generally restricted to providers in the Permanente Medical Groups, affiliated multi-specialty physician groups that provide nearly all the medical services for Kaiser Permanente. The intensified competition from PPOs—in combination with pricing and other tactical errors—damaged Kaiser Permanente's financial results. By 1997 and 1998, Kaiser Permanente faced annual losses of hundreds of millions of dollars.[36] The leadership of Kaiser Permanente decided that telemedicine would be a way out of the crisis and a key to their future success.

Today Kaiser Permanente's use of telemedicine is a formidable competitive advantage. Why haven't other healthcare organizations matched this success as it unfolded over the years? Part of the answer lies in Kaiser Permanente's closely integrated Permanente Medical Groups, which have evolved, over many decades, an organizational culture that can reconcile the professional norms of the practice of medicine with the evolving requirements of the business of healthcare. They have done so by aligning the foundational elements of their business model—pre-paid, group practice—with an ethical vision of the best way to deliver care, a vision that their physicians and their members find compelling. But for the culture of the Permanente Medical Groups, the switchover disruptions of the transition to telemedicine may well have been economically prohibitive. Less integrated health systems without the cultural assets of Kaiser Permanente still find that to be the case.

Regulations as a Barrier to Innovation

The example of telemedicine also illustrates how regulations can act as a barrier to innovation in the health sector. Before March 2020, Medicare could only reimburse for telehealth services in rural areas and only when these services were delivered from a medical facility.[37] Under the Coronavirus Preparedness and Response Supplemental Appropriations Act, as signed into law on March 6, 2020, the Secretary of Health received the authority to waive these and other restrictions on the use of telemedicine. During the emergency, telemedicine was permitted from any location (including a patient's home), on any device that allows audio and video communication, and with reimbursement equal to traditional face-to-face encounters. This permission extended to physicians and nonphysicians such as nurse practitioners, physician assistants, certified nurse midwives, clinical psychologists, and more. These changes had an immediate effect. By April 2020, the number of beneficiaries in fee-for-service Medicare receiving telemedicine services had risen from 13,000 before the emergency to nearly 1.7 million.[38] This effect was not limited to Medicare. An April 2020 survey estimated that the proportion of consumers of healthcare using telemedicine was 78 times higher than it has been two months earlier.[39] Medicare removed an enormous barrier to the adoption of telemedicine by compensating both telemedicine and in-person encounters equally. Similarly, waiving cost-sharing payments for telemedicine removed a significant barrier to patient adoption.

Before the COVID-19 emergency, telemedicine programs confronted a patchwork of reimbursement schemes. Each commercial insurer and state Medicaid agency adopted its rules for telemedicine and its reimbursement. Medicare's emergency policy reduced this fragmentation because most commercial payers and many states followed its lead. Twenty-two states also required more robust telemedicine coverage by insurers regulated in their local markets.[40] Telemedicine began to take shape as a coherent national market opportunity operating under commonly understood rules. Policy changes that permitted telemedicine services across state lines further encouraged the emergence of a national market.

Healthcare providers operate within a network of referrals and handoffs: from home to doctor, from primary care to specialists, from an outpatient visit to a hospital stay, from a hospital stay to a nursing facility, etc. For telemedicine to achieve its full utility, each node in the network must connect to the other nodes. By relaxing privacy regulations to permit the use of "everyday communications technologies," Medicare greatly simplified the task of adopting telemedicine. Providers and patients could now use technologies already in use by the network. The alternative, a local network of providers choosing and implementing a specialized telemedicine platform, would, as in the case of Kaiser Permanente, take years to develop, if it could be implemented at all.

Medicare's emergency regulation also helped reduce professional opposition to telemedicine. Before COVID-19, physicians had questions about telemedicine.[41] Would remote visits degrade the quality of the patient-physician relationship? Could physicians make sound clinical decisions without an in-person physical examination? Would the fragmentation of care delivery worsen if physicians far removed from the patient—perhaps even in other states—became involved in care delivery? Without local oversight, would fraud and abuse increase (for example, in overprescribing narcotics)? These concerns were enshrined in state licensure laws and credentialing practices limiting who may see patients and where. With COVID-19, these concerns became moot, at least during the early days of the crisis. If physicians were to see patients at all, it would have to be via telemedicine. With experience, physicians found telemedicine to be such an effective tool that it might find a permanent place in their practice after the crisis has passed.[42] One study found nearly 60 percent of physicians surveyed had a more favorable view of telemedicine than before the COVID-19 crisis.[43]

The regulatory barriers to telemedicine that existed before the COVID-19 crisis were prohibitive. While they were in place, it was unlikely that new telemedicine-based market entrants could challenge entrenched healthcare delivery systems. These incumbent systems could therefore feel secure in ignoring telemedicine in favor of continuing their business as usual. The removal of these regulatory restraints has contributed to a torrent of new investments in digital health. For example, venture capital investment into the digital health space in the first half of 2021 totaled $14.7 billion, which is nearly twice the investment in 2019 ($7.7 billion).[44]

Professional Resistance to New Entrants

Another set of barriers to innovative new entrants comes from providers themselves. Patients visit a traditional physician practice for a variety of reasons. Some physician visits are for specific, well-understood acute disorders whose diagnosis and treatment do not require sophisticated equipment or advanced training: earaches, pink eye, sore throats. Other visits are more complex. These might include oversight of patients with chronic diseases such as diabetes, high cholesterol, and lupus.[45] Traditionally, both types of visits took place in a physician's office, and care was delivered by a physician or by advanced practice professionals working under a physician's direction.

One way to lower the cost of healthcare is to focus physicians on the more complex visits and to use less highly trained providers for the more straight-forward tasks. This is what retail clinics do. Retail medical clinics offer customers convenience, transparency, low cost, and flexibility. They are open late and on weekends and do not require a prior appointment or medical insurance. At the time of the visit, the clinics charge patients a low flat fee. The menu of services offered at the clinic is limited, and prices are posted for all to see. The large retail clinic chains typically have no physicians on-site. Instead, a nurse practitioner delivers care, supported by a software applica-tion that employs standard care protocols. The first retail clinics appeared in Minnesota grocery stores in the year 2000. By 2006 the two largest such retail clinic companies were acquired by CVS and Walgreens, respectively. There were about 200 such clinics in 2006 and over 1,200 by 2009.[46]

Primary care physicians previously delivered the services now provided by retail clinics. Physicians and the new corporate entrants both had access to the technology of the new business model, and, in principle, either could have profited from them. Indeed, state-level corporate practice of medicine laws prohibiting nonphysicians from owning medical practices would give incumbent physician practices an advantage in introducing the new prac-tice model.

However, in the case of retail clinics, physician practices had weaker incentives to adopt this innovation because features of the model ran counter to established professional norms. Specifically, permitting a nonphysician not under direct physician supervision to treat a patient strikes at the core of a physician's professional identity. The perceived conflict between physi-cian professional identity and the new business model created resistance, and any attempt to overcome this resistance would take time and energy from the leadership of a traditional medical group. Retail pharmacies that are not physician-led did not face this challenge. Consequently, it was easier for them to adopt the innovation.

Rather than adopting the retail clinic model, organized medicine mobilized to stop it. A recent study found that physician organizations responded to the entry of retail clinics by arguing that they were unsafe, immoral, and illegitimate.[47] They argued that the absence of physicians at retail clinics was dangerous for patients because nurse practitioners lacked the training and skills of primary care doctors. In addition, profit-oriented corporations would put commercial interests ahead of the patient's. The final point in their campaign was that medicine ought to be delivered by professionals motivated by patient welfare, not businesses focused on profits. The retail clinics responded to the safety argument by asserting that nurse practitioners are well qualified to treat many primary care conditions. The clinics used sophisticated technology to ensure evidence-based treatments and track outcomes. The defense of retail clinics also had a moral dimension. In the face of rising medical costs and a shortage of primary care physicians, innovations—like retail clinics—that reduce costs and improve access to care were on the side of the angels.

The mobilization against retail clinics has been sufficient to slow, but not stop, the spread of this new model of care. It illustrates how professional norms—often a great good in protecting the interests of patients—can block new entrants and serve as a barrier to disruptive change and innovation.

7

Dilemmas and Opportunities

The U.S. health sector faces two dilemmas. The first dilemma concerns high levels of health expenditures. The United States spends a larger fraction of its national income on healthcare than any other advanced economy.[1] High spending might be acceptable if it produced outstanding outcomes. But health outcomes in the United States do not compare well with those of other wealthy countries.[2]

As discussed in chapter 6, the primary reason for high healthcare expenditures in the United States is the ability of dominant players to mark up their prices far above marginal costs. The exercise of market power makes some firms and individuals richer but makes the nation poorer overall. Addressing the dilemma of high expenditures requires reducing market consolidation, increasing competition, and improving how healthcare markets work.[3]

The second dilemma concerns the *growth* of healthcare spending. Since 1975, U.S. healthcare spending has grown on average 2 percent faster than GDP per year. If these relative growth rates persist for another 75 years—the long-range planning horizon for entitlement programs like Medicare—the health sector will absorb 75 percent of GDP.[4] Such trends seem to point toward a dystopian future where health spending crowds out the consumption of other necessary goods and services.

Conventional wisdom regards these two dilemmas as manifestations of the same problem: overspending on health. However, they result from different economic forces and call for distinct, though sometimes overlapping, responses.

This chapter explains why health expenditures grow faster than GDP and what to do about it. Our answer emphasizes ways to align the incentives for innovation more closely with creating economic value and reducing costs.

Why Not Better and Cheaper? James B. Rebitzer and Robert S. Rebitzer, Oxford University Press.
© Oxford University Press 2023. DOI: 10.1093/oso/9780197603109.003.0007

Growth in Health Expenditures

The phenomenon of healthcare costs growing faster than GDP is not unique to the United States; the share of GDP going to healthcare has increased across all wealthy nations. There are two leading explanations for this: expensive new medical technologies and rising national incomes.

The technology for delivering health services is radically different now than in 1960. However, this flourishing of new technology does not satisfactorily explain why healthcare costs rise faster than GDP. Costly new healthcare technologies need not find a market simply because they are available. This is particularly so if there is good reason to believe—as discussed in previous chapters—that many new technologies do not offer much additional value for patients.[5] We call the new medical technologies explanation of the growth in health spending the *Field of Dreams* theory because its logic echoes the great line from that 1989 film, "If you build it, they will come."

Rising national incomes is the alternative and, in our judgment, the better explanation for why health expenditures grow faster than GDP. Estimates across countries and across regions within countries find that a 1 percent increase in GDP correlates with a 1.6 percent increase in health expenditures.[6] If the percentage increase in health spending exceeds the percent increase in national income, it follows that health spending will constitute a growing share of national income.

But why should more prosperous nations spend an ever-larger proportion of their growing income on health? For most things we buy, more is better. But the additional satisfaction falls with each additional increment consumed. The third donut may taste good, but probably not as good as the first. The same is true for homes. As homebuyers become wealthier, they spend more money on larger houses—but the incremental joy from buying a 3,000 square foot house relative to a 2,500 square foot house is less than moving from a 2,000 square foot house to a 2,500 square foot house.

The psychological tendency for satiation acts as a natural brake on consumption. People may continue to spend more on donuts and living space as they grow more prosperous, but they will also direct their rising income to other goods and services whose marginal value may be higher. No particular good or service should take up a growing share of GDP as societies grow more affluent.

To understand why expenditures on healthcare differ from other expenditures, consider the following thought experiment. Suppose a society was determined to spend exactly the amount on healthcare that would make each of its citizens as well off and satisfied as possible. The optimal healthcare expenditures would be determined by the consequences of taking a percent of GDP away from individual consumption and spending it on healthcare. This reallocation of GDP generates a loss (individuals consume less) and a gain (individuals live longer and healthier lives). If the loss is less than the gain, society will make its members happier by increasing healthcare expenditures as a percent of GDP. Society should continue to allocate more to health so long as the gains from doing so exceed the losses in forgone non-health consumption. Individuals in a poor society may gain more from spending on roads, food, and housing and be better off with a smaller share of GDP going to health. As society grows more affluent, consumers value each additional unit of consumption less. As consumers become increasingly satiated from non-health consumption, the society in our thought experiment will allocate less to non-health goods and services and more to health expenditures that increase the length of life and the quality of life.[7] Based on these tradeoffs and guesses about the growth of U.S. GDP, some estimate that the optimal solution to this thought experiment is for the United States to spend more than 30 percent of GDP on healthcare by the middle of the 21st century.[8]

This result suggests that healthcare costs will constitute a rising share of GDP for decades to come. Indeed, it may be that 30 percent is an underestimate because improvements in healthcare technology over time can increase the desirability of spending even more on healthcare. Consider that since 1970 there has been a dramatic reduction in mortality from heart disease for older individuals—particularly men over age 50.[9] As a result of this improvement in health technology, more people survive heart attacks, increasing the value of other medical services. People who do not die of cardiac disease in their 50s need knee replacements in their 60s and treatment for Alzheimer's in their 70s and 80s. They also place greater value on improvements in the treatment of these conditions. These mutually reinforcing effects of healthcare innovation are not small. One study estimates that reductions in mortality since 1970 have raised the value of further health progress by nearly 20 percent.[10]

Spending a growing share of our national income on health need not be a source of concern. Indeed, under the right circumstances, it increases our prosperity. To explain, let's extend our thought experiment to consider two U.S. healthcare systems: one is the current U.S. system—let's call that

System A. The other is an alternative, hypothetical system, System B, that is identical to System A in all respects except one. System A has implemented technologies and management practices such that a 10 percent increase in health spending improves life expectancy by 1.25 percent. System B, in contrast, requires only a 5 percent increase in health spending to achieve the same increase in life expectancy.

In both System A and System B, demand for healthcare increases as society grows wealthier. However, System B will spend a higher fraction of GDP on its health sector than System A. System B gets more for each additional dollar spent on healthcare, making society more willing to trade reduced consumption growth in other areas for more longevity and a higher quality of life. Healthcare expenditures as a portion of its GDP will grow faster in System B than in System A. But the faster growth rate will not impoverish the nation because System B is better at converting foregone consumption into improved health.

Technologies, practice patterns, and business models that convert resources into health outcomes result from many years of prior discovery and innovation. When the patent system fails to support the development of vaccines or antibiotics while encouraging life-cycle management of existing drugs, when cost-reducing innovations regularly "go missing," the result is a set of technologies and processes that are less efficient at converting national income into desirable health outcomes. These distortions make the United States less well off than it could be, a state of affairs that is neither desirable nor necessary.

Opportunities

The conventional policy stance calls for suppressing the rise of healthcare costs, but this response is a recipe for failure. Restricting healthcare spending by, for example, tying the growth of Medicare to the growth of GDP will not turn off the economic, technical, and psychological forces that cause demand for healthcare to grow faster than national income.[11] A better strategy would be to strengthen incentives for innovations that create economic value and reduce costs. The ideas developed in the preceding chapters offer a guide for pursuing this strategy.

Our recommendations fall into two categories: (1) better aligning the incentives of the patent system with the creation of economic value, and

(2) making it easier for innovators and implementers to make money by reducing the cost of healthcare.

Incentives for Creating Economic Value

We have seen in chapter 2 that for vaccines, cancer drugs, antibiotics, and the life-cycle management of drugs, the incentives inherent in the patent system are not well aligned with creating economic value for patients or society. The heart of the problem is that patents offer innovators time-limited market exclusivity as the primary incentive for innovation and discovery. This incentive is problematic in several ways: monopoly pricing that inhibits the uptake of valuable therapies; time limitations that skew the choice of disease targets for drug development and reward life-cycle management practices; and reliance on "willingness to pay" as the measure of value, which biases innovation toward the health issues of wealthy individuals and countries and which cannot account for benefits not reflected in the market price, such as the "option value" of new antibiotics.

In this section, we discuss ideas to better align patent incentives with the creation of economic value in healthcare. None of these proposals on their own are sufficient—there is no silver bullet—but together they can make a difference.

Subscription Models

Consider the incentives for the inventors of new antibiotics. For the most part, new antibiotics are more expensive substitutes for older antibiotics—until the microbes develop resistance. At that point, new antibiotics become very valuable. The economic value of new antibiotics results from the option they offer in responding to a future contingency. Resistance to current antibiotics may not emerge during the period of market exclusivity, and this uncertainty reduces the value of the patent. Introducing a new antibiotic before resistance to current treatments arise give the bacteria a head start in developing resistance to the new drug. Wise social stewardship ought to push the introduction of new antibiotics as far as possible into the future.[12]

A subscription model would remedy many of the deficiencies of the current system. One recent proposal calls for a fixed recurring payment linked to clinical performance metrics.[13] Such a system pays for the availability of new antibiotics rather than their use, encouraging both innovation and wise stewardship. In this proposal, an expert committee would set criteria for determining participation in the program—presumably focusing on high-need areas for drug development. Next, a proposed antibiotic would be evaluated to determine if it meets the qualification criteria. Then, the manufacturer would work with the Center for Medicare and Medicaid Services (CMS) to agree on the evidentiary basis for demonstrating clinical value, and the FDA would evaluate the drug's efficacy. Finally, CMS would negotiate subscription payments with the drugmaker in exchange for guarantees that the drugmaker will make the antibiotic available when needed. The subscription revenues must be set high enough to induce drugmakers to invest in antibiotic development but not so high as to exceed the value created by the new drug. Hospitals could gain access to the new drug for a low price, but in exchange, they would be required to implement CDC-recommended antimicrobial stewardship protocols, adhere to appropriate use practices, and provide data to allow CMS to monitor performance.[14]

Louisiana used a variation of a subscription model to ensure access to antiviral drugs for hepatitis C for its Medicaid and incarcerated populations. Unlike the subscription proposal for antibiotics, Louisiana's subscription model was not intended to increase incentives for innovation but to increase access by underserved populations to a valuable innovation that would otherwise be priced out of reach. However, both models use a subscription—paying for access, not for use—to address pricing problems arising from the patent system. Hepatitis C is a deadly infectious disease that can be cured by patented antiviral medications such as Sovaldi and Harvoni. These medications are typically sold at a high price—$80,000 per treatment. Treating just the Louisianans with hepatitis C enrolled in Medicaid was estimated to cost $760 million—more than the state spends on K-12 education, Veteran's Affairs, and Corrections combined. Louisiana negotiated an agreement with pharmaceutical companies in which it committed to spending a fixed amount on hepatitis C medication annually in exchange for universal access to the drug for its Medicaid and incarcerated population.[15]

The Louisiana subscription agreement offers an attractive solution to the "monopolist's dilemma," in which a monopolist has to lower its price to sell more. The drugmaker charges monopoly prices to those willing to pay those prices, and the state "subscribes" on behalf of defined populations who cannot pay the total monopoly price. Such an arrangement increases drugmakers' overall revenue because sales to Medicaid and the prison system would be nil without it. Yet Louisiana's agreement is noteworthy because such arrangements are rare. Drugmakers are understandably wary of any intervention with the potential to undermine the monopoly price upon which the value of the patent depends. Subscription agreements might open the door to others who would demand a lower price. In addition, drugs made available at a lower price to one market segment may make their way to other segments that would otherwise pay the full monopoly price.

Advanced Market Commitments

Patents rely on "willingness to pay" measures of value. For most goods and services, consumer willingness to pay is a good enough indicator of social value even though it creates some inequality. It is acceptable, for example, that Tesla entered the car market with vehicles priced and designed for the needs of high-income buyers. However, as we have discussed, high-income individuals and societies are willing to spend more than low-income individuals and societies on better health. They are also eager to spend a considerably higher percentage of their already higher income. Thus in the health sector, a market test based on "willingness to pay" skews the incentives for innovation sharply toward improving the health and longevity of high-income individuals and high-income countries. This skew results in underinvestment in preventives and treatments for diseases affecting poor countries (e.g., malaria) or marginalized populations in the United States (e.g., sickle cell disease or addiction).

An advanced market commitment (AMC) can offset some of these distortions. Under an AMC, sponsors estimate in advance the social value of a treatment with the desired characteristics and commit to paying that value to developers who can meet their specifications. Payments only occur after regulators determine that the treatment is safe and effective. AMCs do not specify any particular technology—any safe and effective treatment that meets requirements is eligible.[16]

The benefit of AMCs is illustrated most clearly in the vaccine market for diseases endemic to poor countries. Research and development (R&D) directed toward health problems in developing countries receives a small portion of the total investment in health R&D globally. A 2005 Center for Global Development report estimated that $6 billion is spent annually on diseases such as malaria, schistosomiasis, or Chagas disease compared to global R&D expenditures of $100 billion. The same report estimated that the total size of the vaccine market in developing countries is $500 million, too small to attract much R&D investment.[17]

In 2007, five countries and the Gates Foundation pledged $1.5 billion toward a pilot AMC targeting pneumococcal conjugate vaccine (PCV).[18] At the start of the project, the World Health Organization estimated that pneumococcus annually killed more than 700,000 children under age five in developing countries.

The AMC launched in 2009 to provide 200 million treatments annually. The design called for firms to agree to 10-year supply contracts capping prices at $3.50 per dose. Firms committing to the agreement would receive a share of the $1.5 billion AMC fund proportionate to the number of doses they supplied, paid out as a per-dose subsidy. In 2010 two drugmakers, GSK and Pfizer, each committed to supplying 30 million doses annually. By 2016, over 50 million children per year were immunized for PVC. In 2019, a third vaccine developed by the Serum Institute of India qualified for the AMC program.[19] The experience with the AMC vaccine suggests that it may have saved 700,000 lives at a very favorable cost.[20] AMCs, in other words, may be a cost-effective way to undo some of the distortions resulting from the "willingness to pay" market test built into the patent system.[21]

The COVID-19 pandemic provides another striking example of the impact of AMCs on vaccine development. Under Operation Warp Speed, a government-sponsored AMC, the United States offered a variety of contracts to manufacturers to spur the development of a COVID-19 vaccine. For example, Pfizer's agreement offered a $2 billion payment contingent on licensure or emergency use authorization for 100 million doses.[22] The result of the program was the development of highly effective vaccines for a novel pathogen, using a new mRNA technology, in less than 12 months.

Two-Part Pricing

A drugmaker that uses its patent monopoly to set prices above marginal cost captures a larger share of a smaller economic pie.[23] If the patent holders sell their new invention at a price equal to marginal cost, they maximize the value created by their treatment. Unfortunately, there is no money left over to reward the innovator at this low price. A well-known solution to this problem is for the patent holder to sell the drug at a price equal to its marginal production cost and then charge a licensing fee for access to the treatment. This licensing fee is the source of funds to compensate the innovator for research and development costs. Because the licensing fee is separate from the price of the drug, the fee does not discourage patients from purchasing the medication. Economists call this pricing strategy two-part pricing because of its two distinct elements: a low price per treatment close to marginal cost and a licensing fee.

The institutional structure of the market for patented drugs in the United States offers a rough approximation to two-part pricing. At the center of this market sit pharmacy benefit managers (PBMs). PBMs operate formularies that make most drugs available to consumers at low copays close to the drug's marginal cost. Insurance premiums constitute the fixed fee portion of two-part pricing. Insurance companies use these premiums to pay PBMs a price per drug that significantly exceeds the copay. PBMs, in turn, use the revenues from the insurers to pay the price (net of rebates) demanded by drugmakers.

A feature of this complicated structure is that the considerable value created by the two-part pricing strategy does not flow to consumers or drugmakers. When the market for PBM services is not very competitive, PBMs can use their position as intermediaries to keep the additional revenue created by the low copays. Consequently, the incentives for innovation are much lower than they could be.[24]

One way to address this inefficiency would be to levy a per-member tax on PBMs and use the revenues collected to invest in discoveries. A well-designed tax on PBMs would not raise copays or distort the flow of funds between insurers, PBMs, and drugmakers. Instead, the tax would extract some surplus from PBMs that could then be used to enhance innovation. The proceeds from a per capita PBM tax could help build an infrastructure to facilitate future research—particularly research on the cost/benefit profile of treatments. We sketch out some of the features of such an infrastructure later in this chapter.

Buyouts and Auctions

Are alternatives to the patent system's "time-limited market exclusivity" conceivable? Yes, according to a proposal inspired by the example of the patent for Daguerreotype photography.[25] The French government purchased this patent in 1839 and placed the technique in the public domain. As a result, Daguerreotype photography was rapidly adopted worldwide and subjected to many subsequent improvements. If the government were to buy out the patent rights to innovations at their estimated private value and then make the innovation freely available, it would eliminate many distorted incentives in today's system. By releasing the discoveries to the public without requiring a licensing fee, this system might also stimulate follow-on innovations built on the patented invention.[26]

A central challenge for any system of patent buyouts is determining the right price. A possible solution to this problem may be an auction. Potential investors would bid on the value of the new technology, and the winning bids would reveal investor willingness to pay. In most cases the winner would not gain ownership of the patent to the technology—the government just uses the winning bid to determine compensation for the inventor. However, to create incentives for bidders to reveal their actual assessment of the innovation, a random sample of the proposed projects would actually be sold to the winning bidders.

A second major challenge is the risk that a government buyer might misuse its purchasing power and force the sale of patents at confiscatory prices. To prevent this, innovators should have the option of selling their patents to the government via auction or using the conventional patent process. In other words, patent buyouts would supplement rather than replace the existing patent system. Additional challenges that a buyout system would need to address include: making reliable information available to bidders in the auction, preventing collusion among bidders, generating government revenue to purchase the patents, and otherwise appropriately structuring the government's role in the innovation process.[27]

Incentives to Make Cost-Reducing Innovation Profitable

It's hard to make money by reducing the cost of healthcare, and this fact shapes the direction of innovation. The essence of the problem is that providers and patients make decisions about care while the benefits of lower costs accrue primarily to the insurer/payer. A simple solution follows logically from the problem: payers should share cost savings with providers and patients. However, this simple solution requires many other changes.

As described in previous chapters, payers often need an outside forcing function, a "jump-start," to offer shared savings contracts to providers. Even when offered, shared savings contracts have inherent limitations and must be complemented by appropriate non-financial motivations shaped by professional and social norms and narratives. In addition, significant investments are needed to improve the overall healthcare data infrastructure so that the costs and benefits of care can be evaluated appropriately. Also, healthcare markets must become more competitive so that complacent incumbents cannot ignore disruptive innovations.

Such wide-ranging changes may seem like a revolutionary overhaul of our entire healthcare system, an overwhelming or even hopeless task. But as the philosopher Karl Popper advised, when faced with fundamental social problems, we must become "piecemeal social engineers" who break the problem into smaller pieces against which we can make incremental progress through trial and error.[28] The following section provides a checklist for the social engineer working to advance cost-reducing healthcare innovations.

Jump-Start Shared Savings

As discussed in chapter 4, providers act as common agents for many payers. Common agency complicates the adoption of shared savings arrangements. The issue is spillovers: incentives provided by one payer also benefit other payers who contract with the provider. Spillovers can lead to an outcome where no shared savings incentives are offered at all. We refer to this outcome as a sticking point equilibrium because all the players are trapped in an undesirable situation that is hard to exit without some external forcing mechanism.[29]

However, sticking points are not economic black holes from which escape is impossible. With bold action, a single large payer can "jump-start" an escape. Suppose a large enough payer adopts aggressive shared savings contracts. In that case, providers may be willing to incur the high start-up costs involved in making their care delivery processes more cost efficient. These improvements will then be available to all the provider's patients, including those whose bills are the responsibility of other payers. Having made the costly transition to new processes, providers are better positioned to respond to cost savings contracts offered by these other payers, which supports the spread of more shared savings contracts throughout the healthcare economy.

One can see an example of jump-starting in a recent study of a trial Comprehensive Care for Joint Replacement (CJR) program.[30] In the trial, conducted on enrollees in traditional Medicare, Medicare replaced its customary fee-for-service payment model with an alternative arrangement in which Medicare paid for hip and knee replacement with a single bundled payment that covered all costs during an episode of care. Providers who keep the cost of hip and knee replacements below the bundled payment get to keep the savings.

The study was possible because Medicare's CJR trial rolled out bundled payments in some randomly selected communities and not others.

Comparing communities with and without CJR, it appears that bundled payments made care more cost effective. Specifically, patients in traditional Medicare were around 10 percent less likely to be discharged from a hospital to expensive post-acute care facilities. Surprisingly, however, the authors also found that introducing the CJR program had almost the same effect on hospital discharges for Medicare Advantage enrollees who were not included in the CJR trial. Similar results were found when the unit of comparison was hospitals rather than communities. Hospitals that were most responsive to CJR, those who made the most significant change in the discharge destination for their traditional Medicare patients, also changed the discharge destination for their Medicare Advantage patients.

Before the CJR, Medicare Advantage plans wanted hospitals to reduce discharges to post-acute care facilities but could not motivate them to alter their practices. However, when traditional Medicare—the nation's largest purchaser of healthcare services—shifted to bundled payments, it suddenly became worthwhile for hospitals to make the necessary changes. This pattern is just what you would expect to see when jump-starting out of a sticking point equilibrium.

Common agency leads to a new view of the federal government's role in shaping the health sector, as "jump-starter" of last resort. Medicare and Medicaid are such large purchasers of services that, with sufficiently bold initiatives, they can stimulate new cost-effective practices throughout the private sector. Effective jump-starts increase the incentives for cost-reducing innovations. Economic models of common agency suggest that jump-starting becomes progressively easier the more a provider's patients are concentrated with a particular payer. Indeed, common agency problems disappear altogether if providers work with only a single payer, as is the case, for example, with Kaiser Permanente, Geisinger Health, and the Veteran's Administration.

Appreciate the Limitations of Financial Incentives
However, even with a jump-start or a single payer, shared savings contracts are only semi-effective ways to create incentives for cost reduction. Information problems, contract design difficulties, and implementation obstacles limit the effectiveness of such contracts.

The most challenging information problems for shared savings contracts concern quality of care and risk adjustment. Consider, for example, the quality issues that emerged in a recent analysis of nursing homes.[31] The nursing home sector has many more for-profit providers than other parts of the healthcare system (about 70 percent). The biggest payers are Medicaid and Medicare, and each program pays a prospectively set amount per day of care. This prospective payment system (PPS) offers providers powerful shared savings incentives—the facility gets to keep every dollar of savings below the per diem payments. Since 2009, private equity (PE) companies have become increasingly active in purchasing nursing homes. PE firms buy existing companies by borrowing money for the acquisition and placing this debt on the purchased firm's balance sheet. PE firms have particularly powerful incentives to reduce costs because their business model generously rewards fund managers who quickly increase the acquired firm's value. Combining powerful managerial incentives with high levels of new debt supercharge economic pressures to improve operational efficiency.

In some settings, the intensive pressures brought by PE stimulate improved management practices. In the case of nursing homes, however, PE does not have such a salutary effect. One study pooled data from about 7.4 million Medicare patients in 18,485 nursing homes between 2000 and 2017, of which PE firms had acquired 1,674. PE ownership of a nursing home increased the probability of death (during the stay or the following 90 days) by 1.7 percentage points. This effect on mortality amounts to a 10 percent increase over the baseline 17 percent mortality rate. These results imply more than 20,000 additional lives lost over the 12 years of the study. An obvious conclusion from these results is that PE acquisition of nursing homes is not a good idea. The sheer magnitude of lives lost, however, raises a deeper question. How could such degradation of quality go unnoticed for so long?

The average overall mortality rate in PE-acquired nursing homes was 0.18, compared to 0.17 for non-PE nursing homes. Under these circumstances, it would take more than 45,000 observations to have an 80 percent chance of detecting the 10 percent difference in mortality between PE and non-PE nursing homes.[32] The typical facility admits around 200 patients per year, so on this basis, it would take more than two decades to detect the excess mortality using facility-level data. Of course, large nursing home operations can pool across many facilities and acquire the needed information more quickly, but aggregation across facilities introduces additional statistical confounders. Detecting the effect of PE ownership required millions of observations and advanced econometric methods. Since big data and mathematical sophistication are not typical of the capabilities one finds in these facilities, managers are probably not cynically trading off deaths and dollars.

A more plausible explanation for the degradation of quality is managerial in-attention facilitated by limited information about the quality of care.

This explanation should not let PE off the hook. Some managers may have been happy not to know if their management practices were raising mortality. More conscientious managers could have tracked the more common and less severe precursors to increased mortality. They might have noticed, for example, an increase in the use of antipsychotics or the incidence of bedsores and used this information to ensure that quality was not degrading. But in an environment with high-powered cost-cutting incentives, such initiatives are not the priority and may be seen as a cause of unnecessary spending. The case of PE in the nursing home sector is a cautionary tale about the risks of powerful shared savings incentives in healthcare.

Risk adjustment poses another informational challenge to shared savings contracts. To illustrate the challenges of risk adjustment, compare compensation in traditional Medicare with Medicare Advantage plans. Physicians in traditional Medicare record diagnoses and the services provided to the patient. They receive a payment from Medicare based on services provided and must be meticulous about recording services with the correct procedure codes.

Compensation is different in Medicare Advantage plans. In this program, the Federal government pays private insurers a per-patient amount based on the prospective costs of the enrollee. Patients with costly chronic diseases tend to be expensive to insure, so prior diagnoses for chronic conditions are used to estimate an enrollee's "risk score." For example, people with diabetes are likely expensive, so that a diabetic may get a higher risk score in a Medicare Advantage plan than a non-diabetic. Insurers who enroll more people with diabetes get more per enrollee.

This PPS amounts to a shared savings contract. If the insurer can find ways to deliver care at less than the expected costs, they can keep the savings. In addition to encouraging cost-effective treatments, the shared savings also creates powerful incentives to ensure that physicians code diagnoses to maximize reimbursements from the Medicare Advantage program. Manipulating diagnosis codes to increase revenues is known as upcoding.

A recent study finds evidence that physicians in Medicare Advantage plans do upcode.[33] The effects of upcoding are substantial. Estimates indicate that upcoding increases the average risk score in Medicare Advantage enrollees by 6–8 percent relative to traditional Medicare. This movement in risk scores is equivalent to 39 percent of enrollees suddenly acquiring a diagnosis of diabetes. How exactly do Medicare Advantage insurers persuade physicians to upcode? They introduce chart reviews and send reminders to nudge physicians to help them remember to investigate and code all the relevant chronic conditions in the medical record. They send nurses to patients' homes to make sure that they document any chronic condition that the physician may have missed. They offer financial rewards to physicians who do a good job at coding for well-compensated chronic conditions. Upcoding also has consequences beyond its direct effect on medical expenditures. Physicians who devote their scarce time and attention to upcoding aren't working on ways to reduce costs.

Risk adjustment can also amplify socially unacceptable health disparities. For example, the Medicaid program in Texas transitioned from a fee-for-service payment system to a managed care system in which insurers received a capitated payment for each enrollee based on historical costs in the locality. In the Medicaid program, the cost of treating Black newborns was more than 80 percent higher than the cost for Hispanic newborns—a difference of more than $4,200 per baby. Because the capitated payments were not "risk-adjusted" to reflect these differences, Medicaid Managed Care plans in Texas could benefit by discouraging Black mothers from enrolling and encouraging Hispanic mothers to enroll. Consistent with this incentive, the rollout of Medicaid managed care programs in Texas appeared to significantly improve the birth outcomes of Hispanic babies but not so for Black babies. In California, where Medicaid managed care operated with less powerful shared savings incentives, there is no evidence that Medicaid Managed Care led to increased disparities between Black and Hispanic infants.[34]

Comparing Texas and California Medicaid offers indirect evidence of unintended consequences from the design of shared savings contracts. More direct evidence of the difficulties of contract design comes from a study of shared savings contracts in long-term care hospitals (LTCH).[35] These were initially created to solve a potential side effect of the PPS for acute care hospitals with unusually long lengths of stay.[36] Before 2002, LTCH were paid their estimated daily cost. However, that year, LTCH were transitioned to a PPS under which they were paid a lump sum based on the patient's diagnosis. Designers of the PPS for LTCH were concerned that these hospitals might take the lump sum payment and discharge the patient too soon. The program established short stay thresholds to discourage premature discharge of patients. The hospitals received a fixed daily amount if stays were shorter than the relevant threshold. After reaching the threshold, payment shifted from a per-day basis to a per-stay basis in which the hospital received a large lump sum to cover the remaining hospitalization costs. This lump sum averaged $13,500 per patient, paid one day after the patient crossed the threshold. Not surprisingly, this induced a significant spike in discharges on precisely the day of the lump sum payment. This discharge pattern did not seem to cause patients harm, but it was quite expensive for Medicare.

This example illustrates that shared savings contracts can be gamed and that efforts to limit such gaming typically create other, unintended distortions. Designing efficient shared savings contracts, in other words, is hard. The contract design problem is greatly compounded when contracts have to share savings that accrue to payers in the future—but this is precisely the contracting that is most useful for encouraging cost-reducing innovations for managing chronic diseases. For these diseases, early actions generate savings that manifest in future years. Neither economists, insurers, nor regulators have workable ideas for managing shared savings contracts geared toward such future costs.[37]

An additional limitation of shared savings contracts concerns implementation within organizations. Many shared savings contracts target entire organizations. For example, Accountable Care Organizations (ACOs) aim to promote process innovations that reduce the cost of care and improve care coordination between providers in the ACO using organization-level shared savings incentives. However, organizational incentives do not directly translate into incentives for those who work in those organizations. As discussed in previous chapters, the free-riding problem in healthcare organizations can dilute gains from shared savings so dramatically that the incentives will not pay for themselves.[38]

High-powered financial incentives can spur innovation. However, such incentives can also lead to unintended and undesirable consequences due to quality measurement issues, risk adjustment, contract design, and other factors. Meaningful non-financial motivators arising from organizational culture or professional norms must therefore accompany financial incentives.[39] We return to the topic of non-financial motivators later in this chapter.

Improve the Data Infrastructure

As we have seen in the case of PE-owned nursing homes, understanding the impact of interventions on the cost and quality of care requires data from large populations of patients. In the heavily fragmented U.S. healthcare sector, few organizations operate at a scale and scope sufficient to support such data collection. One such entity is Medicare, and the widespread availability of Medicare claims data has allowed innovators and researchers to learn a great deal. However, traditional Medicare claims data is limited. For example, it is commonly available only for a random sample of Medicare enrollees. Even when a complete Medicare sample is available, such data leaves out big parts of the health sector, including Medicaid, Medicare Advantage, and private insurance enrollees under age 65. Private insurance claims data, including from the Medicare Advantage program, are generally unavailable for analysis.

Some private initiatives have moved to fill this gap. The Health Care Cost Institute (HCCI) is one of the most noteworthy examples.[40] The HCCI holds data on over 55 million commercially insured individuals from three private insurers (Humana, Kaiser Permanente, and Aetna) as well as a data aggregator and analysis company that uses data from Blue Cross Blue Shield plans (Blue Health Intelligence). Altogether their data covers about one-third of the employer-sponsored insurance population in the United States plus 100 percent of Medicare fee-for-service claims data on roughly 40 million individuals. The data is open to researchers in academic, government, and non-profit research settings for an annual fee of $45,000 per project. The HCCI also publishes public reports on healthcare costs, prices, and utilization. Participation in the HCCI is voluntary, and contributing insurers are free to leave the HCCI—as United Healthcare did in 2019.[41]

Another source of large-scale data is all-payer claims databases (APCDs). These are state-level databases that include medical, pharmacy, and dental claims from private and public payers.[42] Unlike the HCCI data, APCDs have data from most insurance companies operating in any particular state. In some states, contributing data to the APCD is voluntary, but in most states contributing data is mandatory. Mandatory participation enables comprehensive coverage that is very valuable for many study purposes. For example, it makes it possible to study referral networks in ways that HCCI or Medicare data do not.[43] However, to date, most states have not created APCDs.[44]

Claims data from Medicare, the HCCI, and state APCDs are indispensable to developing cost-reducing innovations because they document utilization. Unfortunately, claims data omit much clinically and epidemiologically relevant information.[45]

One way to obtain clinical information not included in healthcare claims is to tap electronic medical records systems. An example of such a program is the Surveillance, Epidemiology, and End Results (SEER) program of the National Cancer Institute. SEER is an authoritative source of information on cancer incidence and survival in the United States; it collects data from state-level cancer registries that cover about 35 percent of the U.S. population. Cancer registries review reported cases, determine whether the information is reportable according to law, and pull information from medical records. The data includes patient demographics, primary tumor site, tumor morphology, stage at diagnosis, the first course of treatment, and follow-up—including mortality.[46] The SEER program makes de-identified information available to researchers and the public. This information can be used to analyze patterns of care, treatment trends by cancer, and treatment disparities. Other registries like SEER have been created that focus on specific disease states or medical interventions such as, for example, joint replacement. Such registries are valuable, but their singular focus limits their utility.

The data infrastructure of U.S. healthcare is an archipelago of data islands. Only a few organizations, such as Kaiser Permanente and the Veteran's Administration, have built bridges across these islands by developing data sets that span insurance categories and geographic jurisdictions, integrating medical records and claims data. Without such information, innovators and implementers seeking to reduce the cost of healthcare are flying blind. Investigators often try to build these bridges themselves in one-off studies that are slow and costly. Alternatively, researchers must tailor their work to the data island to which they have access. These limitations on data availability are a significant drag on the development, adoption, and evaluation of cost-reducing innovations. Investment in a robust national data and analytic infrastructure—including incentives to encourage greater exchange of information between electronic medical records—could facilitate cost-reducing innovation if combined with a suitable catalyst.

What might such a catalyst look like? The UK's National Institute for Health and Care Excellence (NICE) is illustrative. NICE was established in 1999 to support decision-making on new technologies and was asked to consider both costs and benefits of new technologies. Because it was established as part of Britain's National Health Service, its mandate included a commitment to provide the best value for taxpayers' money and the most effective, fair, and sustainable use of finite resources. Where possible NICE calculates a treatment's incremental cost-effectiveness ratio—often expressed as cost per QALY gained. In the UK context, interventions costing less than £20,000 per QALY are considered cost effective. Where the evidence is uncertain, conflicting, insufficient, or not robust, NICE liaises with the research community to investigate the issues. Finally, NICE publishes and disseminates its recommendations and has an implementation strategy to support the adoption of its recommendations.[47] NICE has significant limitations. For instance, it is concerned with building legitimacy with relevant stakeholders, which can cause it to proceed slowly.[48] Nonetheless, it provides essential information for clinicians and policymakers seeking to adopt cost-reducing innovations.

The NICE model is not directly applicable to the United States. Our closest approximation to the UK's National Health Service, Medicare, is legislatively prohibited from developing or deploying a dollars per QALY measure to determine coverage or reimbursement. (Medicare is, however, permitted to consider studies comparing the relative effectiveness of different treatments such as those funded by the government's Patient-Centered Outcomes Research Institute.) Removing these restrictions on Medicare would substantially boost prospects for cost reduction by providing a basis for decision-making backed by Medicare's authority and purchasing power.

A private non-profit organization, the Institute for Clinical and Economic Review (ICER), has attempted to fill the vacuum left by the restrictions on Medicare partially. The ICER was founded in 2006 as an organization within Massachusetts General Hospital but became an independent non-profit in 2013. It conducts evidence-based reviews of healthcare interventions, such as drugs, devices, and diagnostics. ICER's assessment process includes reviewing all available clinical data, comparative effectiveness research, and long-term effectiveness analysis. In addition, the ICER process includes opportunities for stakeholders to engage. At a public meeting, draft reports are discussed with patients, clinical experts, manufacturers, payers, and policy experts. Comments from these public meetings are included in the final assessment.[49]

The example of ICER illustrates the influence of culture and social norms on the trajectory of innovation. The relevant norm, in this case, is the distrust of centralized power that underlies so much of the U.S. political tradition. The same analyses we accept from a private sector organization (ICER) are forbidden when produced by a government agency (Medicare). Such research is a public good. Like all public goods—think education or environmental protection—it is undersupplied by private sector actors alone. Consequently, our social norms result in chronic underinvestment in the information essential for producing and deploying cost-reducing innovations.

Increase Market Competition

There are many ways that society benefits from competitive markets. One underappreciated benefit is the effect of competition on innovation.

Chapter 6 described how high profits from market power increase the cost to incumbent firms of switchover disruptions from innovations. The higher the markups incumbent firms enjoy, the more they have to lose from switchover disruptions. Switchover disruptions cause entrenched incumbents to innovate more slowly and tentatively. More competitive markets reduce markups and thereby reduce the barriers to innovation from switchover disruptions.

However, anti-competitive practices can inhibit innovation even in the absence of switchover disruptions. For example, consider the effect of horizontal mergers on incentives to innovate. Imagine two hospitals offering services that compete for the same customers. Hospital A has a dominant market position, but Hospital B is developing a cost-reducing new process innovation that could allow it to eventually win business that otherwise would have gone to Hospital A. This "business stealing" from A offers B a powerful incentive to pursue the innovation—but only because B needn't consider the costs its success will impose on A. After a horizontal merger between A and B, however, things change. The merged entity will consider the costs of A's lost sales. Suppose A has a sufficiently robust market position pre-merger. In that case, the combined entity may find it most profitable to slow down or stop the development of B's new process to avoid losses to A's existing business.[50]

In addition to horizontal mergers, innovation can be suppressed by exclusionary contracts that restrict market entry, making it difficult for innovative new competitors to challenge incumbents. Consider the case of Johnson and Johnson's biologic drug, Remicade. Johnson and Johnson offered a loyalty rebate program for Remicade. The rebate for purchasing Remicade would only be paid if a hospital bought all related biologics for treating the same conditions from Johnson and Johnson. If the hospital did not comply, it paid the high list price for Remicade and lost the rebate. This program inhibits the entry of biologic products similar to Remicade. Foreseeing this, a potential biosimilar manufacturer might choose not to develop a competitor for Remicade. In this way, exclusionary contracts reduce incentives for innovation and, consequently, R&D investments in biosimilars. The failure to enforce prohibitions against such exclusionary agreements may partly explain why the development of biosimilars in the United States lags behind the EU.[51]

A recent policy review suggests three ways to make healthcare markets more competitive: (1) reduce or eliminate policies that encourage consolidation or that impede entry and competition; (2) strengthen antitrust enforcement; and (3) create an agency responsible for monitoring and intervening in healthcare markets.[52]

Discouraging consolidation may require reform of payment policies used by Medicare and commercial insurers that reimburse physicians more for a procedure performed in an inpatient rather than an outpatient setting.[53] Such policies create incentives for health systems to purchase physician practices. Reform to state laws and regulations can also help.[54] Consider, for example, state Certificate of Need (CON) laws. These laws require a state health planning agency to approve certain significant health investments, such as constructing a new healthcare facility. CON laws aim to inhibit unnecessary or duplicative capital expenditures, but incumbent healthcare providers can also use them to disadvantage potential competitors. Any Willing Provider (AWP) laws, on the books in many states, require health insurers to include any provider in their network who wishes to participate and to pay them at in-network rates. These laws aim to protect consumer choice, but they may also undermine competition among providers for inclusion in a network. State-level laws regulating provider scope of practice and provider licensing may help protect consumers, but they can also be used to squelch innovative new entrants and practices.

Strengthening antitrust enforcement requires improving the capacities of the Antitrust Division of the Department of Justice (DOJ) and the Federal Trade Commission (FTC).[55] In addition to strictly scrutinizing mergers, antitrust regulators should focus more strongly on potential or future threats to competition. Absent such scrutiny, dominant firms may prevent future competition through exclusionary conduct. Congress could strengthen the hand of regulators in this regard by including harms to future competition in antitrust legislation. Such regulatory and legislative changes could be made more impactful by creating a specialized trial court to hear cases brought under federal antitrust laws to ensure that judges with the relevant expertise hear these complex cases. In addition, executive orders and laws could require the government to consider the effects of new bills or regulations on competition and generally promote new firms' entry into markets.[56]

A final proposal to improve competition in healthcare is to create a new federal agency for monitoring, overseeing, and potentially intervening in healthcare markets.[57] The agency would monitor prices, costs, quality, contracts, and access to care, among other variables. When monitoring reveals a potential antitrust or competition problem, the agency will notify the FTC or DOJ. To effectively monitor, the agency will require a much-improved data infrastructure than that which currently exists. Currently, there is no national and publicly available data on total U.S. healthcare costs or prices for specific services and providers.

Mobilize Professional and Social Norms

Imagine a circumstance in which the financial incentives for cost reduction were strong, the data, analytic, and reporting capabilities were state of the art, and anti-competitive behavior was kept to a minimum by vigorous monitoring and enforcement. In such a circumstance, would the skew in innovation away from cost reduction correct itself? We believe the answer is no, not without a change in the professional and social norms at play in the health sector.

Professional norms in healthcare are shaped heavily by the culture of the medical profession. This culture is absorbed early in medical training and is imbued with positive values about service, healing, discipline, and account-ability. However, like all powerful cultures, the culture of medicine also has a dark side. It is factional, hierarchical, exquisitely sensitive to threats to pro-fessional prerogatives, autonomy, and status, and slow to change. At its best, it spurs its adherents to heroic service on behalf of patients, as we have seen during the COVID-19 pandemic. At its worst, it leads physicians to burnout, cynicism, and despair.[58]

Kaiser Permanente's well-developed model of prepaid group practice and its long-term relationships with its members create potent incentives for adopting value-enhancing and cost-reducing innovations. In addition, the organization's extensive patient data and the research capabilities of its Division of Research provide precisely the kind of information infrastructure needed to make evidence-based decisions about the cost and quality of care. However, even in this environment, physicians resisted innovations such as the concentration of surgical volume in a handful of centers of excellence to keep quality up and costs low. The reporting of quality metrics and the development of treatment guidelines also engendered resistance and were characterized as denigrating the "art" of medicine and opening a doorway to second-rate "cookbook" medicine. Implementing these changes took skillful physician leadership and years of careful persuasion.[59]

The example of Kaiser Permanente illustrates that even when innovation is well defined and reinforced with appropriate incentives, people still need clarity about what to do in the face of change.[60] Such clarity generally takes the form of shared understandings and expectations that go far beyond the content of formal job descriptions or standard operating procedures. This informal clarity is the "secret sauce" behind successful organizations and explains why propagating even well-defined innovations can be challenging. Toyota, for example, makes no effort to hide its Toyota Production System methodology, also known as Lean, from competitors because it believes they lack the informal clarity—the organizational culture—needed to make the system work. Professional norms can conceivably be the source of such clarity in healthcare organizations. Often, however, they are not.

Chapter 5 argued that norms could stimulate cost-reducing innovation to the extent that innovations align with ethical commitments and professional obligations. But physician culture does not make clear that stewardship of scarce social resources is a moral duty for the medical profession. Nor does it obligate physicians to lead the design and implementation of cost-reducing innovations, without which such innovations surely struggle. Without clear ethical obligations, innovations often encounter the dark side of physician culture, where concerns over professional turf, status, and autonomy slow or stall innovation.

Changing this reality must begin in medical training. Today, most physicians emerge from their training with little economic understanding of healthcare financing and delivery and the role their decisions play in determining healthcare costs. Time for pursuing scholarly or scientific research is incorporated into medical training, but rarely is such time used to expose trainees to the tools and methods of designing and implementing innovations. Physicians are taught the ethics of caring for individual patients but not the ethics of appropriate stewardship.

Bright spots are emerging to address these gaps in professional training and culture. At Stanford University, for example, the Byers Center for Biodesign teaches interdisciplinary teams of physicians, engineers, and scientists to use design methods to create new medical devices. Similarly, the Stanford Clinical Excellence Research Center (CERC) trains teams of physicians, psychologists, nurse midwives, and other health professionals to work together to design, test, and implement new models of care delivery that safely lower the social cost of healthcare. Texas A&M University's ENMED program trains "physicianeers" in a joint medicine and engineering degree program whose graduates seek to design efficient new medical technologies. Programs like these need to proliferate and become the norm at medical schools and universities across the country.

The blind spots in physician culture that make cost-reducing innovation difficult mirror a more profound confusion in our civic culture about healthcare. Although healthcare is bought and sold like other goods and services, it has a distinct ethical foundation. This foundation is illuminated by a simple question posed by the economist Uwe Reinhardt in the Journal of the American Medical Association in 1997: "Should a child of a poor American family have the same chance of receiving adequate prevention and treatment as the child of a rich family?"[61] In other words, is healthcare a social good that should be available to all on equal terms, or is it a private consumption good whose financing is an individual responsibility? If the former, physicians, hospital administrators, nurses, and related professionals must adopt an ethical commitment to the wise use of the resources needed to meet these social commitments.

* * *

Innovation in healthcare is too often disconnected from value creation and cost reduction. The reasons for this disconnect run deep, and its consequences for our society loom ever larger as healthcare expenditures take up a rising share of our national income. We, as a society, have the opportunity to change this situation, to point innovation in a better direction. To do so, we must act on multiple fronts. Incentives for value creation and cost reduction must be strengthened. We need to invest in a data infrastructure that supports innovators and implementers. Markets must become more competitive to reduce the market power of entrenched incumbents. Finally, professional and social norms need to evolve so that stewardship of scarce healthcare resources becomes an honorable way to care for patients and society.

Does Innovation Respond to Expected Profits?

A fundamental premise of our argument is that inventive activity responds to expected economic rewards. For the casual observer, this seems obvious. From a scientific perspective, however, the response of innovation to expected profits is not a completely settled matter, so it is worth considering the evidence. Consistent with our premise, most evidence suggests that economic rewards *do* stimulate more innovation, but the relationship is subtle, complex, and sometimes surprising.

The causal effects of incentives on innovation are best measured using an experiment in which rewards for some randomly selected areas of investigation are increased relative to others. If we see innovation increasing in the high rewards arm of the experiment, we could then estimate the influence of these high rewards. In the absence of such an experiment, researchers do the next best thing. They study how innovation responds to specific economic conditions (market size and high input prices) and specific institutions (prizes, grants, and patent systems) that make certain areas of investigation more or less profitable.

Market Size

Research and development of new pharmaceuticals require substantial fixed costs, and so, all else equal, the expected rewards to innovation are substantially greater in larger markets. Shifts in population demographics and changes in the provision of health insurance cause large-scale and long-lived increases in the size of markets for some healthcare products and services but not for others. Economists wanting to understand the effects of economic rewards have used these shifts and changes to assess the effect of market size on new drug development.

One influential study examines the effects of demographic shifts on drug development. They reason that as the baby boom generation has aged, the markets for drugs mostly consumed by the young have declined, while the market for drugs used by the middle-aged has increased. They construct age profiles of users for each drug category and compute implied market size from aggregate demographic and income changes given these age profiles. They find that a 1 percent increase in potential market size is associated with a 4 percent growth in the entry of non-generic drugs and new molecular entities whose active ingredients had not been previously marketed in the United States—suggesting that increasing anticipated economic returns stimulates innovation.[1] A later study done by a different set of researchers takes a similar approach, using data from 14 countries, and estimates by how much innovative activity increases with market size.[2] This study found that a 1 percent increase in potential market size increases the number of new treatments by 0.25 percent, directionally similar to the first set of results, but with an effect only one-tenth as large. It is not clear why the magnitude of the results of the two studies differs so dramatically, but a contributing factor may be that the first study focused on the U.S. market where profit margins, and the associated economic incentives, are greater than in the countries included in the later analysis.

Changes in market size can also affect academic medical research, the precursor to developing new treatments. Shifts in the incidence of disease caused by an aging population are associated with more academic publications related to those diseases—even after controlling for the quality of research opportunities.[3]

The size of healthcare markets can also change in response to new public policy or regulations. Such changes can also induce innovation. One study focused on three public policies aimed at increasing the vaccination rates for six diseases.[4] The first two policies were the 1991 CDC recommendations to vaccinate all infants against hepatitis B and the 1993 decision for Medicare to cover the cost of influenza vaccines for Medicare recipients. The third policy was the introduction of the Vaccine Injury Compensation Fund in 1986. This fund reduced the cost of innovation by indemnifying manufacturers from lawsuits resulting from adverse reactions to vaccines for polio, diphtheria-tetanus, measles-mumps-rubella, and pertussis. These policies were associated with a 2.5-fold increase in the number of new vaccine clinical trials. Put differently, a $1 increase in annual expected market revenue stimulated $0.06 in the discounted present value of the investment in the vaccine.

Another policy that expanded the market size for drugs was the introduction of Medicare Part D. Before Part D, Medicare did not cover most classes of drugs. Comparing the number of new clinical trials for drugs heavily used by Medicare patients with those less heavily used, the former had increased R&D activities as measured by the number of Phase I, II, and III clinical trials. The number of Phase 1 trials increased by 2.4–4.7 percent in response to a 1 percent increase in market size. In contrast, the establishment of the Medicare program in 1965—which expanded the availability of health insurance but not drug coverage- did not affect the development of new drugs.[5] The implication seems clear: no change in demand for drugs, no change in drug innovation.

However, the creation of the original Medicare program appears to have had a considerable effect on the demand for the healthcare services it covered and hence on the adoption of new technologies.[6] Upon implementing Medicare in 1966, hospital insurance coverage for the elderly increased instantaneously to almost 100 percent. The result was an increase in hospital admissions of 46 percent and total spending of 28 percent. The increase in the adoption of then-new cardiac technology (open heart surgery facilities and cardiac intensive care units) was greatest in those geographic areas where Medicare had the largest impact on elderly insurance rates.

The introduction of Medicare and Medicaid also shifted the rate of patenting for medical devices.[7] Clemens finds that U.S.-based medical equipment patenting rose by 40–50 percent relative to other U.S. patenting and foreign medical equipment patenting after the passage of the Medicare and Medicaid Act. Increases in patenting activity were largest where Medicare and Medicaid expansions had the largest effect on the number of insured and where the number of physicians per resident was large. Estimates suggest that 25 percent of recent global medical equipment innovation is the result of U.S. insurance expansions.

The rules adopted by private sector actors also influence market size. In the United States, most drug purchases take place through formularies administered by Pharmacy Benefit Managers (PBMs). Beginning in 2012, PBMs began refusing coverage for many newly approved drugs when cheaper alternatives were available. These exclusions affected some classes of drugs more than others. PBMs were interested in using exclusions to reduce drug expenditures for payers without denying members access to important classes of medications. Thus, exclusions were concentrated in drug classes where there were many competing therapeutic options, so it was easy to substitute for the excluded drug. The savings from price reductions were greatest for high volume prescriptions, so exclusions were most likely in drug classes with many patients. Because the PBM industry is heavily concentrated in a small number of firms, each exclusion would sharply reduce the expected volume of sales for the excluded drug. Faced with the prospect of a smaller market, pharmaceutical investments fell markedly in drug classes at high risk of exclusion after 2012. For instance, the total number of drug candidates declined for common conditions such as diabetes and cardiovascular disease for which numerous treatments were already available.[8]

Innovation Induced by Input Prices

The price of inputs to a production process can also motivate innovation. When the price of an input, say labor or land, is relatively high, so the reasoning goes, that will spur innovations that reduce the use of the high-price input. The term of art for this process is "induced" innovation. The idea traces back to Nobel prize-winning economist John Hicks who argued in 1932 that a centuries-long trend of labor-saving innovation in industrial economies resulted from economizing on the use of high-price workers.[9] Other historians similarly argue that high UK wages and low-priced UK coal partially explain why the Industrial Revolution happened first in Britain. These input prices increased the return for substituting steam power for human labor.[10]

Another area where induced innovation from high input prices has attracted attention is environmental policy. A carbon tax will discourage consumption of high carbon energy sources by raising prices. But will it also fuel the future development of new non-carbon energy sources?[11]

One study of the effects of high energy prices on innovation, tracked new, energy-related, patent applications.[12] The results suggest that at least during the 20-year study period (1971–1991), new energy-related patent applications responded rapidly to increases in energy prices and increases in the pre-existing stock of knowledge (as measured by the number of approved patents in the technology class). Changes in the stock of knowledge had significantly larger effects than changes in energy prices, suggesting that while incentives created by input prices matter, the legacy of prior discoveries' also matters. In other words, high input prices may be most successful in inducing innovation when the scientific and technical setting is ripe.

Prizes, Grants, and Procurement

Competitive markets do not, on their own, always provide sufficient incentives for the development of new inventions. For this reason, industrialized societies have used various prizes and grants to create inducements for developing new ideas. One of the more famous examples of such prizes comes from the 1700s and concerns the measurement of longitude.

To pinpoint their location out of sight of land, ships at sea need to know their latitude and longitude. For ship captains, calculating longitude was largely a matter of guesswork.

The longitude problem, as it was known, attracted the attention of top minds and famous scientists—to no avail. In principle, one can calculate longitude by comparing the sun's position at the ship's current location with the time at the ship's point of embarkation (or any other fixed point). This calculation requires a very accurate shipboard clock. However, constructing an accurate marine chronometer was a technical problem that tested the limits of 18th-century engineering. John Harrison ultimately solved the problem. Harrison's research was stimulated by a £20,000 longitude prize offered by the English Parliament in 1714—a sum well in excess of £4,000,000 today. The prize motivated many others as well. Indeed, the board charged with administering the prize was besieged with proposed solutions—many of them ridiculous or at best weakly related to the longitude problem.[13]

But did the prize truly influence the direction or pace of innovation? An obvious difficulty in answering this question is that history offers no counterfactual, no 18th-century England without the longitude prize. Thus we have no direct way to assess whether the solution of the longitude problem would have been meaningfully delayed under a different set of rewards. After all, Harrison's obsession with clocks and the status won by solving the longitude problem might have sustained him in the long discovery process even without the prize. A related possibility is that the accumulated knowledge of metallurgy and watch design combined with the growing importance of sea transport simply made the moment ripe for developing maritime chronometers. In this case, the prize's existence did not *induce* a discovery, but rather the prize is the *result* of the same social, scientific, and technical conditions that made discovery valuable and likely. Finally, we must consider the possibility that the prize delayed the discovery and diffusion of marine chronometers. Harrison's rivals, it appears, took steps to slow the recognition of his solution to give themselves a shot at winning the prize.[14]

Prizes reward a specified innovation. These work well when the prize giver knows enough about the problem to clearly define the criteria for winning and understands how large a prize would be required to attract talented contestants. An alternative that is much more commonly used is to offer grants to innovators with promising projects. These are often run through the National Institute of Health (NIH) or the National Science Foundation (NSF) in the United States. For the most part, NIH and NSF grants aim to promote scientific discovery rather than to achieve a particular outcome. A famous exception, begun in December 1971, was the National Cancer Act that authorized spending enormous sums of money for cancer research and control—a total of $1.5 billion over three years. However, the opinion of many scientists at the time was that the biology of cancer was not sufficiently advanced to support a crash program to defeat the disease. Consistent with this contemporaneous assessment, studies in the 1980s found that the "war on cancer" had most decidedly not been won. These studies found little or very modest progress against the disease, notwithstanding the enormous influx of research dollars.[15]

Despite the failure of the war on cancer, there is evidence that the cumulative effect of grants can under the right circumstances stimulate innovation, even if the efforts sometimes have unintended consequences. One study focuses on the effect of NIH grant activity on the prevention of infant death for at-risk infants from respiratory distress syndrome (RDS), congenital heart defects, and sudden infant death syndrome (SIDS).[16] There has been tremendous innovation in the neonatal treatment of at-risk babies since 1960. This innovation involves hundreds of small changes in clinical care delivery: improved technology for ventilation; improvements in monitoring newborn blood and respiratory function; and synthetic surfactants that can be administered to newborns. NIH research grants were allocated toward diseases that accounted for higher proportions of infant deaths, and these grants were associated with subsequent declines in mortality. Thus grant induced innovation can plausibly be said to have played a role in reducing infant death rates, particularly for RDS. However, because white babies are more likely to have RDS—and at greater severity—this success story had an unintended consequence: increasing racial disparities in infant mortality.

Experience with the Orphan Drug Act (ODA) suggests that patent-like periods of exclusivity combined with tax subsidies can effectively induce innovation. The ODA aims to promote private drug development for rare diseases (with fewer than 200,000 cases per year in the United States). These products are known as orphan drugs. The ODA has two primary incentives: an income tax credit equal to 50 percent of clinical trial expenses and a 7-year market exclusivity. The tax credit incentive is significant because it lowers the costs to pharmaceutical companies of clinical trials, which constitute a large share of the fixed costs of drug development. One study compared the number of clinical trials before and after the implementation of the ODA.[17] It found a substantial increase in the number of trials for orphan drugs relative to the number of trials for other rare diseases not covered by the ODA.

When products are mostly purchased by the government, the policies and standards that determine government procurement can also influence the direction of innovation. One study examined how increases in government purchases of prosthetics during the Civil War and World War 1 altered patenting patterns in the industry. It found that wartime procurement programs were associated with large increases in the volume of prosthetic device patents—consistent with the research reviewed earlier showing that innovation can respond quite strongly to changes in demand. Cost reducing innovation, including efforts to introduce new materials and shed extraneous parts, increased during the Civil War period. The authors attribute this, in part, to the government's Civil War era procurement practice of paying a low, fixed price per prosthetic, which encouraged cost-conscious innovation. In contrast, during the World War I period prosthetic device patents emphasized comfort and appearance. This shift in quality may be linked to changes in demand, because in the World War 1 period government policy and medical advice emphasized veteran rehabilitation and re-employment.[18]

The Strength of the Patent System

Patent systems, despite their imperfections and distortions, provide powerful incentives for innovation. If innovation responds to incentives, one might expect the rate of innovation to accelerate when patents are strengthened. The evidence that stronger patent protections spur greater innovation is, however, very weak. One study examined the effects of changes in patent law in 60 high GDP countries from 1850 until 1997 and found no evidence of a strong positive effect of patent strength on a measure of innovation (patent filing).[19] One reason for the absence of effects could be a lack of statistical power.[20] Estimates of innovation gains could also be biased downward by the difficulty of identifying whether nominal changes in patent regimes alter innovation incentives in a meaningful way.[21]

The effect of stronger patents on innovation is also likely to be unevenly distributed across the economy. For pharmaceutical makers, strengthening patents by moving from a 10-year to a 20-year patent length may be a powerful spur to invention because clinical trials take so long to complete. In contrast, new software innovations go from patent to product much more quickly, and the more rapid pace of software innovation means that the value of patented ideas depreciates more rapidly than in pharmaceuticals. As a result, lengthening patent protections from 10 to 20 years may have less of an incentive effect in software than in drug discovery. This difference in the costs and pace of discovery across sectors may explain why surveys of R&D managers find that managers in chemical and pharmaceutical industries rely heavily on patents while alternative strategies to protect new products and discoveries are viewed as more effective in other sectors.[22]

Sectors may also differ in the importance of downstream innovations building on upstream patents. The presence of an upstream patent has two competing effects on follow-on innovation—one positive and one negative. On the positive side, an expensive upstream patent restricts access and so reduces the number of potential competitors for the downstream innovator. Reduced competition increases the expected downstream profits and so encourages more downstream innovative effort. On the negative side, if the upstream patent holder mistakenly sets the royalty fee too high, it can shut down an entire cascade of valuable downstream innovation efforts. Such mistakes would not occur in an efficient patent system because upstream patent holders would not want to lose out on license revenues. But the system may not be efficient, and mistakes do happen. One influential empirical study found that Celera's establishment of contractual intellectual property on genes reduced follow-on innovation by 30 percent.[23] A later study found no evidence that gene patents inhibited downstream innovation. The difference in the two studies may be due to differences in disclosure requirements. The rules governing gene patenting mandate unusually expansive disclosure of the relevant genetic information, while Celera's contracts kept information about their genes out of the public domain.[24]

Are Innovations Overlooked
in Other Sectors?

In this book, we have asked why value-creating and cost-reducing innovations are so regularly overlooked in the health sector. Readers might rightfully wonder whether overlooked innovations are unique to the health sector or whether they can be found elsewhere in the economy. A complete answer to this question lies beyond the scope of this book. However, recent studies of the effects of the computer revolution on the automation of work raise concerns analogous to the ones we raise in healthcare. These studies suggest that prevailing incentives and social norms lead innovators to produce too much of the wrong sort of innovation. Specifically, too much effort is devoted to using computers to automate jobs rather than augment human capabilities. The result is "mediocre" innovations that displace workers but do not create much additional value for society.

New computer technologies lie behind recent critical advances in automation. Robots, for example, increasingly perform many production tasks previously performed by humans. Incorporating this automation of job tasks into otherwise standard macroeconomic models produces a remarkable result: automation of jobs increases productivity and income, but it also reduces the share of that income accruing to workers.[1] Such redistribution raises obvious social and political problems.[2] It is perhaps less obvious that the redistributive effect of job automation also distorts incentives for innovation.

Consider what might happen if robots were universally less efficient at performing tasks than the people they replace. In this hypothetical example, robots reduce productivity and increase the share of income to investors. If the redistribution effect is large enough, profits for robot makers can be increased by automation even as they make society poorer overall. The point of this example is not that robots make society poorer but rather to illustrate that distributional effects can distort incentives for innovation.

The U.S. tax code also favors investments in automation because labor income is taxed more heavily than capital income. This tax advantage makes innovations that substitute machines for people more profitable than they would otherwise be.

Fortunately, technology can also augment human capabilities rather than simply substitute for humans by automating job tasks. When computers augment human capacities, productivity is increased without moving income away from workers. For example, artificial intelligence (AI)-powered decision support can enhance the productivity of the nurse practioners that Minute Clinics rely on and shift the earnings distribution toward these nonphysician providers.

More generally, AI-powered innovations that augment human capacities have the opposite distributional effect of automation. Human beings are reinstated into the production process and the distribution of the productivity gains from innovation shifts toward labor. However, this pro-labor redistribution reduces the firm's incentives to invest in innovations that augment human capacities.[3] The same features of the tax code that favor new automation end up reducing the profitability of labor augmenting innovations relative to automation because the income of the reinstated workers is more heavily taxed than capital income.

The long-term economic effects of incentives that favor automation over augmentation depend critically on which type of innovation is likely to have a more significant impact on productivity. It is very challenging to predict the productivity gains from yet-to-be-developed technologies, but at least in the context of new AI, some keen observers are willing to take strong positions. Erik Brynjolfsson observes that AI-based augmentation generates far more value than human-like AI designed to substitute for human intelligence.[4] If Brynjolfsson is right, computer-based automation has an innovation problem similar to the one we identify in the health sector. In both cases, prevailing incentives can make mediocre automation more profitable than other innovations offering more significant productivity gains.

Another parallel between computer-based automation and our analysis of healthcare is that social norms influence the projects innovators favor. The relevant norm in AI is the status granted to efforts at building machines with human-like intelligence.[5] This norm manifests in the field's fascination with the famous Turing test of machine intelligence.

The Turing test, named after the computing pioneer Alan Turing, proposes a simple and alluring test of whether a machine has achieved human-like intelligence. Passing the test requires a machine to answer a series of unstructured questions so well that a human observer could not tell a machine was answering. It seems obvious that the Turing test requires participants to build machines that replicate rather than augment human intelligence.

There are many good scientific reasons why Turing and other AI founders might have wanted to build machines that mimic human-level intelligence, but in the years since Turing, scientists and engineers have discovered this is very hard to do. At its core, machine intelligence is very different from human intelligence, and our understanding of it remains at rudimentary stages.[6]

Norms and attitudes amplifying the prestige of AI breakthroughs that mimic human intelligence may have unexpected, adverse economic effects. Google, for example, has made extensive and highly publicized investments in developing sensors and AI capable of driving a car. But at this writing, years of experimentation have failed to produce a self-driving car that can safely and reliably navigate city streets. If Google had instead devoted its resources to new AI that makes human drivers safer, it might have already produced many highly valuable products. Our point is not that self-driving cars are impossible. Rather, it is that the social norms favoring human-like AI may cause technologists to devote too much attention to hard-to-achieve automation rather than easier-to-realize and value-producing augmentation.

In sum, there is good reason to worry that incentives, regulations, and prevailing social norms may move innovators to devote too much attention to the wrong types of AI innovation in the workplace. This conclusion is analogous to our findings regarding health sector innovation. In both cases, scientifically dynamic fields fail to realize their full potential to improve the human condition. This parallel points to a more general question: Can profit motives and market forces alone be relied upon to generate the "right types" of innovation? If not, what interventions and institutions are needed to put innovation on a better path?[7]

Acknowledgments

This project began with the stories we told each other from our respective perches as an economist and a management consultant. Jim would like to thank David Weil for persuading him that writing a book was a good thing for an economist to do. Jim began work on this project as a visiting scholar at the Brocher Foundation and thanks them for their support. He also received critical research support from Boston University's Questrom School of Business and benefited greatly from conversations with Keith Ericson and Frank Levy. Jim also thanks Kathleen Engel for her thoughtful questions and enthusiastic, loving support throughout this long project. Bob would like to thank Mark Smith, Ian Morrison, Sam Karp, Arnie Milstein, and Bill Bernstein for sharpening his thinking and broadening his perspective on healthcare and on innovation. He'd also like to thank Jackie Schneider for reminding him to "keep the story deep and brief" and for her unwavering love and encouragement. Bob and Jim would like to thank Frank Levy, Ken Kimmell, and Eden Engel-Rebitzer for reading drafts of the book proposal. Victor Fuchs, Eran Politzer, Magnum Shahzad, and Tal Gross gave detailed comments on the draft manuscript, and we benefited enormously from their astute observations and suggestions.

Notes

Chapter 1

1. Meyer, Gregg S., Akinluwa A. Demehin, Xiu Liu, and Duncan Neuhauser. 2012. "Two Hundred Years of Hospital Costs and Mortality—MGH and Four Eras of Value in Medicine." *The New England Journal of Medicine*, 366(23): 2147–2149.
2. Catillon, Maryaline, David Cutler, and Thomas Getzen. 2018. "Two Hundred Years of Health and Medical Care: The Importance of Medical Care for Life Expectancy Gains." National Bureau of Economic Research Working Paper Series, No. 25330.
3. Murphy, Kevin M., and Robert H. Topel. 2006. "The Value of Health and Longevity." *Journal of Political Economy*, 114(5): 871–904.
4. Nordhaus, William D. 1996. "Do Real-Output and Real-Wage Measures Capture Reality? the History of Lighting Suggests Not." In *The Economics of New Goods*, ed. Timothy F. Bresnahan and Robert J. Gordon, 27–70. Chicago: University of Chicago Press.
5. Delong, Brad. 2019. "The Lighting Budget of Thomas Jefferson." Delong's Grasping Reality, https://www.bradford-delong.com/2019/02/the-lighting-budget-of-thomas-jefferson.html (accessed June 22, 2021).
6. Table 1.4 in Nordhaus. "Do Real-Output and Real-Wage Measures Capture Reality? the History of Lighting Suggests Not."
7. For a review see Goldstein, Joseph L., and Michael S Brown. 2015. "A Century of Cholesterol and Coronaries: From Plaques to Genes to Statins." *Cell*, 161(1): 161–172.
8. Goldman, Dana P., Karen Van Nuys, Jakub P. Hlavka, Luca Pani, Sylvain Chassang, and Erik Snowberg. 2018. "A New Model for Pricing Drugs of Uncertain Efficacy." *The New England Journal of Medicine Catalyst*, https://catalyst.nejm.org/doi/full/10.1056/CAT.18.0035.
9. Shrank, William H., Teresa L. Rogstad, and Natasha Parekh. 2019. "Waste in the US Health Care System: Estimated Costs and Potential for Savings." *JAMA*, 322(15): 1501.
10. The problem of cost-reduction is often confused with the problem of high prices and high levels of expenditures in U.S. healthcare. However, the two issues are distinct and have very different economic implications. We discuss this topic at greater length in chapter 7.
11. A number of studies have examined how market size alters the direction of pharmaceutical innovations. See Acemoglu, Daron, and Joshua Linn. 2004. "Market Size in Innovation: Theory and Evidence from the Pharmaceutical Industry." *Quarterly Journal of Economics*, 119(3): 1049–1090; and Dubois, Pierre, Olivier de Mouzon, Fiona Scott-Morton, and Paul Seabright. 2015. "Market Size and Pharmaceutical Innovation." *RAND Journal of Economics*, 46(4): 844–871. Much less attention has

been given to the effect of shared savings incentives on innovation. For an important exception see Weisbrod, Burton A. 1991. "The Health Care Quadrilemma: An Essay on Technological Change, Insurance, Quality of Care, and Cost Containment" *Journal of Economic Literature*, 29(2): 523–552. Weisbrod's analysis, however, was written without the benefit of recent advances in contract theory and behavioral economics that greatly enhance our understanding of the specific problems shared savings arrangements must overcome in the health sector.

12. Plackett, Benjamin. 2020. "Why Big Pharma Has Abandoned Antibiotics" *Nature*, 586(7830): S50.

13. Kremer, Michael, and Christopher M. Snyder. 2015. "Prentatives versus Treatments" *Quarterly Journal of Economics*, 130(3): 1167–1239.

14. Budish, Eric, Benjamin N. Roin, and Heidi Williams. 2015. "Do Firms Underinvest in Long-Term Research? Evidence from Cancer Clinical Trials" *American Economic Review*, 105(7): 2044–2085.

15. Richards, Kevin T., Kevin J. Hickey, and Erin H. Ward. 2020. "Drug Pricing and Pharmaceutical Patenting Practices" Congressional Research Service.

16. Conti, Rena M., Brigham Frandsen, Michael L. Powell, and James B. Rebitzer. 2021. "Common Agent or Double Agent? Pharmacy Benefit Managers in the Prescription Drug Market" National Bureau of Economic Research Working Paper Series, No. 28866.

17. Dranove, David, Craig Garthwaite, and Manuel Hermosilla. 2014. "Pharmaceutical Profits and the Social Value of Innovation" National Bureau of Economic Research Working Paper Series, No. 20212.

18. Chandra, Amitabh, and Jonathan Skinner. 2012. "Technology Growth and Expenditure Growth in Health Care" *Journal of Economic Literature*, 50(3): 645–680.

19. Weisbrod. "The Health Care Quadrilemma: An Essay on Technological Change, Insurance, Quality of Care, and Cost Containment."

20. Frandsen, Brigham, Michael Powell, and James B. Rebitzer. 2019. "Sticking Points: Common Agency Problems and Contracting in the US Healthcare System" *RAND Journal of Economics*, 50(2): 251–285.

21. Cebul, Randall D., James B. Rebitzer, Lowell J. Taylor, and Mark E. Votruba. 2011. "Unhealthy Insurance Markets: Search Frictions and the Cost and Quality of Health Insurance" *American Economic Review*, 101(5): 1842–1871.

22. Kaplan, Robert M. 2019. *More than Medicine*. Cambridge: Harvard University Press; and Pryor, Katherine, and Kevin Volpp. 2018. "Deployment of Preventive Interventions—Time for a Paradigm Shift" *The New England Journal of Medicine*, 378(19): 1761–1763.

23. Fisher, Elliott S., Mark B. McClellan, John Bertko, Steven M. Lieberman, Julie J. Lee, Julie L. Lewis, and Jonathan S. Skinner. 2009. "Fostering Accountable Health Care: Moving Forward in Medicare" *Health Affairs*, 28(2): W219–W231.

24. Roth, Alvin E. 2007. "Repugnance as a Constraint on Markets" *The Journal of Economic Perspectives*, 21(3): 37–58.

25. Elías, Julio J., Nicola Lacetera, and Mario Macis. 2015. "Markets and Morals: An Experimental Survey Study" *PloS one*, 10(6): e0127069.

26. Bowles, Samuel, and Sandra Polania-Reyes. 2012. "Economic Incentives and Social Preferences: Substitutes or Complements?" *Journal of Economic Literature*, 50(2): 368–425; and Bowles, Samuel. 2016. *The Moral Economy*. New Haven: Yale University Press.

27. Bowles. *The Moral Economy*.

28. Akerlof, George A., and Rachel E. Kranton. 2000. "Economics and Identity" *Quarterly Journal of Economics*, 115(3): 715–753.

29. Akerlof, George A., and Rachel E. Kranton. 2010. *Identity Economics*. Princeton: Princeton University Press.

30. Shiller, Robert J. 2019. *Narrative Economics*. Princeton; Oxford: Princeton University Press.

31. Mokyr, Joel. 2016. *A Culture of Growth*. Princeton: Princeton University Press.

32. Shapiro, Carl. 2012. "Competition and Innovation: Did Arrow Hit the Bull's Eye?" In *The Rate and Direction of Innovative Activity Revisited*, ed. Josh Lerner and Scott Stern, 361–404. Chicago: University of Chicago Press.

33. Arrow, Kenneth. 1962. "Economic Welfare and the Allocation of Resources for Invention." In *The Rate and Direction of Inventive Activity: Economic and Social Factors*, ed. Universities-National Bureau Committee for Economic Research, Committee on Economic Growth of the Social Science Research Council, 609–626. Princeton: Princeton University Press.

34. Federico, Giulio, Fiona S. Morton, and Carl Shapiro. 2020. "Antitrust and Innovation: Welcoming and Protecting Disruption." In *Innovation Policy and the Economy*, Vol. 20, ed. Josh Lerner and Scott Stern, 125–190. Chicago: University of Chicago Press.

35. Aghion, Philippe, Nick Bloom, Richard Blundell, Rachel Griffith, and Peter Howitt. 2005. "Competition and Innovation: An Inverted-U Relationship" *Quarterly Journal of Economics*, 120(2): 701–728.

36. Holmes, Thomas J., and James A. Schmitz. 2010. "Competition and Productivity: A Review of Evidence" *Annual Review of Economics*, 2(1): 619–642.

37. Holmes, Thomas J., David K. Levine, and James A. Schmitz. 2012. "Monopoly and the Incentive to Innovate when Adoption Involves Switchover Disruptions" *American Economic Journal: Microeconomics*, 4(3): 1–33. Holmes, Levine, and Schmitz. "Monopoly and the Incentive to Innovate when Adoption Involves Switchover Disruptions."

38. The theory of switchover disruption has some surface similarity to Clay Christensen's theory of disruptive innovation popularized in the *Innovator's Dilemma* and other books (Christensen, Clayton M. 2013. *The Innovator's Dilemma*, 1st ed. Reprint Edition. Boston: Harvard Business Review Press). But as we detail in chapter 6, the economic logic is quite different and it emphasizes different mechanisms of action than those at work the health sector. Christensen's account has been subject to harsh empirical criticism by some scholars of the technology industries he studied.

39. Christensen, Clayton M., Jerome H. Grossman, and Jason Hwang. 2009. *The Innovator's Prescription: A Disruptive Solution for Health Care*. New York: McGraw-Hill; and Robinson, James C. 2020. "Slouching towards Disruptive Innovation" *Health*

Affairs Blog, https://www.healthaffairs.org/do/10.1377/forefront.20200227.395178/full/ (accessed February 28, 2020).

40. Morgenson, Getchen. 2017. "A Costly Drug, Missing a Dose of Disclosure" *New York Times*.

41. Cunningham, Colleen, Florian Ederer, and Song Ma. 2021. "Killer Acquisitions" *The Journal of Political Economy*, 129(3): 649–702.

42. Frandsen, Powell, and Rebitzer. "Sticking Points: Common Agency Problems and Contracting in the US Healthcare System."

43. Gottlieb, J. D., A. H. Shapiro, and A. Dunn. 2018. "The Complexity of Billing and Paying for Physician Care" *Health Affairs*, 37(4): 619–626.

Chapter 2

1. Mukherjee, Siddhartha. 2010. *The Emperor of all Maladies: A Biography of Cancer*. New York: Scribner.

2. As we detail in an appendix 1, a substantial body of research supports this conclusion.

3. Taylor, Timothy. 2018. "What's the Value of a QALY?" *Conversable Economist*, http://conversableeconomist.blogspot.com/2018/06/whats-value-of-qaly.html?m=1. For a discussion of the historical evolution of the value of a QALY see Neumann, Peter J., Joshua T. Cohen, and Milton C. Weinstein. 2014. "Updating Cost-Effectiveness—the Curious Resilience of the $50,000-Per-QALY Threshold" *The New England Journal of Medicine*, 371(9): 796–797.

4. The calculation is 0.1 QALY*$100,000/$50,000 = 0.2.

5. In perfectly competitive markets, prices are driven down to marginal cost. In a long-run equilibrium where marginal cost equals average cost, this leaves nothing leftover to reward innovators (Vollrath, Deitrich. 2015. "Market Power versus Price-Taking in Economic Growth" *Growth Economics Blog*, https://growthecon.com/feed/2015/06/06/market-power-versus-price-taking-in-economic-growth.html (accessed February 4, 2021)). If intense competition can reduce or eliminate incentives for innovation, the reverse does not hold true. Market power and monopoly can also inhibit incentives for innovation—a point we take up in later chapters.

6. Advanced Market Commitments by private and public donors can also mitigate the underpricing problem. Donors committed $1.5 billion for a pilot program to help purchase pneumococcal vaccine for distribution to children in low-income countries. Three vaccines have been developed under this program, 150 million children were immunized, and an estimated 700,000 lives were saved (Kremer, Michael, Jonathan D. Levin, and Christopher M. Snyder. 2020. "Advance Market Commitments: Insights from Theory and Commitments" National Bureau of Economic Research Working Paper, No. 26775).

7. Abi Younes, George, Charles Ayoubi, Omar Ballester, Gabriele Cristelli, Gaétan de Rassenfosse, Dominique Foray, Patrick Gaulé, Gabriele Pellegrino, Matthias van den Heuvel, Elizabeth Webster, et al. 2020. "COVID-19: Insights from Innovation Economists" *Science & Public Policy*, 47(5): 733–745.

8. Kremer, Michael, and Christopher M. Snyder. 2015. "Preventatives versus Treatments" *Quarterly Journal of Economics*, 130(3): 1167–1239.

9. This example is taken from Kremer and Snyder. 2015. "Preventatives versus Treatments."

10. The value of a vaccine for the 95 percent of patients with only a 5 percent chance of contracting the disease would be 0.05*$1M = $50K. Selling the vaccine for $50K to everyone at risk of the disease would thus generate revenues of $50K*1,000= $50M per year. However, 5 percent of the population has a 95 percent chance of getting the disease and this population is willing to pay 0.95*$1M =$950K. At this price, total revenues for the vaccine maker would be $950K*50 = $47.5M. High-risk people have a value for the vaccine that is almost 20 times more than low-risk people, but high risks are so scarce in the population that pricing a vaccine for them earns less in revenue than setting the price of the vaccine at a level everyone is willing to pay. If the vaccine maker in this example had to choose, it would sell the vaccine at a low price to everyone and earn $50M rather than sell the vaccine at a high price only to those likely to get sick, but in either case revenues are higher with a treatment. This example illustrates a more general point: treatments are favored over equally effective vaccines when treatments enable more effective market segmentation. People who are already sick with the disease identify themselves as a market segment willing to pay a very high price for treatment. Suppose instead that we allowed the vaccine maker to identify low and high risks and sell at a different price to both market segments. Allowing this sort of effective market segmentation would support maximum vaccine revenues of $97.5M—more than the $95M revenues from a treatment.

11. Kremer and Snyder. 2015. "Preventatives versus Treatments."

12. A different distribution of risks can overturn this result. The human papilloma virus (HPV) is spread more uniformly through the population and, in this case, the benefits of an HPV vaccine will exceed the profit-maximizing price for many more potential patients. The higher take-up rate for the HPV vaccine at the profit-maximizing price makes developing an HPV vaccine more profitable relative to treatment (Kremer and Snyder. 2015. "Preventatives versus Treatments").

13. Kremer and Snyder. 2015. "Preventatives versus Treatments."

14. McNeil, Donald G., Jr. 2019a. "200,000 Uninsured Americans to Get Free H.I.V.-Prevention Drugs" *New York Times*.

15. As we discuss below, health insurers rarely require their members to pay the full list price of a patented drug. For the population most likely to benefit from PrEP, however, access to health insurance itself poses a prohibitive barrier. Many lack private insurance or find commercial insurance premiums prohibitive. Navigating the bureaucracy involved in Medicare and Medicaid and establishing a regular relationship with a provider also inhibits take up. Other reasons for slow diffusion include inertia in provider treatment attitudes, concerns that failure to regularly take Truvada would expose users to HIV and perhaps also encourage drug resistance, and fear that by reducing the risk of HIV the preventative may also encourage riskier behaviors and spread other sexually transmitted diseases (Tuller, David. 2018. "HIV Prevention Drug's Slow Uptake Undercuts its Early Promise" *Health Affairs*, 37(2): 178–180).

16. Lin, Jennifer S., Margaret A. Piper, Leslie A. Perdue, Carolyn M. Rutter, Elizabeth M. Webber, Elizabeth O'Connor, Ning Smith, and Evelyn P. Whitlock. 2016. "Screening for Colorectal Cancer: Updated Evidence Report and Systematic Review for the US Preventive Services Task Force" *JAMA*, 315(23): 2576–2594.

17. Small average mortality reductions have led some researchers to argue that screening technologies like colonoscopies and flexible sigmoidoscopies just don't create much value for patients (see Kaplan, Robert M. 2019. *More than Medicine*. Cambridge: Harvard University Press). But this reasoning does not consider the substantial value that early treatment resulting from early detection provides for patients likely to go on to develop colorectal cancer. Depending on the distribution of risk, the profit-maximizing strategy for screening technologies might be to charge a high price so that only those in high-risk subgroups will use the screening test.

18. Budish, Eric, Benjamin N. Roin, and Heidi Williams. 2015. "Do Firms Underinvest in Long-Term Research? Evidence from Cancer Clinical Trials" *American Economic Review*, 105(7): 2044–2085.

19. This finding does not entirely close the case. Some argue that the difference between blood cancers and solid tumors may be due to differences in how the two types of cancer can be treated (Prasad, Vinay, and Stephan Lindner. 2018. "Why is Research in Early-Stage Cancer Research So Low?" *Journal of Cancer Policy*, 17: 4–8).

20. Outterson, Kevin, and Anthony McDonnell. 2016. "Funding Antibiotic Innovation with Vouchers: Recommendations on How to Strengthen a Flawed Incentive Policy" *Health Affairs*, 35(5): 784–790.

21. Teillant, Aude, Sumanth Gandra, Devra Barter, Daniel J. Morgan, and Ramanan Laxminarayan. 2015. "Potential Burden of Antibiotic Resistance on Surgery and Cancer Chemotherapy Antibiotic Prophylaxis in the USA: A Literature Review and Modelling Study" *The Lancet Infectious Diseases*, 15(12): 1429–1437.

22. Outterson, Kevin, Unni Gopinathan, Charles Clift, Anthony D. So, Chantal M. Morel, and John-Arne Røttingen. 2016. "Delinking Investment in Antibiotic Research and Development from Sales Revenues: The Challenges of Transforming a Promising Idea into Reality" *PLOS Medicine*, 13(6): e1002043.

23. Plackett, Benjamin. 2020. "Why Big Pharma Has Abandoned Antibiotics" *Nature*, 586(7830): S50.

24. Stoner, Isaac. 2020. "Saving Lives Should Be Good Business. Why Doesn't that Apply to Finding New Antibiotics?" *STAT*, https://www.statnews.com/2020/03/18/saving-lives-should-be-good-business-why-doesnt-that-apply-to-finding-new-antibiotics/.

25. Most antibiotics do not come to market with demonstrated superiority in efficacy or safety. Many antibiotics approved in the 1980s and 1990s had difficulty competing against already approved drugs (Outterson, Kevin, John H. Powers, Gregory W. Daniel, and Mark B. McClellan. 2015. "Repairing the Broken Market for Antibiotic Innovation" *Health Affairs*, 34(2): 277–285).

26. Outterson, Powers, Daniel, and McClellan. 2015. "Repairing the Broken Market for Antibiotic Innovation."

27. Stoner. 2020. "Saving Lives Should Be Good Business. Why Doesn't that Apply to Finding New Antibiotics?"

28. This section relies heavily on Richards, Kevin T., Kevin J. Hickey, and Erin H. Ward. 2020. "Drug Pricing and Pharmaceutical Patenting Practices" Congressional Research Service.

29. See page 16 of Richards, Hickey, and Ward. 2020. "Drug Pricing and Pharmaceutical Patenting Practices."

30. See page 21 of Richards, Hickey, and Ward. 2020. "Drug Pricing and Pharmaceutical Patenting Practices."

31. McNeil, Donald G., Jr. 2019. "Gilead Will Donate Truvada to U.S. for H.I.V. Prevention" *New York Times*.

32. See page 30 of Richards, Hickey, and Ward. 2020. "Drug Pricing and Pharmaceutical Patenting Practices."

33. See page 26 and footnote 256 of Richards, Hickey, and Ward. 2020. "Drug Pricing and Pharmaceutical Patenting Practices."

34. Dranove, David, Craig Garthwaite, and David Besanko. 2016. "Insurance and the High Prices of Pharmaceuticals" National Bureau of Economic Research Working Paper Series, No. 22353.

35. Conti, Rena M., Brigham Frandsen, Michael L. Powell, and James B. Rebitzer. 2021. "Common Agent or Double Agent? Pharmacy Benefit Managers in the Prescription Drug Market" National Bureau of Economic Research Working Paper Series, No. 28866.

36. As an empirical matter, little is known about the effects of PBMs on innovation and some recent studies point in the other direction. Agha, Kim, and Li (2022) studied the consequences for innovation when PBMs began refusing coverage for new drugs when cheaper alternatives were available. They found that this shift in PBM policy reduced development of drug candidates in drug classes with more pre-existing therapies. The implication of this result is that the enhanced willingness of PBMs to exclude drugs from formularies when cheaper alternatives were available encouraged more scientifically novel research (Agha, Leila, Soomi Kim, and Danielle Li. 2022. "Insurance Design and Pharmaceutical Innovation" *AER: Insights*, 4(2): 191–208).

37. Garthwaite, Craig, Manuel I. Hermosilla, and David Dranove. 2020. "Expected Profits and the Scientific Novelty of Innovation" National Bureau of Economic Research Working Paper, No. 27093.

38. This perspective on innovation comes from Chandra, Amitabh, and Jonathan Skinner. 2012. "Technology Growth and Expenditure Growth in Health Care" *Journal of Economic Literature*, 50(3): 645–680.

39. Robinson, James C. 2015. *Purchasing Medical Innovation: The Right Technology, for the Right Patient, at the Right Price*. Oakland: University of California Press.

40. We are not suggesting that the FDA should necessarily be charged with making these judgements. Our point, rather, is that a system where nobody is making these judgments is likely to influence innovative effort.

41. Robinson. 2015. *Purchasing Medical Innovation*.

42. Spatz, Erica S. 2014. "Implantable Cardioverter-Defibrillator." In *Redirecting Innovation in U.S. Health Care: Options to Decrease Spending and Increase Value: Case Studies*, ed. Steven Garber, Susan M. Gates, Emmett B. Keeler, Mary E. Vaiana,

Andrew W. Mulcahy, Christopher Lau, and Arthur L. Kellermann, 63–82. Rand Corporation.

43. See page 73 of Spatz. 2014. "Implantable Cardioverter-Defibrillator."

44. ICDs are examples of Category Two or Category Three technologies. The therapy has an unfavorable cost-effectiveness ratio that varies considerably across patients. Consistent with the permissiveness of the U.S. payment model, only about one-fifth as many eligible patients receive ICD therapy in Canada compared to the United States.

45. Roman, Benjamin R. 2014. "Avastin for Metastatic Breast Cancer." In *Redirecting Innovation in U.S. Health Care: Options to Decrease Spending and Increase Value*, ed. Steven Garber, Susan M. Gates, Emmett B. Keeler, Mary E. Vaiana, Andrew W. Mulcahy, Christopher Lau, and Arthur L. Kellerman, 1–12. Rand Corporation.

46. Of course, drug makers set their prices in response to the institutional environment in which they operate. A policy environment that links QALY evaluation to reimbursement would put downward pressure on transaction prices. Figuring out the right link between QALYs and price is a more subtle exercise than is commonly supposed. Regulators may want to pay a premium above the QALY value of a drug to encourage certain avenues of research. To the extent that a new innovation reduces future health risks, conventional methods may understate the value of new innovations. Lakdawalla et al. (2016) present a numerical exercise demonstrating how the value of insurance from physical risks offered by new technologies may exceed the financial spending on the risks that they pose (Lakdawalla, Darius, Anup Malani, and Julian Reif. 2017. "The Insurance Value of Medical Innovation" *Journal of Public Economics*, 145: 94–102).

47. Kyle, Margaret, and Heidi Williams. 2017. "Is American Health Care Uniquely Inefficient? Evidence from Prescription Drugs" *American Economic Review*, 107(5): 486–490.

Chapter 3

1. A potentially important set of missing innovations concerns medical procedures. A great deal of technological innovation takes the form of new procedures such as less invasive surgeries for heart attacks, new mental health treatments, and improvements in the diagnosis and treatment of strokes. There are more than 10,000 Current Procedural Terminology (CPT) codes in the codebook maintained by the American Medical Association. Like new patented medications, developing new procedures involves a substantial upfront investment and ultimate approval involves a complex regulatory process that, on average, takes more than 10 years to successfully complete. Unlike pharmaceuticals, however, approved new procedures do not offer their inventors well-defined intellectual property rights or market exclusivity. Medical societies have not supported procedure patents, and courts are reluctant to uphold procedure patents independent of the patent for an associated medical device. We might expect that the absence of intellectual property protection would weaken

incentives to develop innovative procedures. In addition, most procedures are reimbursed on the basis of provider costs. This form of reimbursement likely biases the direction of innovation against cost reduction. As Dranove et al. (2022) write in their analysis of innovation in medical procedures, "Under a fee-for-service system where reimbursement is based on provider costs, providers attempting to maximize profits should have cost-increasing, quality improving technologies rather than cost reducing ones." Unfortunately, the data needed to investigate this claim about missing cost-reducing innovations in medical procedures is currently lacking. For a comprehensive discussion of all these issues see Dranove, David, Craig Garthwaite, Christopher Heard, and Bingxiao Wu. 2022. "The Economics of Medical Procedure Innovation." *Journal of Health Economics*, 81: 102549.

2. Page 3 of The National Commission on Physician Payment Reform. 2013. "Report of the National Commission on Physician Payment Reform."

3. Weisbrod, Burton A. 1991. "The Health Care Quadrilemma: An Essay on Technological Change, Insurance, Quality of Care, and Cost Containment." *Journal of Economic Literature*, 29(2): 523–552; and Chandra, Amitabh, and Jonathan Skinner. 2012. "Technology Growth and Expenditure Growth in Health Care." *Journal of Economic Literature*, 50(3): 645–680.

4. Roberts, John. 2004. *The Modern Firm: Organizational Design for Performance and Growth*. Oxford: Oxford University Press.

5. Gaynor, Martin, James B. Rebitzer, and Lowell J. Taylor. 2004. "Physician Incentives in Health Maintenance Organizations." *Journal of Political Economy*, 112(4): 915–931.

6. Zuvekas, Samuel H., and Joel W. Cohen. 2016. "Fee-for-Service, while Much Maligned, Remains the Dominant Payment Method for Physician Visits." *Health Affairs*, 35(3): 411.

7. California Health Care Almanac. 2021. https://www.chcf.org/wp-content/uploads/2019/05/CAHealthInsurersAlmanac2019.pdf (accessed July 9, 2021).

8. Robinson, James C. 2015. *Purchasing Medical Innovation: The Right Technology, for the Right Patient, at the Right Price*. Oakland: University of California Press.

9. Cutler, David M., and Richard J. Zeckhauser. 2000. "The Anatomy of Health Insurance." In *Handbook of Health Economics*, Vol. 1, ed. Anthony J. Culyer and Joseph P. Newhouse, 563–643. N.p.: Elsevier.

10. Cutler, David M., Jonathan Skinner, Ariel D. Stern, and David Wennberg. 2019. "Physician Beliefs and Patient Preferences: A New Look at Regional Variation in Health Care Spending." *American Economic Journal: Economic Policy*, 11(1): 192–221.

11. Finkelstein, Amy, Matthew Gentzkow, and Heidi Williams. 2016. "Sources of Geographic Variation in Health Care: Evidence from Patient Migration." *Quarterly Journal of Economics*, 131(4): 1681–1726.

12. Kaplan, Robert M. 2019. *More than Medicine*. Cambridge: Harvard University Press.

13. Chandra, Amitabh, and Douglas O. Staiger. 2007. "Productivity Spillovers in Health Care: Evidence from the Treatment of Heart Attacks." *Journal of Political Economy*, 115(1): 103–140.

14. Cutler, Skinner, and Wennberg. "Physician Beliefs and Patient Preferences."

15. Starr, Paul. 1984. *The Social Transformation of American Medicine*. New York: Basic Books; Robinson, James C. 1999. *The Corporate Practice of Medicine: Competition and Innovation in Health Care*. Berkeley: University of California Press.

16. See Table 1 in Baker, Laurence, Kate Bundorf, and Anne Royalty. 2018. "Measuring Physician Practice Competition Using Medicare Data." In *Measuring and Modeling Health Care Costs*, ed. Ana Aizcorbe, Colin Baker, Ernst R. Berndt, and David M. Cutler, 351–378. Chicago: University of Chicago Press.

17. See Table 2 in National Ambulatory Care Survey: 2010 Summary Tables. http://www. cdc.gov/nchs/data/ahcd/namcs_summary/2010_namcs_web_tables.pdf.

18. Cebul, Randall, James B. Rebitzer, Lowell J. Taylor, and Mark Votruba. 2008. "Organizational Fragmentation and Care Quality in the US Health Care System" *Journal of Economic Perspectives*, 22(4): 93–113; Burns, L. R., and M. V. Pauly. 2018. "Transformation of the Health Care Industry: Curb Your Enthusiasm?" *The Milbank Quarterly*, 96(1): 57–109; and Rebitzer, James B., and Mark E. Votruba. 2011. "Organizational Economics and Physician Practices" National Bureau of Economic Research Working Paper #17535.

19. Burns, Lawton R., Jeff C. Goldsmith, and Aditi Sen. 2013. "Horizontal and Vertical Integration of Physicians: A Tale of Two Tails" *Advances in Health Care Management*, 15: 39.

20. Robinson. *Purchasing Medical Innovation*.

21. The type of process improvements adopted by the large multi-specialty groups were also shaped by financial incentives. Hoag, which was paid per surgical case, optimized throughput of patients through their system. Kaiser Permanente, which is paid on a capitated rate, also sought to maximize surgical throughput but at the same time invested in other improvements, such as a joint registry and non-surgical alternatives for patients with joint pain, geared toward lowering the total cost of treating these patients.

22. Institute Of Medicine Committee on Quality of Health Care in America. 2001. *Crossing the Quality Chasm: A New Health Care System for the 20th Century*. Washington, DC: National Academy Press.

23. For case studies see Milstein, Arnold, and Elizabeth Gilbertson. 2009. "American Medical Home Runs" *Health Affairs*, 28(5): 1317–1326; and Simon, M., N. K. Choudhry, J. Frankfort, D. Margolius, J. Murphy, L. Paita, T. Wang, and A. Milstein. 2017. "Exploring Attributes of High-Value Primary Care" *Annals of Family Medicine*, 15(6): 529–534. The statistical studies find that costs are higher in settings where care coordination is more challenging. For example, a number of studies have found that patients whose care is spread across more providers—with all the attendant coordination problems—appear to use significantly more resources than patients relying on fewer providers. Here is a sample of these studies: Agha, Leila, Brigham Frandsen, and James B. Rebitzer. 2019. "Fragmented Division of Labor and Healthcare Costs: Evidence from Moves across Regions" *Journal of Public Economics*, 169: 144–159; Hussey, Peter S., Eric C. Schneider, Robert S. Rudin, Steven Fox, Julie Lai, and Craig E. Pollack. 2014. "Continuity and the Costs of Care for Chronic Disease" *JAMA Internal Medicine*, 174(5): 742–748; Nyweide, D. J., D. L. Anthony, J. P. Bynum, R.

L. Strawderman, W. B. Weeks, L. P. Casalino, and E. S. Fisher. 2013. "Continuity of Care and the Risk of Preventable Hospitalization in Older Adults" *JAMA Internal Medicine*, 173(20): 1879–1885; Baicker, Katherine, and Amitabh Chandra. 2004. "The Productivity of Physician Specialization: Evidence from the Medicare Program" *American Economic Review*, 94(2): 357–361; and Romano, M. J., J. B. Segal, and C. E. Pollack. 2015. "The Association between Continuity of Care and the Overuse of Medical Procedures" *JAMA Internal Medicine*, *175*(7): 1148–1154.

24. Mehrotra, Ateev, Christopher B. Forrest, and Caroline Y. Lin. 2011. "Dropping the Baton: Specialty Referrals in the United States" *The Milbank Quarterly*, 89(1): 39–68.

25. Agha, Leila, Keith M. Ericson, Kimberley H. Geissler, and James B. Rebitzer. 2022. "Team Relationships and Performance: Evidence from Healthcare Referral Networks" *Management Science*, 68(5): 3735–3754.

26. An exception to this is a study of referrals across organizational borders. For reasons of interoperability of IT systems and also sociology, informational flows across organizational boundaries are often problematic. When Medicare referrals are concentrated *within* an organization, utilization falls and there are improvements in some aspects of care quality (Agha, Leila, Keith M. Ericson, and Xiaoxi Zhao. Forthcoming. "The Impact of Organizational Boundaries on Healthcare Coordination and Utilization" *American Economic Journal: Economic Policy*).

27. A specific form such market power can take would be if primary care physicians face inducements to refer within the group. Specialist referrals within a group can increase costs or reduce efficiency if external specialists are cheaper or are a better match for the referred patient (Brot-Goldberg, Zarek C. and Mathijs de Vaan. 2018. "Intermediation and Vertical Integration in the Market for Surgeons" Unpublished working paper; and Kowalzyck, Liz. 2018. "Steward Health Care Pressured Doctors to Restrict Referrals Outside Chain, Suit Says" *Boston Globe*).

28. McWilliams, J. M., M. E. Chernew, and B. E. Landon. 2017. "Medicare ACO Program Savings Not Tied to Preventable Hospitalizations or Concentrated among High-Risk Patients" *Health Affairs*, 36(12): 2085–2093; McWilliams, J. M., L. A. Hatfield, M. E. Chernew, B. E. Landon, and A. L. Schwartz. 2016. "Early Performance of Accountable Care Organizations in Medicare" *The New England Journal of Medicine*, 374(24): 2357–2366.

29. Javitt, Jonathan C., James B. Rebitzer, and Lonnie Reisman. 2008. "Information Technology and Medical Missteps: Evidence from a Randomized Trial" *Journal of Health Economics*, 27(23): 585–602.

30. Blumenthal, David. 2011a. "Wiring the Health System—Origins and Provisions of a New Federal Program" *The New England Journal of Medicine*, 365(24): 2323–2329; Blumenthal, David. 2011b. "Implementation of the Federal Health Information Technology Initiative" *The New England Journal of Medicine*, 365(25): 2426–2431.

31. Page 50 in DesRoches, Catherine M., Eric G. Campbell, Sowmya R. Rao, Karen Donelan, Timothy G. Ferris, Ashish Jha, Rainu Kaushal, Douglas E. Levy, Sara Rosenbaum, Alexandra E. Shields, et al. 2008. "Electronic Health Records in Ambulatory Care—A National Survey of Physicians" *The New England Journal of Medicine*, 359(1): 10–50.

32. Page 1631 in Jha, Ashish K., Catherine M. DesRoches, Eric G. Campbell, Karen Donelan, Sowmya R. Rao, Timothy G. Ferris, Alexandra Shields, Sara Rosenbaum, and David Blumenthal. 2009. "Use of Electronic Health Records in U.S. Hospitals" *The New England Journal of Medicine*, 360(16): 1628–1638.

33. Blumenthal, David. 2009. "Stimulating the Adoption of Health Information Technology" *The New England Journal of Medicine*, 360(15): 1477–1479.

34. Gold, Marsha, and Catherine Mclaughlin. 2016. "Assessing HITECH Implementation and Lessons: 5 Years Later" *The Milbank Quarterly*, 94(3): 654–687.

35. Blumenthal. "Stimulating the Adoption of Health Information Technology."

36. Adler-Milstein, Julia, and Ashish K. Jha. 2017. "HITECH Act Drove Large Gains in Hospital Electronic Health Record Adoption" *Health Affairs Web Exclusive*, 36(8): 1416–1422.

37. Furukawa, M. F., J. King, V. Patel, C. J. Hsiao, J. Adler-Milstein, and A. K. Jha. 2014. "Despite Substantial Progress in EHR Adoption, Health Information Exchange and Patient Engagement Remain Low in Office Settings" *Health Affairs*, 33(9): 1672–1679.

38. A survey of hospitals in 2014 found that only 21 percent had interoperable systems (Holmgren, A. J., Vaishali Patel, Dustin Charles, and Julia Adler-Milstein. 2016. "US Hospital Engagement in Core Domains of Interoperability" *The American Journal of Managed Care*, 22(12): 1).

39. Some also argue that hospitals gain market power by blocking easy information sharing. See Savage, Lucia, Martin Gaynor, and Julia Adler-Milstein. 2019. "Digital Health Data and Information Sharing: A New Frontier for Health Care Competition?" *Antitrust Law Journal*, 82(2): 593–621; and Lin, Sunny C., Jordan Everson, and Julia Adler-Milstein. 2018. "Technology, Incentives, or Both? Factors Related to Level of Hospital Health Information Exchange" *Health Services Research*, 53(5): 3285–3308.

40. Brynjolfsson, Erik, and Andrew McAfee. 2014. *The Second Machine Age: Work, Progress, and Prosperity in a Time of Brilliant Technologies*, 1st ed. New York: W.W. Norton and Company.

41. Buntin, Melinda B., Matthew F. Burke, Michael C. Hoaglin, and David Blumenthal. 2011. "The Benefits of Health Information Technology: A Review of the Recent Literature Shows Predominantly Positive Results" *Health Affairs*, 30(3): 464–471.

42. Agha, Leila. 2014. "The Effects of Health Information Technology on the Costs and Quality of Medical Care" *Journal of Health Economics*, 34: 19–30; McCullough, Jeffrey S., Stephen T. Parente, and Robert Town. 2016. "Health Information Technology and Patient Outcomes: The Role of Information and Labor Coordination" *RAND Journal of Economics*, 47(1): 207–236.

43. In 1987, for example, Nobel laureate Robert Solow observed "you can see the computer age everywhere but in the productivity statistics" (Solow, Robert S. 1987. "We'd Better Watch Out" *New York Times Book Review*). His aphorism neatly summarized the state of economic knowledge about information technology in the 1980s and 1990s.

44. Gee, Emily, and Topher Spiro. 2019. "Excess Administrative Costs Burden the U.S. Health Care System" Center for American Progress, https://www. americanprogress

.org/issues/healthcare/reports/2019/04/08/468302/excess-administrative-costsburden-us-health-care-system.

45. Papanicolas, I., L. R. Woskie, and A. K. Jha. 2018. "Health Care Spending in the United States and Other High-Income Countries" *JAMA*, 319(10): 1024–1039.

46. Gee and Spiro. "Excess Administrative Costs Burden the U.S. Health Care System."

47. Frandsen, Brigham, Michael Powell, and James B. Rebitzer. 2019. "Sticking Points: Common Agency Problems and Contracting in the US Healthcare System" *RAND Journal of Economics*, 50(2): 251–285.

48. Gottlieb, J. D., A. H. Shapiro, and A. Dunn. 2018. "The Complexity of Billing and Paying for Physician Care" *Health Affairs*, 37(4): 619–626.

49. Gans, Joshua. 2016. *The Disruption Dilemma*. Cambridge, MA: The MIT Press.

50. Fuchs, Victor R. 2019. "Does Employment-Based Insurance Make the US Medical Care System Unfair and Inefficient?" *JAMA*, 321(21): 2069.

51. This example was suggested to us by David Molitor.

52. Hult, Kristopher J., Sonia Jaffe, and Tomas J. Philipson. 2018. "How Does Technological Change Affect Quality-Adjusted Prices in Health Care? Systematic Evidence from Thousands of Innovations" *American Journal of Health Economics*, 4(4): 433–425.

53. Nelson, A. L., J. T. Cohen, D. Greenberg, and D. M. Kent. 2009. "Much Cheaper, Almost as Good: Decrementally Cost-Effective Medical Innovation" *Annals of Internal Medicine*, 151(9): 662–667.

54. Watchful waiting produced savings of $2,721 versus a QALY loss of $194,331 for a cost-effectiveness ratio of 0.0140. Percutaneous coronary intervention saved $4,944 and lost $3,210,306 QALY, yielding an effectiveness ratio of 0.0015 (Nelson, Cohen, Greenberg, and Kent. "Much Cheaper, Almost as Good.").

55. Diabetes Prevention Program Research Group. 2002. "Reduction in the Incidence of Type 2 Diabetes with Lifestyle Intervention or Metformin" *The New England Journal of Medicine*, 346(6): 393–403.

56. Volpp, Kevin G., Andrea B. Troxel, Mark V. Pauly, Henry A. Glick, Andrea Puig, David A. Asch, Robert Galvin, Jingsan Zhu, Fei Wan, Jill DeGuzman, et al. 2009. "A Randomized, Controlled Trial of Financial Incentives for Smoking Cessation" *The New England Journal of Medicine*, 360(7): 699–709.

57. Diabetes Prevention Program Research Group. "Reduction in the Incidence of Type 2 Diabetes with Lifestyle Intervention or Metformin."

58. Kaplan. *More than Medicine*; Pryor, Katherine, and Kevin Volpp. 2018. "Deployment of Preventive Interventions—Time for a Paradigm Shift" *The New England Journal of Medicine*, 378(19): 1761–1763.

59. Kaplan. *More than Medicine*.

60. Chandra, Amitabh, Anupam B. Jena, and Jonathan S. Skinner. 2011. "The Pragmatist's Guide to Comparative Effectiveness Research" *The Journal of Economic Perspectives*, 25(2): 27–46.

61. Powell, Michael. 2016. "Comparative Effectiveness Testing," unpublished working paper.

62. This is because substantial investments in comparative effectiveness research creates large fixed (or sunk) costs. In the presence of these fixed costs, average costs exceed marginal costs. In highly competitive markets, price is driven down to marginal costs and so cannot cover fixed costs. Put differently, any firm that invested heavily in comparative effectiveness research would lose money in a perfectly competitive market.

63. Ollove, Michael. 2019. "Drug-Price Debate Targets Pharmacy Benefit Managers" *Stateline.org.*

64. Page 1 in Seeley, Elizabeth, and Aaron S. Kesselheim. 2019. "Pharmacy Benefit Managers: Practices, Controversies, and What Lies Ahead" Commonwealth Fund Issue Brief, PMID: 30990594.

Chapter 4

1. Weisbrod, Burton A. 1991. "The Health Care Quadrilemma: An Essay on Technological Change, Insurance, Quality of Care, and Cost Containment" *Journal of Economic Literature*, 29(2): 523–552.

2. Our discussion of common-agency problems in this section is taken from Frandsen, Brigham, Michael Powell, and James B. Rebitzer. 2019. "Sticking Points: Common Agency Problems and Contracting in the US Healthcare System" *RAND Journal of Economics*, 50(2): 251.

3. A famous economic study illustrates the difference between first-best and second-best incentives (Levitt, Steven D., and Chad Syverson. 2008. "Market Distortions When Agents are Better Informed: The Value of Information in Real Estate Transactions" *The Review of Economics and Statistics*, 90(4): 599–611). The study compared home sales price when real estate agents sell other people's homes to the sales price when the agent sells her own home. Similar homes owned by real estate agents sold for 3.7 percent more than other houses and stayed on the market 9.5 days longer. When realtors sell their own homes, they are operating under first-best incentives and so are willing to wait longer to get a better offer. When realtors are hired as the agents for others, they typically operate with second-best incentives. This means they are less willing to wait for a better deal because they only get a fraction of the marginal benefits from improving the deal. The better results when realtors sell their own homes demonstrates the economic differences between first-best and second-best incentives.

4. There are other explanations that go beyond risk. These rely on costs or distortions created by the incentives themselves. The logic of incentive design requires a savvy principal to choose a level of incentive where the marginal benefit to the principal of more powerful incentives equals the marginal cost. When incentives themselves do not create costs or distortions, the principal will choose incentives that are intense enough that the marginal benefit to the principal of additional effort equals the marginal cost of that effort to the agent. This logic produces the first-best incentive arrangement where agents get 100 percent of the value created by their additional efforts. When incentives themselves create costs and distortions, the marginal costs

of increasing incentives goes up and the optimal level of performance pay goes down. The result is second-best incentives in which agents get only a fraction of the value produced by their marginal effort. In original formulations of the principal-agent model, the costs of incentives are often the same as those we discuss in our real estate example—agent risk aversion. Subsequent research uncovered many other costs and distortions arising from performance pay. Some of these costs emerge from psychological or sociological factors acting on agents, but others emerge from the nature of production technology. For a review and discussion of these issues see Rebitzer, James B., and Lowell J. Taylor. 2011. "Extrinsic Rewards and Intrinsic Motives: Standard and Behavioral Approaches to Agency in Labor Markets." In *Handbook of Labor Economics*, ed. Orley Ashenfelter and David Card, 701–772. Vol. 4. Amsterdam: North-Holland.

5. See Frandsen, Powell, and Rebitzer. 2019. "Sticking Points: Common Agency Problems and Contracting in the US Healthcare System"; Glazer, Jacob, and Thomas G. McGuire. 2002. "Multiple Payers, Commonality and Free-Riding in Health Care: Medicare and Private Payers" *Journal of Health Economics*, 21(6): 1049–1069; and Bernheim, B., D. and Michael D. Whinston. 1986. "Common Agency" *Econometrica*, 54(4): 923–942.

6. Direct evidence for spillovers between payers comes from a study of Medicare's attempt to warn doctors to curtail overuse of antipsychotics. In 2015, Medicare randomized warning letters to doctors and found that these letters also reduced prescriptions for commercially insured patients not mentioned in the letter (Barnett, Michael L., Andrew Olenski, and Adam Sacarny. 2021. "Common Practice: Spillovers from Medicare on Private Health Care" http://sacarny.com/wp-content/uploads/2021/06/BOS-Spillovers-2021–06.pdf). Accessed September 1, 2021.

7. Third-best incentive systems, as the name implies, give agents an even smaller share of the marginal value created by their efforts than do second-best incentives. To understand why common-agency produces third-best incentives, remember the decision rule discussed above—that a savvy principal will choose an incentive where the marginal benefit to them of more powerful incentives equals the marginal cost of incentives. Common-agency weakens incentives relative to standard models because no single principal can capture the marginal benefits from incentives that spill over to other principals. Thus optimal incentives under common-agency are third-best—even though they are the best the principal can do under the circumstances of common-agency.

8. Frandsen, Powell, and Rebitzer. 2019. "Sticking Points: Common Agency Problems and Contracting in the US Healthcare System."

9. To see how this works, let us return to the example of the electronic health record system. Suppose that in order to make the system interoperable, the physician has to purchase new hardware and also hire consultants to install the system and transfer data from the old system. From the perspective of the physician, these are one-time setup costs. If the shared savings incentives from the two payers don't cover at least these setup costs, physicians will simply not upgrade their system. If Payer 1 believes that Payer 2 won't cover the start-up costs, the only way to get the physician to install the improved system would be for Payer 1 to offer payments generous enough to

cover these costs. If this up-front expense is prohibitively large for Payer 1, then the best strategy for Payer 1 is to offer no shared saving incentives at all. The same reasoning applies to Payer 2. Thus unless there was a way for the two payers to coordinate their incentives for physicians, neither payer will offer any shared savings incentives at all and the physician will not make the investment.

10. Bundorf, M. K. 2016. "Consumer-Directed Health Plans: A Review of the Evidence" *Journal of Risk and Insurance*, 83(1): 9–41 .

11. Bundorf. 2016. "Consumer-Directed Health Plans: A Review of the Evidence."

12. Brot-Goldberg, Zarek, Amitabh Chandra, Benjamin R. Handel, and Jonathan T. Kolstad. 2017. "What Does a Deductible do? The Impact of Cost-Sharing on Health Care Prices, Quantities, and Spending Dynamics" *Quarterly Journal of Economics*, 132(3): 1261–1318.

13. Chandra, Amitabh, Evan Flack, and Ziad Obermeyer. 2021. "The Health Costs of Cost-Sharing" National Bureau of Economic Research Working Paper Series, No. 28439.

14. Chernew, Michael, Zack Cooper, Eugene Larsen-Hallock, and Fiona S. Morton. 2018. "Are Health Care Services Shoppable? Evidence from the Consumption of Lower-Limb MRI Scans" National Bureau of Economic Research Working Paper Series, No. 24869.

15. McWilliams, J. M., Ellen Meara, Alan M. Zaslavsky, and John Z. Ayanian. 2007. "Health of Previously Uninsured Adults After Acquiring Medicare Coverage" *JAMA*, 298(24): 2886–2894.

16. Fang, Hanming, and Alessandro Gavazza. 2011. "Dynamic Inefficiencies in an Employment-Based Health Insurance System: Theory and Evidence" *American Economic Review*, 101(7): 3047–3077.

17. The magnitudes of the effects reported in the study are substantial. All else equal, a one standard deviation increase in job tenure increases pre-retirement expenditures on medical care by about $500 per year while reducing medical spending in retirement by more than $4,000 per year. Assuming that individuals work for 45 years and live for 15 years in retirement, the increase in job tenure leads to gains of more than $20,000 when working and reductions of more than $60,000 in retirement. In other words, an additional dollar of health expenditures during working years yields nearly $3 of savings in retirement. These estimates are approximations. They omit many important costs and returns from investment, and there is no direct observation of investments in future health. They nevertheless raise the possibility that the returns from investments in future health may be substantial if insurers can count on long-term relationships with their beneficiaries.

18. Cochrane, John H. 1995. "Time-Consistent Health Insurance" *Journal of Political Economy*, 103(3): 445–473; and Handel, Benjamin R., Igal Hendel, and Michael D. Whinston. 2017. "The Welfare Effects of Long-Term Health Insurance Contracts" National Bureau of Economic Research Working Paper Series, No. 23624.

19. Mukherjee, Siddhartha. 2019. "New Blood: The Promise and Price of Cellular Therapies" *New Yorker*, 95(20), https://www.newyorker.com/magazine/2019/07/22/the-promise-and-price-of-cellular-therapies.

20. Cebul, Randall D., James B. Rebitzer, Lowell J. Taylor, and Mark E. Votruba. 2011. "Unhealthy Insurance Markets: Search Frictions and the Cost and Quality of Health Insurance" *American Economic Review*, 101(5): 1842–1871.

21. This discussion is taken largely from Frandsen, Brigham, and James B. Rebitzer. 2014. "Structuring Incentives within Accountable Care Organizations" *Journal of Law, Economics, and Organization*, 31(S1): 77–103.

22. The problem we discuss in this paragraph is a question of statistical power, but there are other reasons why quality measurement is very difficult in the health sector. First, quality is multidimensional, and it is hard to know how to weigh its different dimensions in coming up with an overall quality score. Second, the science of care quality is complex and evolving, so it is sometimes hard to know what constitutes quality care. Third, in many instances patients can't directly assess the quality of their care, so experts have to make inferences about what aspects of care their patients would want if they knew enough to make these judgements. Finally, to the extent that incentives depend on quality measures built from the reports of self-interested providers, the incentives can distort quality measures.

23. Nyweide, David J., William B. Weeks, Daniel J. Gottlieb, Lawrence P. Casalino, and Elliott S. Fisher. 2009. "Relationship of Primary Care Physicians' Patient Caseload with Measurement of Quality and Cost Performance" *JAMA*, 302(22): 2444–2450.

24. Fisher, Elliott S., Mark B. McClellan, John Bertko, Steven M. Lieberman, Julie J. Lee, Julie L. Lewis, and Jonathan S. Skinner. 2009. "Fostering Accountable Health Care: Moving Forward in Medicare" *Health Affairs*, 28(2): W219–W231.

25. Frandsen and Rebitzer. 2014. "Structuring Incentives within Accountable Care Organizations."

26. Shortell, Stephen M, Carrie H. Colla, Valerie A. Lewis, Elliott Fisher, Eric Kessell, and Patricia Ramsay. 2015. "Accountable Care Organizations: The National Landscape" *Journal of Health Politics, Policy and Law*, 40(4): 647–668.

27. This discussion of Baystate Health comes from Heath, Jermaine, Ellen Meara, and Eric Wadsworth. 2018. "Baystate Health: Navigating a Path between Volume and Value" *Dartmouth College*, unpublished teaching case.

Chapter 5

1. About Palliative Care. 2022. https://www.capc.org/about/palliative-care/?clickthrough_doc_id=core.contentpage.549&clickthrough_req_id=9Jmt9PGuQKCK_RnsoUR XrA&clickthrough_query=About%20palliative%20care (accessed August 10, 2021).

2. Meier, Diane E. 2009. "Finding My Place" *Journal of Palliative Medicine*, 12(4): 331–335.

3. Morrison, Sean R., Diane E. Meir, Maggie Rogers, Allison Silvers, Stacie Sinclair, and Rachael Heitner. 2020. "America's Care of Serious Illness" *Center to Advance Palliative Care*, 1–39, https://reportcard.capc.org/wp-content/uploads/2020/05/CAPC_State-by-State-Report-Card_051120.pdf.

4. As of this writing, there are no large scale prospective, randomized studies indicating that palliative care is cheaper than conventional care. A meta analysis of observational studies has estimated savings as high as 28 percent on hospital costs for some types of seriously ill patients. Patients who received palliative care consultations within three days of hospitalization had a $3,237 reduction in direct hospital costs off of a base of $11,661 for those receiving usual care. The effects were larger than this for cancer patients and for patients with 4 + comorbidities (May, Peter, Charles Normand, J. Brian Cassel, Egidio Del Fabbro, Robert L. Fine, Reagan Menz, Corey A. Morrison, Joan D. Penrod, Chessie Robinson, and R. S. Morrison. 2018. "Economics of Palliative Care for Hospitalized Adults with Serious Illness: A Meta-Analysis" *JAMA Internal Medicine*, 178(6): 820–829). Any assessment of the incremental value of palliative care also depends on the value of the care it is displacing.

5. Meier. 2009. "Finding My Place."

6. *The Surgical Palliative Care Podcast*. Episode 5. "Dr. Diane Meier: Founder of the Center to Advance Palliative Care (CPAP), 2022."

7. Meier. 2009. "Finding My Place."

8. Meier. 2009. "Finding My Place."

9. See page 26 of US Renal Data System. 2019. "Annual Data Report: Epidemiology of Kidney Disease in the United States. Executive Summary."

10. See page 43 of US Renal Data System. 2019. "Annual Data Report: Epidemiology of Kidney Disease in the United States. Executive Summary."

11. See page 46 of US Renal Data System. 2019. "Annual Data Report: Epidemiology of Kidney Disease in the United States. Executive Summary."

12. Roth, Alvin E. 2007. "Repugnance as a Constraint on Markets" *The Journal of Economic Perspectives*, 21(3): 37–58.

13. Elías, Julio J., Nicola Lacetera, and Mario Macis. 2019. "Paying for Kidneys? A Randomized Survey and Choice Experiment" *American Economic Review*, 109(8): 2855–2888.

14. See Figure 5 in Elías, Lacetera, and Macis. 2019. "Paying for Kidneys? A Randomized Survey and Choice Experiment."

15. Starr, Paul. 1984. *The Social Transformation of American Medicine*. New York: Basic Books.

16. Robinson, James C. 1999. *The Corporate Practice of Medicine: Competition and Innovation in Health Care*. Berkeley: University of California Press.

17. Friedman, Milton. 1970. "The Social Responsibility of Business is to Increase its Profits" *New York Times Magazine*. September 13.

18. See Hart, Oliver, and Luigi Zingales. 2017. "Companies Should Maximize Shareholder Welfare Not Market Value" *Journal of Law, Finance and Accounting*, 2(2): 247–275. Hart and Zingales find that ethics become irrelevant only in an exceptional circumstance: when the economic cost of the ethical decision equals the social cost of the non-ethical choice. The economic cost of solar power is the loss of profits relative to oil production. The social cost of oil production is the environmental damage resulting from the additional investment in oil. In the special case where the loss of profits from solar power equals the environmental harm from oil, even the most

environmentally concerned investor, one who completely internalizes the social costs of environmental damage, would be indifferent between the two technologies. Only in this special case do ethical concerns have no bearing on the decision to maximize shareholder value.

19. Consistent with this idea, there is some evidence that shared savings programs in physician-integrated ACOs were able to reduce per patient expenditures more than hospital-integrated ACOs (McWilliams, J. M., Laura A. Hatfield, Bruce E. Landon, Pasha Hamed, and Michael E. Chernew. 2018. "Medicare Spending after 3 Years of the Medicare Shared Savings Program." *The New England Journal of Medicine*, 379(12): 1139–1149). An alternative interpretation of this result is that the incentives differed across these two governance structures. Hospital ACOs lose revenues when in-patient spending is reduced, while physician-integrated ACOs do not.

20. Roth. 2007. "Repugnance as a Constraint on Markets."

21. Satz, Debra. 2010. *Why Some Things Should Not be for Sale*. New York: Oxford University Press.

22. Blendon, R. J., M. Brodie, J. M. Benson, D. E. Altman, L. Levitt, T. Hoff, and L. Hugick. 1998. "Understanding the Managed Care Backlash." *Health Affairs*, 17(4): 80–94.

23. 1Day Sooner.Org. 2020. https://1daysooner.org/ (accessed May 26, 2021).

24. Bowles, Samuel, and Sandra Polania-Reyes. 2012. "Economic Incentives and Social Preferences: Substitutes or Complements?" *Journal of Economic Literature*, 50(2): 368–425.

25. Bowles and Polania-Reyes. 2012. "Economic Incentives and Social Preferences: Substitutes or Complements?"

26. Lacetera, Nicola, Mario Macis, and Robert Slonim. 2013. "Economic Rewards to Motivate Blood Donations." *Science*, 340(6135): 927–928.

27. A related field experiment studied recruitment for healthcare positions in Zambia. It examined whether increasing the salience of career benefits in recruiting attracted more talented applicants at the expense of prosocial motivation. The treatment arm of the experiment featured recruiting ads that emphasized career benefits of the job while the control arm advertisements emphasized helping the community as the main benefit of the job. The treatment arm applicants were more talented on average and less prosocially motivated—but the extrinsic recruiting effort did not crowd out intrinsic motives. The reason is that the most talented applicants in the treatment arm also had the best alternative job options. They were interested in the relatively low status healthcare job because it also appealed to their strong prosocial motives. The government hired based on observed talent, so those hired from the treatment arm were at least as prosocial as those in the control arm. In this experiment, prosocial motives were not crowded out by the promise of extrinsic rewards. The government got the benefits of more talented and more prosocially motivated health workers who delivered more health services with a remarkably positive health impact. These results suggest that the identity associated with the job can affect those drawn to it and this selection can improve performance. Ashraf, Nava, Oriana Bandiera, Edward Davenport, and Scott S. Lee. 2020. "Losing Prosociality in the Quest for Talent?

Sorting, Selection, and Productivity in the Delivery of Public Services" *The American Economic Review*, 110(5): 1355–1394.

28. Bowles and Polania-Reyes. 2012. "Economic Incentives and Social Preferences: Substitutes or Complements?"

29. The experiments involve games in which individuals have to decide how many resources to share with others at some cost to themselves, including: Trust, Ultimatum, Public Goods, Third Party Punishment, Common Pool Resource, Gift Exchange, and Principal-Agent games.

30. Akerlof, George A., and Rachel E. Kranton. 2000. "Economics and Identity" *Quarterly Journal of Economics*, 115(3): 715–753; and Akerlof, George A., and Rachel E. Kranton. 2010. *Identity Economics*. Princeton: Princeton University Press.

31. Akerlof and Kranton. 2010. *Identity Economics*. Princeton, New Jersey.

32. Harrington, Brooke. 2021. "The Anti-Vaccine Con Job is Becoming Untenable" *The Atlantic*. August 1, https://www.theatlantic.com/ideas/archive/2021/08/vaccine-refusers-dont-want-blue-americas-respect/619627/.

33. This can be seen, for example, in the introduction of certain evidence-based treatment guidelines and the concentration of surgical volume in centers of excellence. See Pearl, Robert. 2021. *Uncaring: How the Culture of Medicine Kills Doctors and Patients*. Public Affairs. Depending on group norms, the desire to earn the respect from peers can also induce physicians to seek to excel relative to others in their reference group. One paper studied mortality rates in coronary artery bypass graft (CABG) procedures. The introduction of CABG report cards allowed surgeons to compare their mortality rates with the expected mortality had the average surgeon in their state handled the case. Physicians who learned from the report cards that their outcomes differed from the average surgeon managed to reduce mortality rates. These peer comparisons had a much bigger effect on mortality rates than pecuniary incentives for improving outcomes (Kolstad, Jonathan T. 2013. "Information and Quality when Motivation is Intrinsic: Evidence from Surgeon Report Cards" *The American Economic Review*, 103(7): 2875–2910.)

34. Successes have been noted in the use of comparisons to reduce the inappropriate use of antibiotics in primary care and to improve patient ratings of physician quality. However, unintended consequences also occur. Navathe, Amol S., and Ezekiel J. Emanuel. 2016. "Physician Peer Comparisons as a Nonfinancial Strategy to Improve the Value of Care" *JAMA*, 316(17): 1759–1760.

35. Liao, J. M., L. A. Fleisher, and A. S. Navathe. 2016. "Increasing the Value of Social Comparisons of Physician Performance Using Norms" *JAMA*, 316(11): 1151–1152.

36. Shiller, Robert J. 2019. *Narrative Economics*. Princeton; Oxford: Princeton University Press.

37. See for example Mukherjee, Siddhartha. 2010. *The Emperor of All Maladies*. New York: Scribner.

38. Mokyr, Joel. 2016. *A Culture of Growth*. Princeton: Princeton University Press.

39. Leonhardt, David. 2009. "If Healthcare is Going to Change His Ideas Will Change It" *New York Times*.

40. Meier. 2009. "Finding My Place."

41. Reinhardt, Uwe E. 1997. "Wanted: A Clearly Articulated Social Ethic for American Health Care." *JAMA: The Journal of the American Medical Association*, 278(17): 1446–1447.

Chapter 6

1. Three percentage points may not seem significant, but the difference is equivalent to nearly one-third of the total improvement in survival over the 18 years covered by the study. Skinner, Jonathan, and Douglas Staiger. 2015. "Technology Diffusion and Productivity Growth in Health Care." *The Review of Economics and Statistics*, 97(5): 951–964.

2. Chandra, Amitabh, Amy Finkelstein, Adam Sacarny, and Chad Syverson. 2016. "Health Care Exceptionalism? Performance and Allocation in the US Health Care Sector." *The American Economic Review*, 106(8): 2110–2144.

3. David Cutler remarked on the apparent absence of organizational innovation in the health sector and touches on some of the same themes we develop in this chapter (Cutler, David M. 2011. "Where are the Health Care Entrepreneurs? The Failure of Organizational Innovation in Health Care." *Innovation Policy and the Economy*, 11(1): 1–28).

4. A remarkable study of British hospitals finds some direct evidence that heightened competition improves managerial practices and hospital performance. The hospital system in England is controlled by the central government. As a result, the number of hospitals in an area is influenced by political considerations. Since having more hospitals serve a community is politically popular, the government allows for more hospitals in areas where they expect a tight political race. When political considerations add an additional hospital to a local area, competition increases, and this change allows for a clean test of the effect of competition on hospital performance. It turns out that increased competition improves both management and quality of care. Specifically, adding a rival hospital to a market increases the quality of hospital management practices and improves survival rates from emergency heart attacks. These results suggest that in the context of the British National Health Service, the incentives to implement quality enhancing and cost—reducing management methods increase with the degree of market competition (Bloom, N., C. Propper, S. Seiler, and J. Van Reenen. 2015. "The Impact of Competition on Management Quality: Evidence from Public Hospitals." *The Review of Economic Studies*, 82(2 (291)): 457–489).

5. Canadian mines were subject to similar competitive pressures and, like the U.S. mines, altered production processes. In his detailed study of the episode, Schmitz (2005) estimates that in both U.S. and Canadian industries, labor productivity doubled in a few years. (Schmitz, James A., Jr. 2005. "What Determines Productivity? Lessons from the Dramatic Recovery of the U.S. and Canadian Iron Ore Industries Following their Early 1980s Crisis." *Journal of Political Economy*, 113(3): 582–625).

6. We interpret our example of work rules in the Mesabi mines as illustrating the interaction of inefficient bargaining and market power. There is no theoretical reason to believe that the Mesabi bargaining was efficient, but work rules can also emerge as the result of efficient bargaining, specifically efforts to enhance employment relative to the inefficient level that emerges from monopoly model of union bargaining (see Espinosa, Maria P., and Changyong Rhee. 1989. "Efficient Wage Bargaining as a Repeated Game." *The Quarterly Journal of Economics*, 104(3): 565–588).

7. Shapiro, Carl. 2012. "Competition and Innovation: Did Arrow Hit the Bull's Eye?" In *The Rate and Direction of Innovative Activity Revisited*, ed. Josh Lerner and Scott Stern, 361–404. Chicago: University of Chicago Press.

8. Shapiro. 2012. "Competition and Innovation: Did Arrow Hit the Bull's Eye?"

9. Firms in highly competitive markets generally tend to under invest in innovation but they do not tend to underinvest in other sorts of economic goods and services. Most economic goods and services are rivalrous, meaning that if they are consumed by one party they are not available for others to consume. New ideas, however, are nonrivalrous—their use by one party doesn't prevent others from using the same idea. This feature means that without some sort of intellectual property rights or equivalent protection, innovators cannot capture most of the returns from new ideas and so innovation is depressed. In the extreme case of perfect competition, "rival goods" like labor and capital earn a return that leaves organizations with no money left to pay the inventors of "nonrival goods." This means that in a perfectly competitive market equilibrium, there will be no resources available to compensate an innovator with a new idea, plan or technology (Vollrath, Deitrich. 2015. "Market Power versus Price-Taking in Economic Growth." *Growth Economics Blog*, https://growthecon.com/blog/market-power-versus-price-taking-in-economic-growth/ (accessed January 7, 2021)).

10. Arrow's analysis focuses on the incentives for innovators (see Arrow, Kenneth. 1962. "Economic Welfare and the Allocation of Resources for Invention." In *The Rate and Direction of Inventive Activity: Economic and Social Factors*, ed. Universities-National Bureau Committee for Economic Research, Committee on Economic Growth of the Social Science Research Council, 609–626. Princeton: Princeton University Press). He compares the profit maximizing royalties an independent inventor can charge for a cost-reducing innovation to the profits a monopoly producer would earn from adopting the same innovation. He finds that the monopolist firm always gains less from the innovation than the independent inventor and so concludes that monopoly power reduces innovation incentives. What explains this result? The independent innovator charges royalties that capture the full monopoly value produced by the cost-reducing innovation. The monopolist firm also captures the full monopoly value produced by the cost-reducing innovation, but the firm was already earning some monopoly profits prior to the innovation. The marginal benefit of the invention is thus smaller, and the monopolist has weaker innovation incentives than other actors in the economy.

11. Holmes, Thomas J., David K. Levine, and James A. Schmitz. 2012. "Monopoly and the Incentive to Innovate When Adoption Involves Switchover Disruptions." *American*

Economic Journal: Microeconomics, 4(3): 1–33; and Gilbert, Richard J., and David M. G. Newbery. 1982. "Preemptive Patenting and the Persistence of Monopoly." *The American Economic Review*, 72(3): 514–526.

12. Gilbert and Newbery. 1982. "Preemptive Patenting and the Persistence of Monopoly."

13. Gans, Joshua. 2016. *The Disruption Dilemma*. Cambridge, MA: The MIT Press. Gans. 2016. *The Disruption Dilemma*.

14. Holmes, Levine, and Schmitz. 2012. "Monopoly and the Incentive to Innovate When Adoption Involves Switchover Disruptions." The switchover cost model of disruption is quite distinct from Clay Christensen's widely discussed theory of *disruptive innovation*. In Christensen's theory, dominant firms succeed by tightly focusing on the product attributes demanded by their core customers. This focus causes incumbents to pass over innovations that lower costs at the expense of product features important to established customers. These promising innovations are instead developed by rivals to the dominant incumbents and eventually become more attractive alternatives for the incumbent's core customers. From the perspective of Christensen's model, the iPhone was unlikely to be a disruptive innovation because it was a high-price new product with expanded features (page 34 in Gans. 2016. *The Disruption Dilemma*). In contrast to Christensen's emphasis on customer demand, the switchover disruption theory emphasizes the effects of new innovations on the dominant firm's production processes and business models. In short, it is a supply side perspective.

15. Anderson, Gerard F., Uwe E. Reinhardt, Peter S. Hussey, and Varduhi Petrosyan. 2003. "It's the Prices, Stupid: Why the United States is so Different from Other Countries." *Health Affairs*, 22(3): 89–105.

16. Papanicolas, I., L. R. Woskie, and A. K. Jha. 2018. "Health Care Spending in the United States and Other High-Income Countries." *JAMA*, 319(10): 1024–1039.

17. For example, a recent study compared utilization and other features of healthcare systems across 11 wealthy Organization for Economic Cooperation and Development (OECD) countries. The data shows that the United States ranks in the middle of the pack for per capita hospitalizations for MIs, pneumonia, chronic obstructive pulmonary diseases, and hip replacements. It is number one or number two for some services such as magnetic resonance imaging (MRIs), computer tomography (CT scans), cardiovascular procedures, knee replacements, cataract operations, and cesarean deliveries. Yet even for these services, the differences in how much we consume don't appear all that large compared to other wealthy countries. For example, the United States performs 33 cesarean deliveries per 100 live births, but it is tied with Switzerland in this, while Australia and Canada perform 32 and 31 per 100 live births respectively. (Papanicolas, Woskie, and Jha. 2018. "Health Care Spending in the United States and Other High-Income Countries").

18. The United States ranks below the median in the per capita number of physicians, primary care physicians, nurses, and hospital beds. It ranks number three for the per capita number of specialists, matching those of Japan, and has only two fewer specialists per thousand population than the UK. It is, however, geared up to provide more imaging, ranking second in per capita MRI units, third in CT units, and first

in mammography machine units (Papanicolas, Woskie, and Jha. 2018. "Health Care Spending in the United States and Other High-Income Countries").

19. Anderson, Reinhardt, Hussey, and Petrosyan. 2003. "It's the Prices, Stupid: Why the United States is so Different from Other Countries."

20. Papanicolas, Woskie, and Jha. 2018. "Health Care Spending in the United States and Other High-Income Countries."

21. The average nightly hospital price in 2014 exceeded $5,200 in the United States, $4,700 in Switzerland, and $750 in Australia. Larger international price differentials also exist for specific procedures. For example, the average price of angioplasty was nearly $32,000 in the United States compared with $10,000 in Switzerland. Similar comparisons for coronary bypass surgery were approximately $78,000 in the United States versus $34,000 in Switzerland. As noted previously, the United States performs the same number of cesareans per 100 live births as Switzerland, but the average price of a cesarean in the United States exceeded $16,000 compared to about $10,000 in Switzerland. High U.S. prices are not limited to surgical procedures. The average price of an MRI in the United States was about $1,000 compared to more than $780 in the UK, $500 in Switzerland and $200 in Australia (Papanicolas, Woskie, and Jha. 2018. "Health Care Spending in the United States and Other High-Income Countries"). The average salary of a generalist physician in the United States is nearly $220,000 per year—63 percent above the mean across a set of 11 rich countries. For specialists, the average U.S. salary is even higher in both absolute and relative terms: more than $310,000 per year and 73 percent above the cross-country average. Nurses are also paid more, but not by as much. Average U.S. nursing salaries were about $74,000, 43 percent above the international average (Papanicolas, Woskie, and Jha. 2018. "Health Care Spending in the United States and Other High-Income Countries"). Not only are average salaries higher in the United States but professional fees for specific procedures are also higher. For example, Laugesen and Glied (2011) reported that in 2008, public payers in Australia paid surgeons nearly 64 percent of what U.S. public payers did for hip replacements. Similar ratios in other countries were Canada, 40 percent; France, 41 percent; Germany, 77 percent; and the UK, 72 percent (Exhibit 3 in Laugesen, Miriam J., and Sherry A. Glied. 2011. "Higher Fees Paid to US Physicians Drive Higher Spending for Physician Services Compared to Other Countries" *Health Affairs*, 30(9): 1647–1656).

22. For example, U.S. physicians may be more productive than their counterparts and, for this reason, earn more. Social factors such as a wider income distribution in the United States can also play a role. If, for example, you need to pay physicians at the ninety-fifth percentile of a nation's income distribution, then nations with more unequal distributions will pay their physicians more. The fact that U.S. physicians finance their own education through student loans also drives up salaries compared to other nations that pay for the education of physicians.

23. Martin, Anne B., Micah Hartman, David Lassman, and Aaron Catlin. 2021. "National Health Care Spending in 2019: Steady Growth for the Fourth Consecutive Year" *Health Affairs Web Exclusive*, 40(1): 14–24.

24. Cooper, Zack, Stuart V. Craig, Martin Gaynor, and John Van Reenen. 2018. "The Price Ain't Right? Hospital Prices and Health Spending on the Privately Insured" *The Quarterly Journal of Economics*, 134(1): 51–107.

25. Page 66 in Cooper, Craig, Gaynor, and Van Reenen. 2018. "The Price Ain't Right? Hospital Prices and Health Spending on the Privately Insured."

26. Frakt, Austin. 2017. "Hospitals Don't Shift Costs from Medicare or Medicaid to Private Insurers" *JAMA Forum Archive*, A6(1), https://jamanetwork.com/channels/health-forum/fullarticle/2760166.

27. Cooper, Craig, Gaynor, and Van Reenen. 2018. "The Price Ain't Right? Hospital Prices and Health Spending on the Privately Insured."

28. Private payers play an unusually important role in the delivery of healthcare in the United States. According to data from the American Community Survey compiled by the Kaiser Family Foundation, more than 56 percent of Americans with insurance obtain their insurance through the commercial insurance market. These figures understate the importance of commercial insurance plans because of the large fraction of Medicare beneficiaries who also purchase private supplemental plans (Kaiser Family Foundation. 2016. "Kaiser Family Foundation: State HMO Penetration Rate" KFF.org., http://kff.org/other/state-indicator/hmo-penetration-rate/?currentTimefr ame=0 (accessed February 22, 2021).

29. Dafny (2010) analyzed data from a set of large, fully insured employers. She found that when employer profits rose, so did their health insurance premiums, and this increase was most pronounced in local markets where there were six or fewer competing health plans. In a competitive insurance market, premiums would be determined by costs, not by the profitability—and the presumed capacity to pay—of employers (Dafny, Leemore. 2010. "Are Health Insurance Markets Competitive?" *The American Economic Review*, 100(4): 1399–1431).

30. Large mergers, such as the 1999 merger of Aetna and Prudential, altered the degree of competition across many markets. Consistent with the presence of insurer market power, one study found that the reduction in competition resulting from the insurance mergers caused an increase in insurance premiums paid by large employers (Dafny, Leemore, Mark Duggan, and Subramaniam Ramanarayanan. 2012. "Paying a Premium on Your Premium?" *The American Economic Review*, 102(2): 1161–1185).

31. Ericson, Keith M. 2014. "Consumer Inertia and Firm Pricing in the Medicare Part D Prescription Drug Insurance Exchange" *American Economic Journal: Economic Policy*, 6(1): 38–64.

32. In a competitive market, competition causes equivalent products to sell for the same price. However, if information about insurance products is difficult to obtain or hard to understand, this law of one price breaks down, and firms can thrive by adopting diverse markup strategies for identical policies. An insurer operating with a small markup will sell many policies because consumers discover that this is a good deal while an insurer operating with a high markup will sell to the smaller number of customers who have not yet discovered the lower markup offering. The degree to which high and low markup-pricing strategies coexist in the same market reveals how hard it is to comparison shop. Applying this indicator to the small group

insurance market suggests that prices could rise to nearly 30 percent above costs (Cebul, Randall D., James B. Rebitzer, Lowell J. Taylor, and Mark E. Votruba. 2011. "Unhealthy Insurance Markets: Search Frictions and the Cost and Quality of Health Insurance" *The American Economic Review*, 101(5): 29–1871).

33. Medicare Payment Advisory Commission. 2016. "Report to Congress: Medicare and the Health Care Delivery System. Congressional Publications" https://www.medpac. gov/document/http-www-medpac-gov-docs-default-source-reports-june-2016-rep ort-to-the-congress-medicare-and-the-health-care-delivery-system-pdf/.

34. At Kaiser Permanente, telehealth includes a variety of options including phone, email, doctor-to-doctor consults, and two-way video. All these contacts are mediated through their electronic medical record (EMR) system. In 2017, Kaiser reported 133,935 video visits and that 59 percent of their "touches" with patients were EMR enabled telehealth (Kaiser Permanente Institute for Health Policy. 2017. "Transforming Care Delivery with Telehealth at Kaiser Permanent" Kaiser Permanente Institute for Health Policy, https://www.kpihp.org/wp-content/uploads/ 2018/11/Telehealth_FactSheet_040318_230pm-.pdf (accessed July 28, 2021)).

35. "Kaiser Permanente's Big EHR Bet Paying Off" 2012. *Health Data Management*, https:// aushealthit.blogspot.com/2012/03/kaiser-permanente-just-seems-to-be.html.

36. See Crosson, Francis. 1999. "Permanente Medicine: The Path to a Sustainable Future" *Permanente Journal*, 3(1): 56–59; and Robertson, Kathy. 1999. "Reversal for Kaiser: Keep Morse Ave. Hospital" *Sacramento Business Journal*, 15(50): 1.

37. Verma, Seema. 2020. "Early Impact of CMS Expansion of Medicare Telehealth during COVID-19" *Health Affairs Blog*, https://www.healthaffairs.org/do/10.1377/forefr ont.20200715.454789/.

38. Verma. 2020. "Early Impact of CMS Expansion of Medicare Telehealth during COVID-19."

39. Cordina, Jenny, Jennifer Fowkes, Rupal Malani, and Laura Medford-Davis. 2022. "Patients Love Telehealth—Physicians are Not so Sure" *McKinsey Insights*. February 2022, https://search.proquest.com/docview/2637157597.

40. Volk, JoAnn, Dania Palanker, Madeline O'Brien, and Christina L. Goe. 2021. "States' Actions to Expand Telemedicine Access during COVID-19 and Future Policy Considerations" *Commonwealth Fund*, https://search.datacite.org/works/10.26099/ r95z-bs17.

41. Dorsey, E. R., and Eric J. Topol. 2016. "State of Telehealth" *The New England Journal of Medicine*, 375(2): 154–161.

42. Srinivasan, Malathi, Steven Asch, Stacie Vilendrer, Samuel C. Thomas, Rika Bajra, Linda Barman, Lauren M. Edwards, Heather Filipowicz, Lena Giang, Olivia Jee, et al. 2020. "Qualitative Assessment of Rapid System Transformation to Primary Care Video Visits at an Academic Medical Center" *Annals of Internal Medicine*, 173(7): 527–535.

43. Bestsennyy, Oleg, Greg Gilbert, Alex Harris, and Jennifer Rost. 2020. "Telehealth: A Quarter-Trillion-Dollar Post-Covid-19 Reality?" McKinsey.com, https://www.mckin sey.com/~/media/McKinsey/Industries/Healthcare%20Systems%20and%20S ervices/Our%20Insights/Telehealth%20A%20quarter%20trillion%20dollar%20p

ost%20COVID%2019%20reality/Telehealth-A-quarter-trilliondollar-post-COVID-19-reality.pdf (accessed July 28, 2021).

44. Bestsennyy, Gilbert, Harris, and Rost. 2020. "Telehealth: A Quarter-Trillion-Dollar Post-Covid-19 Reality?"

45. Christensen, Clayton M., Jerome H. Grossman, and Jason Hwang. 2009. *The Innovator's Prescription: A Disruptive Solution for Health Care*. New York: McGraw-Hill.

46. Galperin, Roman V. 2020. "Organizational Powers: Contested Innovation and Loss of Professional Jurisdiction in the Case of Retail Medicine." *Organization Science*, 31(2): 508–534.

47. Galperin. 2020. "Organizational Powers: Contested Innovation and Loss of Professional Jurisdiction in the Case of Retail Medicine."

Chapter 7

1. Heffler, Stephen K., Todd G. Caldis, Sheila D. Smith, and Gig A. Cuckler. 2020. "The Long-Term Projection Assumptions for Medicare and Aggregate National Health Expenditures." Department of Health and Human Services, Centers for Medicare and Medicaid Services.

2. Compared to other rich countries, the United States has low life expectancy. It also has a higher chronic disease burden, higher rates of hospitalization from preventable causes such as diabetes and hypertension, and higher rates of avoidable deaths from causes that are considered preventable with timely access to effective medical care. (Tikkanen, Roosa, and Melinda K. Abrams. 2020. "U.S. Health Care from a Global Perspective, 2019: Higher Spending, Worse Outcomes?" https://www.commonwealthfund.org/publications/issue-briefs/2020/jan/us-health-care-global-perspective-2019). How much of this poor relative performance is due to the U.S. healthcare itself as opposed to high rates of poverty and generally poor social support in the United States is a difficult matter currently subject to intense debate (Price, Gary, and Tim Norbeck. 2018. "U.S. Health Outcomes Compared to Other Countries are Misleading." *Forbes*. April 9, https://www.forbes.com/sites/physiciansfoundation/2018/04/09/u-s-health-outcomes-compared-to-other-countries-are-misleading/?sh=326046401232). A powerful illustration of this comes from Case, Anne, and Angus Deaton. 2015. "Rising Morbidity and Mortality in Midlife among White Non-Hispanic Americans in the 21st Century." *Proceedings of the National Academy of Sciences*, 112(49): 15078–15083. They document a marked increase in the all-cause mortality of middle-aged white non-Hispanic men and women in the United States between 1999 and 2013. This increase for whites was largely accounted for by increasing death rates from drug and alcohol poisonings, suicide, and chronic liver diseases and cirrhosis. Individuals with a high-school degree or less experienced the greatest increases. The proximate cause of many of these excess deaths lies directly in the role the healthcare system played in promoting the use of opioids. The vulnerability of so many to addiction, however, is also due to broader social forces such as falling labor force participation and wage rates for less educated workers.

3. Gaynor, Martin. 2020. "What to do about Health-Care Markets? Policies to Make Health-Care Markets Work" *Policy Brief Series (Hamilton Project)*, (10): 1–36.

4. Heffler, Caldis, Smith, and Cuckler. 2020. "The Long-Term Projection Assumptions for Medicare and Aggregate National Health Expenditures."

5. Hall, Robert E., and Charles I. Jones. 2007. "The Value of Life and the Rise in Health Spending" *The Quarterly Journal of Economics*, 122(1): 39–72.

6. Heffler, Caldis, Smith, and Cuckler. 2020. "The Long-Term Projection Assumptions for Medicare and Aggregate National Health Expenditures." Other estimates range between 1.4 and 1.7 (Smith, Sheila, Joseph P. Newhouse, and Mark S. Freeland. 2009. "Income, Insurance, and Technology: Why Does Health Spending Outpace Economic Growth?" *Health Affairs*, 28(5): 1276–1284).

7. In the static model presented in Hall and Jones (2007), "the health share rises over time as income grows if the marginal utility of consumption falls sufficiently rapidly relative to the joy of living an extra year and the ability of health spending to generate that extra year" (page 48 of Hall and Jones. 2007. "The Value of Life and the Rise in Health Spending.").

8. Hall and Jones. 2007. "The Value of Life and the Rise in Health Spending."

9. Cutler, David M. 2004. *Your Money or Your Life: Strong Medicine for America's Health Care System*. Oxford: Oxford University Press; and Murphy, Kevin M., and Robert H. Topel. 2006. "The Value of Health and Longevity" *Journal of Political Economy*, 114(5): 871–904.

10. Murphy and Topel. 2006. "The Value of Health and Longevity."

11. This is not to say there is no role at all for price caps to deal with market imperfections. A recent policy paper, for example, proposes to cap the maximum price of a procedure in a market at five times the price at the 20th percentile of the price distribution for that procedure. The authors estimate that such caps may save 8.7 percent of inpatient spending (Chernew, Michael E., Leemore S. Dafny, and Maximilian J. Pany. 2020. "A Proposal to Cap Provider Prices and Price Growth in the Commercial Health-Care Market" *Policy Brief Series (Hamilton Project)*, (8): 1–28. The proposal also caps the rate of growth of this price cap. This plan aims primarily to limit the scope for the exercise of market power within local markets.

12. Outterson, Kevin, and Anthony McDonnell. 2016. "Funding Antibiotic Innovation with Vouchers: Recommendations on How to Strengthen a Flawed Incentive Policy" *Health Affairs (Project Hope)*, 35(5): 784–790.

13. Schneider, Monika, Gregory W. Daniel, Nicholas R. Harrison, and Mark B. McClellan. 2020. "Delinking US Antibiotic Payments through a Subscription Model in Medicare" Margolis Center for Health Policy, Duke University, https://healthpolicy.duke.edu/sites/default/files/2020-02/margolis_subscription_model_14jan2020.pdf.

14. Schneider, Daniel, Harrison, and McClellan. 2020. "Delinking US Antibiotic Payments through a Subscription Model in Medicare."

15. Gee, Rebekah E. 2019. "Louisiana's Journey toward Eliminating Hepatitis C" *Health Affairs Blog*, https://www.healthaffairs.org/do/10.1377/forefront.20190327.603623/ (accessed September 1, 2020); and Schneider, Daniel, Harrison, and McClellan. 2020. "Delinking US Antibiotic Payments through a Subscription Model in Medicare."

16. Kremer, Michael, Jonathan D. Levin, and Christopher M. Snyder. 2020. "Advance Market Commitments: Insights from Theory and Commitments" National Bureau of Economic Research Working Paper, No. 26775.

17. Barder, Owen, Michael Kremer, and Ruth Levine. 2005. *Making Markets for Vaccines: Ideas to Action*. Washington: Center for Global Development. Poor countries benefit enormously from modern pharmaceuticals and vaccines, but most of these were developed in response to incentives for innovation in rich countries. Little private research and development is targeted toward the diseases of poor countries: malaria, TB, schistosomiasis, or Chagas disease. One can see a similar bias in diseases that affect both rich and poor countries. For example, private sector HIV/AIDs research is focused on drug treatments. Treatments make sense for rich countries where the majority of patients are covered by private or government insurance and so are not directly exposed to high prices. A vaccine for HIV/AIDs would carry a lower price tag than a treatment and would not require ongoing interactions with a provider. Vaccines for HIV/AIDs would therefore save more lives than treatments in low-income countries where access to providers and insurance is limited or nonexistent (page 25 of Kremer, Michael and Rachel Glennerster. 2004. *Strong Medicine*. Princeton; Oxfordshire: Princeton University Press).

18. The description of this AMC comes from Kremer, Levin, and Snyder. 2020. "Advance Market Commitments: Insights from Theory and Commitments."

19. The first two manufacturers initially priced their product at $3.50 per dose but were forced by public pressure to reduce their prices down to $2.90 per dose. The Serum Institute will be pricing its vaccine at $2 per dose.

20. A vaccine covering strains in developed countries already existed. PCVs focused on strains in developing countries that were in late-stage clinical trials—so advanced market commitments would primarily help ensure adequate manufacturing and distribution.

21. Kremer and Glennerster (2004) sketch what an AMC would look like in the case of malaria (Kremer and Glennerster. 2004. *Strong Medicine*). Considering the difficulties of developing a malaria vaccine, Kremer and Glennerster estimate a pharmaceutical company would need to generate approximately $2.3 billion in sales in 2004 dollars to match the return on investment from other R&D projects of similar difficulty. A coalition of NGOs and governments could pre-commit to pay $15 per treatment in real terms for the first 200 million people immunized with a new vaccine that cleared predetermined efficacy and safety standards. In return, the innovator would agree to provide and sell the vaccine to all comers at a price of $1 per person. This price would prevail even after the 200 million-person threshold is reached. Kremer and Glennerster estimate that such a hypothetical vaccine pre commitment for malaria would cost about $15 per QALY saved. Assuming a very low value of $100 per QALY for very low-income countries, the hypothetical vaccine generates a great deal of economic value and is very cost effective. Without these pre-commitments, savvy investors would place their bets on other challenges where conventional market-based assessments of "willingness to pay" are higher even though their effect on social welfare may be lower.

22. Kremer, Levin, and Snyder. 2022. "Designing Advance Market Commitments for New Vaccines."

23. The value lost from sales that don't happen under monopoly pricing create what economists call a deadweight loss to society.

24. Conti, Rena M., Brigham Frandsen, Michael L. Powell, and James B. Rebitzer. 2021. "Common Agent or Double Agent? Pharmacy Benefit Managers in the Prescription Drug Market." National Bureau of Economic Research Working Paper Series, No. 28866.

25. Michael Kremer. 1998. "Patent Buyouts: A Mechanism for Encouraging Innovation." *The Quarterly Journal of Economics*, 113(4): 1137–1167.

26. There is evidence, for example, that when Bell labs was forced to license all its existing patents royalty-free by a consent decree, a lasting increase in innovation followed. There was an increase in both citations of these patents and in patenting activity overall. Most of the increase centered on young and small companies, suggesting that patents held by a dominant firm can be a barrier to entry for small firms (Watzinger, Martin, Thomas Fackler, Markus Nagler, and Monika Schnitzer. 2020. "How Antitrust Enforcement Can Spur Innovation: Bell Labs and the 1956 Consent Decree." *American Economic Journal: Economic Policy*, 12(4): 328–359).

27. The Federal government's central role can have both positive and negative effects on incentives for innovation. On the positive side, the government can adjust the bids to move the incentives for innovators closer to the value created by the innovation. This adjustment might be helpful because the bids on the patents would not include the value that accrues to consumers in the form of consumer surplus. Kremer (1998) suggests that consumer surplus is large enough that the government ought to commit to doubling the winning bid (Kremer. 1998. "Patent Buyouts: A Mechanism for Encouraging Innovation"). The negative effect of government discretion stems from credibility issues. If one government commits to purchasing patents at twice the winning auction bid, a subsequent government can undo this commitment. Projects that made economic sense under the first set of commitments may not make sense if the commitments are withdrawn. Government discretion can thus introduce fragility into the proposed auction system and this fragility can undermine innovation incentives. (Kremer, Michael, and Heidi Williams. 2010. "Incentivizing Innovation: Adding to the Tool Kit." *Innovation Policy and the Economy*, 10(1): 1–17).

28. Popper, Karl R. 2020. *The Open Society and its Enemies*. Princeton: Princeton University Press.

29. Frandsen, Brigham, Michael Powell, and James B. Rebitzer. 2019. "Sticking Points: Common Agency Problems and Contracting in the US Healthcare System." *RAND Journal of Economics*, 50(2): 251.

30. Einav, Liran, Amy Finkelstein, Yunan Ji, and Neale Mahoney. 2020. "Randomized Trial Shows Healthcare Payment Reform Has Equal-Sized Spillover Effects on Patients Not Targeted by Reform." *Proceedings of the National Academy of Sciences*, 117(32): 18939–18947.

31. Gupta, Atul, Abhinav Gupta, Sabrina T. Howell, and Constantine Yannelis. 2021. "Does Private Equity Investment in Healthcare Benefit Patients? Evidence from

Nursing Homes" National Bureau of Economic Research Working Paper Series, No. 28474.

32. The power calculations were made using a sample size calculator at ClinCalc.com under the assumptions that alpha is 0.05, power is 80 percent, the PE mortality rate is 18 percent, and the non-private equity mortality rate is 17 percent. (Sample Size Calculator. https://clincalc.com/stats/samplesize.aspx (accessed July 30, 2021)).

33. Specifically, it finds that in counties where Medicare Advantage plans are more prevalent, the overall patient risk scores are higher across *both* Medicare Advantage and traditional Medicare enrollees. This is what would happen if Medicare Advantage plans were assigning more expensive diagnoses to their enrollees than under traditional Medicare (Geruso, Michael and Timothy Layton. 2020. "Upcoding: Evidence from Medicare on Squishy Risk Adjustment" *The Journal of Political Economy*, 128(3): 984–1026).

34. The analysis of the rollout of the Texas managed care program is from Kuziemko, Ilyana, Katherine Meckel, and Maya Rossin-Slater. 2018. "Does Managed Care Widen Infant Health Disparities? Evidence from Texas Medicaid" *American Economic Journal. Economic Policy*, 10(3): 255–283. They found that as a result of the managed care roll out, Black mortality and preterm births increased by 15 percent and 7 percent respectively, while Hispanic mortality and preterm births decreased by 22 percent and 7 percent.

35. Einav, Finkelstein, Ji, and Mahoney. 2020. "Randomized Trial shows Healthcare Payment Reform has Equal-Sized Spillover Effects on Patients Not Targeted by Reform."

36. Prospective Payment Systems (PPS) offer a kind of shared savings contracts in which hospitals are paid on the basis of the diagnosis of the patient (as expressed in the patient's Diagnostic Related Group codes or DRGs) and not on the costs incurred treating the patients. Thus a hospital admitting a patient for a heart attack gets a fixed payment, regardless of the amount spent by the hospital in treating the patient. If the hospital can deploy care pathways that deliver care at a lower cost, the hospital keeps the difference. When regulators set up the PPS system for acute care hospitals, they realized that some hospitals with long length of stays would not be viable under the PPS system. They therefore carved out a separate category of hospitals that had an average inpatient length of stay of at least 25 days. These became long-term care hospitals.

37. A noteworthy exception to this generalization is Cochrane, John H. 1995. "Time-Consistent Health Insurance" *Journal of Political Economy*, 103(3): 445–473. It focuses on the problem of providing long-term health insurance contracts in place of the single year contracts that currently dominate the market. This analysis replaces the long-term contract between enrollee and insurer with a sequence of short-term contracts where the health status of the patient is continually "marked to market" in a special account. If a patient becomes sicker, their premiums go up in a way that compensates the insurer for higher expected costs. If a patient becomes healthier, premiums fall. The proposed contract design is complex and requires information about current and prospective patient costs that is simply unavailable. Its value is in illustrating the deep design challenges posed by long-term contracts.

38. Frandsen, Brigham, and James B. Rebitzer. 2014. "Structuring Incentives within Accountable Care Organizations" *Journal of Law, Economics, and Organization* 31(S1): 77–103.

39. Robert Pearl, former CEO of The Permanente Medical Group, outlines the power of physician culture as a motivating force in healthcare in his memoir/manifesto (Pearl, Robert. 2021. *Uncaring: How the Culture of Medicine Kills Doctors and Patients.* New York City: PublicAffairs). In the book he describes instances in which cultural sensitivities made the difference between adoption and rejection of innovations.

40. Information in this paragraph comes from the Health Care Cost Institute web page (Health Care Cost Institute, https://healthcostinstitute.org/ (accessed June 18, 2021)).

41. Herman, Bob. 2019. "Blue Cross Blue Shield Replaces United in Health Data-Sharing Deal" *Axios*. November 12, 2020 https://search.proquest.com/docview/2428567196.

42. All-Payer Claims Databases. 2021. https://www.ahrq.gov/data/apcd/index.html (accessed June 21, 2021).

43. Agha, Leila, Keith M. Ericson, Kimberley H. Geissler, and James B. Rebitzer. 2022. "Team Relationships and Performance: Evidence from Healthcare Referral Networks" *Management Science*, 68(5): 3735–3754.

44. As of early 2019, 20 states have implemented or are in the process of implementing APCDs (Chernew, Dafny, and Pany. 2020. "A Proposal to Cap Provider Prices and Price Growth in the Commercial Health-Care Market").

45. Another problem is that none of these databases include prices from the entire health sector. The Supreme Court has held that the participation of self-insured groups in APCDs is voluntary and so some of these groups have stopped participating. A comprehensive APCD would seem to require federal legislation mandating reporting by all payers (Chernew, Dafny, and Pany. 2020. "A Proposal to Cap Provider Prices and Price Growth in the Commercial Health-Care Market").

46. Overview of the SEER Program. https://seer.cancer.gov/about/overview.html (accessed June 18, 2021).

47. The Principles that Guide the Development of NICE Guidance and Standards. https://www.nice.org.uk/about/who-we-are/our-principles (accessed June 18, 2021).

48. Timmins, Nicholas, Michael Rawlins, and John Appleby. 2016. *A Terrible Beauty: A Short History of NICE, the National Institute for Health and Care Excellence.* Bangkok: Amarin Printing and Publishing Public Co., Ltd.

49. Institute for Clinical and Economic Review. "Methods and Process" ICER: Institute for Clinical and Economic Review, https://icer.org/our-approach/methods-process/ (accessed June 18, 2021).

50. The tendency of horizontal mergers to reduce incentives for innovation is quite general and applies to any desirable new product or process—not simply those new products that have lower costs. In the language of economics, B's innovation imposes a negative externality on A, and the merged entity internalizes the externality. The analysis is complicated if provider A is also engaged in innovation, but the basic conclusion that horizontal mergers can reduce incentives to innovate remains. It is also possible that the merger creates synergies that can support innovations. For example,

rivals to an innovative firm may be able to partially imitate its new product and so reduce returns to the innovator. A new entity that merged the rivals would be able to internalize these spillovers and so have greater incentives to innovate. Another innovation synergy might occur if the merged entity increases the scale over which the innovation may be deployed. Finally, innovation synergies may result if the merged firms' development team becomes more efficient post merger. Mergers can also result in R&D dis-synergies by reducing the diversity of approaches to an innovation problem. For a general overview of these and other points relating to innovation and competition see Federico, Giulio, Fiona S. Morton, and Carl Shapiro. 2020. "Antitrust and Innovation: Welcoming and Protecting Disruption." In *Innovation Policy and the Economy*, ed. Josh Lerner and Scott Stern, 125–190. Vol. 20. Chicago: The University of Chicago Press.

51. Federico, Morton, and Shapiro. 2020. "Antitrust and Innovation: Welcoming and Protecting Disruption." It seems plausible that such exclusionary payment practices can discourage new entry, but it is not clear how the loyalty rebate itself—which is more generous to hospitals—can be self-financing. If all hospitals agree to accept the more generous loyalty rebate, how does the drugmaker get the funds to pay the rebates? Is entry precluded so that the drugmaker can charge non hospitals more for the drug and use this to fund the loyalty rebates?

52. Gaynor. 2020. "What to do about Health-Care Markets? Policies to Make Health-Care Markets Work."

53. Medicare's 340B program, which was implemented to make cheap drugs available to hospitals treating low-income patients, turns out to have a similar effect. It creates an artificial incentive for oncologists and others who administer expensive drugs to become employed by a hospital (page 19 of Gaynor. 2020. "What to do about Health-Care Markets? Policies to Make Health-Care Markets Work").

54. Gaynor. 2020. "What to do about Health-Care Markets? Policies to Make Health-Care Markets Work."

55. Gaynor (2020), for example, suggests $156.75 million per year to support antitrust enforcement and to help them keep pace with a rising tide of mergers (Gaynor. 2020. "What to do about Health-Care Markets? Policies to Make Health-Care Markets Work.").

56. The suggestions in this paragraph are described by Baker, Jonathan B., and Fiona Scott Morton. 2019. "Confronting Rising Market Power" *Economists for Inclusive Prosperity*, https://econfip.org/wp-content/uploads/2019/05/Confronting-Rising-Market-Power.pdf.

57. This proposal comes from Gaynor. 2020. "What to do about Health-Care Markets? Policies to Make Health-Care Markets Work." His idea was inspired by two existing monitoring agencies: the Massachusetts Health Policy Commission and the Dutch Healthcare Authority.

58. Pearl. 2021. *Uncaring: How the Culture of Medicine Kills Doctors and Patients.*

59. Pearl. 2021. *Uncaring: How the Culture of Medicine Kills Doctors and Patients.*

60. Gibbons, Robert, and Rebecca Henderson. 2012. "Relational Contracts and Organizational Capabilities" *Organizational Science*, 23(5): 1350–1364.

61. Reinhardt, Uwe E. 1997. "Wanted: A Clearly Articulated Social Ethic for American Health Care." *JAMA*, 278(17): 1446–1447.

Appendix 1

1. Acemoglu, Daron, and Joshua Linn. 2004. "Market Size in Innovation: Theory and Evidence from the Pharmaceutical Industry." *Quarterly Journal of Economics*, 119(3): 1049–1090.

2. Dubois, Pierre, Olivier de Mouzon, Fiona Scott-Morton, and Paul Seabright. 2015. "Market Size and Pharmaceutical Innovation." *RAND Journal of Economics*, 46(4): 844–871.

3. See columns 5 and 6 in Table 1 of Bhattacharya, Jay, and Mikko Packalen. 2011. "Opportunities and Benefits as Determinants of the Direction of Scientific Research." *Journal of Health Economics*, 30(4): 603–615.

4. Finkelstein, Amy. 2004. "Static and Dynamic Effects of Health Policy: Evidence from the Vaccine Industry." *Quarterly Journal of Economics*, 119(2): 527–564.

5. Acemoglu, Daron, David Cutler, Amy Finkelstein, and Joshua Linn. 2006. "Did Medicare Induce Pharmaceutical Innovation?" *American Economic Review*, 96(2): 103–107.

6. Finkelstein, Amy. 2007. "The Aggregate Effects of Health Insurance: Evidence from the Introduction of Medicare." *Quarterly Journal of Economics*, 122(1): 1–37.

7. Clemens, Jeffrey. 2013. "The Effect of U.S. Health Insurance Expansions on Medical Innovation." National Bureau of Economic Research Working Paper Series, No. 19761.

8. This discussion of the effects of PBM exclusions on innovation comes from Kim, Soomi, Danielle Li, and Leila Agha. 2020. "Insurance Design and Pharmaceutical Innovation." National Bureau of Economic Research Working Paper Series, No. 27563.

9. Brugger, Florian, and Christian Gehrke. 2017. "The Neoclassical Approach to Induced Technical Change: From Hicks to Acemoglu." *Metroeconomica*, 68(4): 730–776.

10. See, for example, the account in Allen, Robert C. 2011. *Global Economic History: A Very Short Introduction.* New York: Oxford University Press. There is evidence that high prices for inputs in healthcare can cause a substitution toward lower-cost inputs. The implementation of diagnostic related groupings (DRGs) in 1983 caused an increase in the cost of labor to hospitals relative to capital. Labor became relatively expensive because the DRG payment system made hospitals fully responsible for the marginal costs of labor. In contrast, marginal capital expenditures were partially subsidized. (This feature of DRG reimbursement has since changed.) The shift in relative input costs likely caused an increase in demand for capital intensive treatments (Acemoglu, Daron, and Amy Finkelstein. 2008. "Input and Technology Choices in Regulated Industries: Evidence from the Health Care Sector." *Journal of Political Economy*, 116(5): 837–880).

11. Some models suggest that induced innovation likely has only a small effect on energy consumption relative to simply substituting less expensive for more expensive energy sources. See Nordhaus, William D. 2002. "Modeling Induced Innovation

in Climate-Change Policy." In *Technological Change and the Environment*, ed. A. Grubler, N. Nakicenovic, and W. D. Nordhaus, 182–209. Routledge.

12. Popp, D. 2002. "Induced Innovation and Energy Prices." *The American Economic Review*, 92(1): 160–180.

13. Sobel, Dava. 1995. *Longitude*, Repr. ed. Harmondsworth: Penguin Books.

14. The private sector can also offer prizes to reward innovators. Recently some companies, such as Innocentive and Kaggle, have attempted to use web-based contests to stimulate innovations, but this model does not yet appear to have taken off (Van Alstyne, Marshall W., Allesandro Di Fiore, and Simon Schneider. 2017. "4 Mistakes that Kill Crowdsourcing Efforts." *Harvard Business Review Digital Articles*, https://hbr.org/2017/07/4-mistakes-that-kill-crowdsourcing-efforts).

15. Mukherjee, Siddhartha. 2010. *The Emperor of all Maladies: A Biography of Cancer*. New York: Scribner.

16. Cutler, David M., Ellen Meara, and Seth Richards-Shubik. 2012. "Induced Innovation and Social Inequality: Evidence from Infant Medical Care." *Journal of Human Resources*, 47(2): 456–492.

17. Yin, Wesley. 2008. "Market Incentives and Pharmaceutical Innovation." *Journal of Health Economics*, 27(4): 1060–1077.

18. Clemens, Jeffrey, and Parker Rogers. 2020. "Demand Shocks, Procurement Policies, and the Nature of Medical Innovation: Evidence from Wartime Prosthetic Device Patents," National Bureau of Economic Research Working Paper Series, No. 26679. https://www.nber.org/papers/w26679.

19. With the exception that foreign entities filed more patents in countries where patents were stronger. Lerner, Josh. 2009. "The Empirical Impact of Intellectual Property Rights on Innovation: Puzzles and Clues." *The American Economic Review*, 99(2): 343–348.

20. Williams, Heidi L. 2017. "How Do Patents Affect Research Investments?" *Annual Review of Economics*, 9(1): 441–469.

21. See for example, the introduction of a new patent regime in India Duggan, Mark, Craig Garthwaite, and Aparajita Goyal. 2016. "The Market Impacts of Pharmaceutical Product Patents in Developing Countries: Evidence from India." *The American Economic Review*, 106(1): 99–135.

22. Williams. 2017. "How Do Patents Affect Research Investments?"

23. Williams, Heidi L. 2013. "Intellectual Property Rights and Innovation: Evidence from the Human Genome." *Journal of Political Economy*, 121(1): 1–27.

24. Sampat, Bhaven, and Heidi L. Williams. 2019. "How Do Patents Affect Follow-on Innovation? Evidence from the Human Genome." *The American Economic Review*, 109(1): 203–236.

Appendix 2

1. The productivity effects of automation also determine the demand for labor. As productivity increases, firms produce products and services more cheaply, and the net demand for labor consequently grows. Whether overall demand for labor goes up or

down depends on the relative magnitude of productivity and displacement effects. Automation that brings with it sizable displacement effects but only modest productivity gains can reduce overall labor demand. Some recent studies of the use of robots find that industries into which industrial robots are introduced experience declines in labor demand for production workers because displacement effects exceed productivity effects (Acemoglu, Daron, and Pascual Restrepo. 2019. "Automation and New Tasks" *The Journal of Economic Perspectives*, 33(2): 3–30).

2. One could, in principle, use the political system to redistribute the benefits from automation more widely. However, sufficiently widespread automation may leave the beneficiaries of such redistribution in a weak position to influence the political system. The resulting increase in the concentration of wealth and power may create what Erik Brynjolfsson calls the "Turing Trap"—a political and economic equilibrium in which those disempowered by automation have no way to improve their material situation (Brynjolfsson, Erik. 2022. "The Turing Trap: The Promise & Peril of Human-Like Artificial Intelligence" *Daedalus*, 151(2): 272–287).

3. An analogue to this argument is found in Richard Freeman and Edward Lazear's analysis of the economics of works councils. They suggest that works councils increase worker productivity while reducing the share of income going to capital. For this reason, employer incentives to introduce works councils are too weak and mandated works councils could improve overall efficiency. See Freeman, Richard B., and Edward P. Lazear. 1995. "An Economic Analysis of Works Councils." In *Works Councils: Consultation, Representation, and Cooperation Industrial Relations*, ed. Joel Rogers and Wolfgang Streeck, 27–52. Chicago: University of Chicago Press.

4. Brynjolfsson. 2022. "The Turing Trap: The Promise & Peril of Human-Like Artificial Intelligence."

5. This history is extensively reviewed and discussed by Erik J. Larson in his book, *The Myth of Artificial Intelligence* (Larson, Erik J. 2021. *The Myth of Artificial Intelligence*. Cambridge, MA; London: The Belknap Press of Harvard University Press).

6. Larson. 2021. *The Myth of Artificial Intelligence*.

7. For a symposium discussing how to move the direction of AI innovation in a more socially productive direction see the special issue of Boston Review, AI's Future Doesn't Have to Be Dystopian. 2022, https://bostonreview.net/forum/ais-future-doesnt-have-to-be-dystopian/ (accessed May 18, 2022).

References

1daysooner.Org. 2020. https://1daysooner.org/ (accessed May 26, 2021).

Abi Younes, George, Charles Ayoubi, Omar Ballester, Gabriele Cristelli, Gaétan de Rassenfosse, Dominique Foray, Patrick Gaulé, Gabriele Pellegrino, Matthias van den Heuvel, Elizabeth Webster, et al. 2020. "COVID-19: Insights from Innovation Economists." *Science & Public Policy*, 47(5): 733–745.

About Palliative Care. 2022. https://www.capc.org/about/palliative-care/?clickthrough _doc_id=core.contentpage.549&clickthrough_req_id=9Jmt9PGuQKCK_RnsoUR XrA&clickthrough_query=About%20palliative%20care (accessed August 10, 2021).

Acemoglu, Daron, David Cutler, Amy Finkelstein, and Joshua Linn. 2006. "Did Medicare Induce Pharmaceutical Innovation?" *The American Economic Review*, 96(2): 103–107.

Acemoglu, Daron, and Amy Finkelstein. 2008. "Input and Technology Choices in Regulated Industries: Evidence from the Health Care Sector." *Journal of Political Economy*, 116(5): 837–880.

Acemoglu, Daron, and Joshua Linn. 2004. "Market Size in Innovation: Theory and Evidence from the Pharmaceutical Industry." *Quarterly Journal of Economics*, 119(3): 1049–1090.

Acemoglu, Daron, Andrea Manera, and Pascual Restrepo. 2020. "Does the US Tax Code Favor Automation?" *Brookings Papers on Economic Activity*, 2020(1): 231–285.

Acemoglu, Daron, and Pascual Restrepo. 2019. "Automation and New Tasks." *The Journal of Economic Perspectives*, 33(2): 3–30.

Acemoglu, Daron, and Pascual Restrepo. 2020. "The Wrong Kind of AI? Artificial Intelligence and the Future of Labour Demand." *Cambridge Journal of Regions, Economy and Society*, 13(1): 25–35.

Adler-Milstein, Julia, and Ashish K. Jha. 2017. "HITECH Act Drove Large Gains in Hospital Electronic Health Record Adoption." *Health Affairs Web Exclusive*, 36(8): 1416–1422.

Agha, Leila. 2014. "The Effects of Health Information Technology on the Costs and Quality of Medical Care." *Journal of Health Economics*, 34: 19–30.

Agha, Leila, Keith M. Ericson, Kimberley H. Geissler, and James B. Rebitzer. 2022. "Team Relationships and Performance: Evidence from Healthcare Referral Networks." *Management Science*, 68(5): 3735–3754.

Agha, Leila, Keith M. Ericson, and Xiaoxi Zhao. Forthcoming. "The Impact of Organizational Boundaries on Healthcare Coordination and Utilization." *American Economic Journal: Economic Policy*.

Agha, Leila, Brigham Frandsen, and James B. Rebitzer. 2019. "Fragmented Division of Labor and Healthcare Costs: Evidence from Moves across Regions." *Journal of Public Economics*, 169: 144–159.

Agha, Leila, Soomi Kim, and Danielle Li. 2022. "Insurance Design and Pharmaceutical Innovation." *AER: Insights*, 4(2): 191–208.

Aghion, Philippe, Nick Bloom, Richard Blundell, Rachel Griffith, and Peter Howitt. 2005. "Competition and Innovation: An Inverted-U Relationship." *Quarterly Journal of Economics*, 120(2): 701–728.

AI's Future Doesn't Have to Be Dystopian. 2022. https://bostonreview.net/forum/ais-fut ure-doesnt-have-to-be-dystopian/ (accessed May 18, 2022).

Akerlof, George A., and Rachel E. Kranton. 2010. *Identity Economics*. Princeton: Princeton University Press.

Akerlof, George A., and Rachel E. Kranton. 2000. "Economics and Identity." *Quarterly Journal of Economics*, 115(3): 715–753.

Akerlof, George A., and Brian G. M. Main. 1981. "An Experience-Weighted Measure of Employment and Unemployment Durations." *The American Economic Review*, 71(5): 1003–1011.

All-Payer Claims Databases. 2021. https://www.ahrq.gov/data/apcd/index.html (accessed June 21, 2021).

Allen, Robert C. 2011. *Global Economic History: A Very Short Introduction*. New York: Oxford University Press.

Anderson, Gerard F., Uwe E. Reinhardt, Peter S. Hussey, and Varduhi Petrosyan. 2003. "It's the Prices, Stupid: Why the United States is so Different from Other Countries." *Health Affairs*, 22(3): 89–105.

Arrow, Kenneth. 1962. "Economic Welfare and the Allocation of Resources for Invention." In *The Rate and Direction of Inventive Activity: Economic and Social Factors*, ed. Universities-National Bureau Committee for Economic Research, Committee on Economic Growth of the Social Science Research Council, 609–626. Princeton: Princeton University Press.

Ashraf, Nava, Oriana Bandiera, Edward Davenport, and Scott S. Lee. 2020. "Losing Prosociality in the Quest for Talent? Sorting, Selection, and Productivity in the Delivery of Public Services." *The American Economic Review*, 110(5): 1355–1394.

Baicker, Katherine, and Amitabh Chandra. 2004. "The Productivity of Physician Specialization: Evidence from the Medicare Program." *The American Economic Review*, 94(2): 357–361.

Baker, Jonathan B., and Fiona Scott Morton. 2019. "Confronting Rising Market Power." *Economists for Inclusive Prosperity*. https://econfip.org/wp-content/uploads/2019/05/ Confronting-Rising-Market-Power.pdf.

Baker, Laurence, Kate Bundorf, and Anne Royalty. 2018. "Measuring Physician Practice Competition Using Medicare Data." In *Measuring and Modeling Health Care Costs*, ed. Ana Aizcorbe, Colin Baker, Ernst R. Berndt, and David M. Cutler, 351–378. Chicago: University of Chicago Press.

Barder, Owen, Michael Kremer, and Ruth Levine. 2005. *Making Markets for Vaccines: Ideas to Action*. Washington: Center for Global Development.

Barnett, Michael L., Andrew Olenski, and Adam Sacarny. 2021. "Common Practice: Spillovers from Medicare on Private Health Care." http://sacarny.com/wp-content/uploads/2021/06/BOS-Spillovers-2021–06.pdf (accessed September 1, 2021).

Bernheim, B. D., and Michael D. Whinston. 1986. "Common Agency." *Econometrica*, 54(4): 923–942.

Bestsennyy, Oleg, Greg Gilbert, Alex Harris, and Jennifer Rost. 2020. "Telehealth: A Quarter-Trillion-Dollar Post-Covid-19 Reality?" McKinsey.com. https://www.mckin sey.com/~/media/McKinsey/Industries/Healthcare%20Systems%20and%20Services/ Our%20Insights/Telehealth%20A%20quarter%20trillion%20dollar%20post%20CO

VID%2019%20reality/Telehealth-A-quarter-trilliondollar-post-COVID-19-reality. pdf (accessed July 28, 2021).

Bhattacharya, Jay, and Mikko Packalen. 2011. "Opportunities and Benefits as Determinants of the Direction of Scientific Research." *Journal of Health Economics*, 30(4): 603–615.

Biller-Andorno, Nikola, and Thomas H. Lee. 2013. "Ethical Physician Incentives— from Carrots and Sticks to Shared Purpose." *The New England Journal of Medicine*, 368(11): 980–982.

Blendon, R. J., M. Brodie, J. M. Benson, D. E. Altman, L. Levitt, T. Hoff, and L. Hugick. 1998. "Understanding the Managed Care Backlash." *Health Affairs*, 17(4): 80–94.

Bloom, N., C. Propper, S. Seiler, and J. Van Reenen. 2015. "The Impact of Competition on Management Quality: Evidence from Public Hospitals." *The Review of Economic Studies*, 82(2 (291)): 457–489.

Blumenthal, David. 2011a. "Implementation of the Federal Health Information Technology Initiative." *New England Journal of Medicine*, 365(25): 2426–2431.

Blumenthal, David. 2011b. "Wiring the Health System—Origins and Provisions of a New Federal Program." *New England Journal of Medicine*, 365(24): 2323–2329.

Blumenthal, David. 2009. "Stimulating the Adoption of Health Information Technology." *The New England Journal of Medicine*, 360(15): 1477–1479.

Boldrin, Michele and David K. Levine. 2013. "The Case against Patent." *The Journal of Economic Perspectives*, 27(1): 3–22.

Bowles, Samuel. 2016. *The Moral Economy*. New Haven: Yale University Press.

Bowles, Samuel, and Sandra Polania-Reyes. 2012. "Economic Incentives and Social Preferences: Substitutes or Complements?" *Journal of Economic Literature*, 50(2): 368–425.

Brot-Goldberg, Zarek, Amitabh Chandra, Benjamin R. Handel, and Jonathan T. Kolstad. 2017. "What Does a Deductible do? the Impact of Cost-Sharing on Health Care Prices, Quantities, and Spending Dynamics." *Quarterly Journal of Economics*, 132(3): 1261–1318.

Brot-Goldberg, Zarek C., and Mathijs de Vaan. 2018. "Intermediation and Vertical Integration in the Market for Surgeons." Unpublished working paper.

Brugger, Florian, and Christian Gehrke. 2017. "The Neoclassical Approach to Induced Technical Change: From Hicks to Acemoglu." *Metroeconomica*, 68(4): 730–776.

Brynjolfsson, Erik. 2022. "The Turing Trap: The Promise & Peril of Human-Like Artificial Intelligence." *Daedalus*, 151(2): 272–287.

Brynjolfsson, Erik, and Andrew McAfee. 2014. *The Second Machine Age: Work, Progress, and Prosperity in a Time of Brilliant Technologies*, 1st ed. New York: WW Norton & Company.

Budish, Eric, Benjamin N. Roin, and Heidi Williams. 2015. "Do Firms Underinvest in Long-Term Research? Evidence from Cancer Clinical Trials." *The American Economic Review*, 105(7): 2044–2085.

Bundorf, M. K. 2016. "Consumer-Directed Health Plans: A Review of the Evidence." *Journal of Risk and Insurance*, 83(1): 9–41.

Buntin, Melinda B., Matthew F. Burke, Michael C. Hoaglin, and David Blumenthal. 2011. "The Benefits of Health Information Technology: A Review of the Recent Literature Shows Predominantly Positive Results." *Health Affairs*, 30(3): 464–471.

Bureau of Labor Statistics. 2018. "Employee Tenure in 2018." *Bureau of Labor Statistics*. https://www.bls.gov/news.release/archives/tenure_09202018.htm#:~:text=Med

ian%20tenure%20for%20women%2C%20at,See%20tables%201%20and%203 (accessed June 2019).

Burns, L. R., and M. V. Pauly. 2018. "Transformation of the Health Care Industry: Curb Your Enthusiasm?" *The Milbank Quarterly*, 96(1): 57–109.

Burns, Lawton R., Jeff C. Goldsmith, and Aditi Sen. 2013. "Horizontal and Vertical Integration of Physicians: A Tale of Two Tails" *Advances in Health Care Management*, 15: 39.

California Health Care Almanac. 2021. https://www.chcf.org/wp-content/uploads/2019/05/CAHealthInsurersAlmanac2019.pdf (accessed July 9, 2021).

Case, Anne, and Angus Deaton. 2015. "Rising Morbidity and Mortality in Midlife among White Non-Hispanic Americans in the 21st Century" *Proceedings of the National Academy of Sciences*, 112(49): 15078–15083.

Catillon, Maryaline, David Cutler, and Thomas Getzen. 2018. "Two Hundred Years of Health and Medical Care: The Importance of Medical Care for Life Expectancy Gains" National Bureau of Economic Research Working Paper Series, No. 25330.

Cebul, Randall D., James B. Rebitzer, Lowell J. Taylor, and Mark E. Votruba. 2011. "Unhealthy Insurance Markets: Search Frictions and the Cost and Quality of Health Insurance" *The American Economic Review*, 101(5): 1842–1871.

Cebul, Randall, James B. Rebitzer, Lowell J. Taylor, and Mark Votruba. 2008. "Organizational Fragmentation and Care Quality in the US Health Care System" *The Journal of Economic Perspectives*, 22(4): 93–113.

Chandra, Amitabh, Amy Finkelstein, Adam Sacarny, and Chad Syverson. 2016. "Health Care Exceptionalism? Performance and Allocation in the US Health Care Sector" *The American Economic Review*, 106(8): 2110–2144.

Chandra, Amitabh, Evan Flack, and Ziad Obermeyer. 2021. "The Health Costs of Cost-Sharing" National Bureau of Economic Research Working Paper Series, No. 28439.

Chandra, Amitabh, Anupam B. Jena, and Jonathan S. Skinner. 2011. "The Pragmatist's Guide to Comparative Effectiveness Research" *The Journal of Economic Perspectives*, 25(2): 27–46.

Chandra, Amitabh, and Jonathan Skinner. 2012. "Technology Growth and Expenditure Growth in Health Care" *Journal of Economic Literature*, 50(3): 645–680.

Chandra, Amitabh, and Douglas O. Staiger. 2007. "Productivity Spillovers in Health Care: Evidence from the Treatment of Heart Attacks" *Journal of Political Economy*, 115(1): 103–140.

Chernew, Michael, Zack Cooper, Eugene Larsen-Hallock, and Fiona S. Morton. 2018. "Are Health Care Services Shoppable? Evidence from the Consumption of Lower-Limb MRI Scans" National Bureau of Economic Research Working Paper Series, No. 24869.

Chernew, Michael E., Leemore S. Dafny, and Maximilian J. Pany. 2020. "A Proposal to Cap Provider Prices and Price Growth in the Commercial Health-Care Market" *Policy Brief Series (Hamilton Project)*, (8): 1–28. https://www.hamiltonproject.org/assets/files/CDP_PP_WEB_FINAL.pdf.

Christensen, Clayton M. 2013. *The Innovator's Dilemma*, 1st ed. Reprint Edition. Boston: Harvard Business Review Press.

Christensen, Clayton M., Jerome H. Grossman, and Jason Hwang. 2009. *The Innovator's Prescription: A Disruptive Solution for Health Care*. New York: McGraw-Hill.

Clemens, Jeffrey. 2013. "The Effect of U.S. Health Insurance Expansions on Medical Innovation" National Bureau of Economic Research Working Paper Series, No. 19761.

Clemens, Jeffrey, and Parker Rogers. 2020. "Demand Shocks, Procurement Policies, and the Nature of Medical Innovation: Evidence from Wartime Prosthetic Device Patents" National Bureau of Economic Research Working Paper Series, No. 26679.

Cochrane, John H. 1995. "Time-Consistent Health Insurance" *Journal of Political Economy*, 103(3): 445–473.

Conti, Rena M., Brigham Frandsen, Michael L. Powell, and James B. Rebitzer. 2021. "Common Agent or Double Agent? Pharmacy Benefit Managers in the Prescription Drug Market" National Bureau of Economic Research Working Paper Series, No. 28866.

Cooper, Zack, Stuart V. Craig, Martin Gaynor, and John Van Reenen. 2018. "The Price Ain't Right? Hospital Prices and Health Spending on the Privately Insured" *The Quarterly Journal of Economics*, 134(1): 51–107.

Cordina, Jenny, Jennifer Fowkes, Rupal Malani, and Laura Medford-Davis. 2022. "Patients Love Telehealth—Physicians Are Not so Sure" *McKinsey Insights*. February 22, https://search.proquest.com/docview/2637157597.

Crosson, Francis. 1999. "Permanente Medicine: The Path to a Sustainable Future" *Permanente Journal*, 3(1): 56–59.

Cunningham, Colleen, Florian Ederer, and Song Ma. 2021. "Killer Acquisitions" *The Journal of Political Economy*, 129(3): 649–702.

Cutler, David M. 2011. "Where are the Health Care Entrepreneurs? The Failure of Organizational Innovation in Health Care" *Innovation Policy and the Economy*, 11(1): 1–28.

Cutler, David M. 2004. *Your Money or Your Life: Strong Medicine for America's Health Care System.* Oxford: Oxford University Press.

Cutler, David M., Ellen Meara, and Seth Richards-Shubik. 2012. "Induced Innovation and Social Inequality: Evidence from Infant Medical Care" *Journal of Human Resources*, 47(2): 456–492.

Cutler, David M., Jonathan Skinner, Ariel D. Stern, and David Wennberg. 2019. "Physician Beliefs and Patient Preferences: A New Look at Regional Variation in Health Care Spending" *American Economic Journal: Economic Policy*, 11(1): 192–221.

Cutler, David M., and Richard J. Zeckhauser. 2000. "The Anatomy of Health Insurance." In *Handbook of Health Economics*, Vol. 1, ed. Anthony J. Culyer and Joseph P. Newhouse, 563–643. N.p.: Elsevier.

Dafny, Leemore S. 2010. "Are Health Insurance Markets Competitive?" *The American Economic Review*, 100(4): 1399–1431.

Dafny, Leemore, Mark Duggan, and Subramaniam Ramanarayanan. 2012. "Paying a Premium on Your Premium?" *The American Economic Review*, 102(2): 1161–1185.

Delong, Brad. 2019. "The Lighting Budget of Thomas Jefferson" Delong's Grasping Reality. https://www.bradford-delong.com/2019/02/the-lighting-budget-of-thomas-jefferson.html (accessed June 22, 2021).

DesRoches, Catherine M., Eric G. Campbell, Sowmya R. Rao, Karen Donelan, Timothy G. Ferris, Ashish Jha, Rainu Kaushal, Douglas E. Levy, Sara Rosenbaum, Alexandra E. Shields, et al. 2008. "Electronic Health Records in Ambulatory Care—A National Survey of Physicians" *New England Journal of Medicine*, 359(1): 10–50.

Diabetes Prevention Program Research Group. 2002. "Reduction in the Incidence of Type 2 Diabetes with Lifestyle Intervention or Metformin" *The New England Journal of Medicine*, 346(6): 393–403.

Dorsey, E. R., and Eric J. Topol. 2016. "State of Telehealth." *The New England Journal of Medicine*, 375(2): 154–161.

Dranove, David, Craig Garthwaite, and David Besanko. 2016. "Insurance and the High Prices of Pharmaceuticals." National Bureau of Economic Research Working Paper Series, No. 22353.

Dranove, David, Craig Garthwaite, Christopher Heard, and Bingxiao Wu. 2022. "The Economics of Medical Procedure Innovation." *Journal of Health Economics*, 81: 102549.

Dranove, David, Craig Garthwaite, and Manuel Hermosilla. 2014. "Pharmaceutical Profits and the Social Value of Innovation." National Bureau of Economic Research Working Paper Series, No. 20212.

Dubois, Pierre, Olivier de Mouzon, Fiona Scott-Morton, and Paul Seabright. 2015. "Market Size and Pharmaceutical Innovation." *RAND Journal of Economics*, 46(4): 844–871.

Duggan, Mark, Craig Garthwaite, and Aparajita Goyal. 2016. "The Market Impacts of Pharmaceutical Product Patents in Developing Countries: Evidence from India." *The American Economic Review*, 106(1): 99–135.

Einav, Liran, Amy Finkelstein, Yunan Ji, and Neale Mahoney. 2020. "Randomized Trial shows Healthcare Payment Reform Has Equal-Sized Spillover Effects on Patients Not Targeted by Reform." *Proceedings of the National Academy of Sciences*, 117(32): 18939–18947.

Einav, Liran, Amy Finkelstein, Sehndhil Mullainathan, and Ziad Obermeyer. 2018. "Predictive Modeling of U.S. Healthcare Spending in Late Life." *Science*, 36-: 1462–1465.

Elías, Julio J., Nicola Lacetera, and Mario Macis. 2019. "Paying for Kidneys? A Randomized Survey and Choice Experiment." *The American Economic Review*, 109(8): 2855–2888.

Elias, Julio J., Nicola Lacetera, and Mario Macis. 2015. "Markets and Morals: An Experimental Survey Study." *PloS One*, 10(6): e0127069.

Ericson, Keith M. 2014. "Consumer Inertia and Firm Pricing in the Medicare Part D Prescription Drug Insurance Exchange." *American Economic Journal: Economic Policy*, 6(1): 38–64.

Espinosa, Maria P., and Changyong Rhee. 1989. "Efficient Wage Bargaining as a Repeated Game." *The Quarterly Journal of Economics*, 104(3): 565–588.

Fang, Hanming, and Alessandro Gavazza. 2011. "Dynamic Inefficiencies in an Employment-Based Health Insurance System: Theory and Evidence." *The American Economic Review*, 101(7): 3047–3077.

Federico, Giulio, Fiona S. Morton, and Carl Shapiro. 2020. "Antitrust and Innovation: Welcoming and Protecting Disruption." In *Innovation Policy and the Economy*, ed. Josh Lerner and Scott Stern, 125–190. Vol. 20. Chicago: The University of Chicago Press.

Finkelstein, Amy. 2007. "The Aggregate Effects of Health Insurance: Evidence from the Introduction of Medicare." *Quarterly Journal of Economics*, 122(1): 1–37.

Finkelstein, Amy. 2004. "Static and Dynamic Effects of Health Policy: Evidence from the Vaccine Industry." *Quarterly Journal of Economics*, 119(2): 527–564.

Finkelstein, Amy, Matthew Gentzkow, and Heidi Williams. 2016. "Sources of Geographic Variation in Health Care: Evidence from Patient Migration." *Quarterly Journal of Economics*, 131(4): 1681–1726.

Fisher, Elliott S., Mark B. McClellan, John Bertko, Steven M. Lieberman, Julie J. Lee, Julie L. Lewis, and Jonathan S. Skinner. 2009. "Fostering Accountable Health Care: Moving Forward in Medicare." *Health Affairs*, 28(2): W219–W231.

Frakt, Austin. 2017. "Hospitals Don't Shift Costs from Medicare or Medicaid to Private Insurers" *JAMA Forum Archive*, A6(1). https://jamanetwork.com/channels/health-forum/fullarticle/2760166.

Frandsen, Brigham, Karen E. Joynt, James B. Rebitzer, and Ashish K. Jha. 2015. "Care Fragmentation, Quality, and Costs among Chronically Ill Patients" *American Journal of Managed Care*, 21(5): 355–326.

Frandsen, Brigham, Michael Powell, and James B. Rebitzer. 2019. "Sticking Points: Common Agency Problems and Contracting in the US Healthcare System" *RAND Journal of Economics*, 50(2): 251–285.

Frandsen, Brigham, and James B. Rebitzer. 2014. "Structuring Incentives within Accountable Care Organizations" *Journal of Law, Economics, and Organization*, 31(S1): 77–103.

Freeman, Richard B., and Edward P. Lazear. 1995. "An Economic Analysis of Works Councils." In *Works Councils: Consultation, Representation, and Cooperation Industrial Relations*, ed. Joel Rogers and Wolfgang Streeck, 27–52. Chicago: University of Chicago Press.

Friedman, Milton. 1970. "The Social Responsibility of Business is to Increase its Profits" *New York Times Magazine*. September 13. https://www.nytimes.com/1970/09/13/archives/a-friedman-doctrine-the-social-responsibility-of-business-is-to.html.

Fuchs, Victor R. 2019. "Does Employment-Based Insurance make the US Medical Care System Unfair and Inefficient?" *JAMA*, 321(21): 2069.

Furukawa, M. F., J. King, V. Patel, C. J. Hsiao, J. Adler-Milstein, and A. K. Jha. 2014. "Despite Substantial Progress in EHR Adoption, Health Information Exchange and Patient Engagement Remain Low in Office Settings" *Health Affairs*, 33(9): 1672–1679.

Galperin, Roman V. 2020. "Organizational Powers: Contested Innovation and Loss of Professional Jurisdiction in the Case of Retail Medicine" *Organization Science*, 31(2): 508–534.

Gans, Joshua. 2016. *The Disruption Dilemma*: Cambridge, MA: The MIT Press.

Garthwaite, Craig, Manuel I. Hermosilla, and David Dranove. 2020. "Expected Profits and the Scientific Novelty of Innovation" National Bureau of Economic Research Working Paper, #27093.

Gaynor, Martin. 2020. "What to do about Health-Care Markets? Policies to Make Health-Care Markets Work" *Policy Brief Series (Hamilton Project)* (10): 1–36.

Gaynor, Martin, James B. Rebitzer, and Lowell J. Taylor. 2004. "Physician Incentives in Health Maintenance Organizations" *Journal of Political Economy*, 112(4): 915–931.

Gee, Emily, and Topher Spiro. 2019. "Excess Administrative Costs Burden the U.S. Health Care System" Center for American Progress. https://www.americanprogress.org/issues/healthcare/reports/2019/04/08/468302/excess-administrative-costsburden-us-health-care-system.

Gee, Rebekah E. 2019. "Louisiana's Journey toward Eliminating Hepatitis C" *Health Affairs Blog*.

Geruso, Michael, and Timothy Layton. 2020. "Upcoding: Evidence from Medicare on Squishy Risk Adjustment" *The Journal of Political Economy*, 128(3): 984–1026.

Gibbons, Robert, and Rebecca Henderson. 2012. "Relational Contracts and Organizational Capabilities" *Organizational Science*, 23(5): 1350–1364.

Gilbert, Richard J., and David M. G. Newbery. 1982. "Preemptive Patenting and the Persistence of Monopoly" *The American Economic Review*, 72(3): 514–526.

Glazer, Jacob, and Thomas G. McGuire. 2002. "Multiple Payers, Commonality and Free-Riding in Health Care: Medicare and Private Payers" *Journal of Health Economics*, 21(6): 1049–1069.

Gold, Marsha, and Catherine Mclaughlin. 2016. "Assessing HITECH Implementation and Lessons: 5 Years Later" *The Milbank Quarterly*, 94(3): 654–687.

Goldman, Dana P., Karen Van Nuys, Jakub P. Hlavka, Luca Pani, Sylvain Chassang, and Erik Snowberg. 2018. "A New Model for Pricing Drugs of Uncertain Efficacy" *New England Journal of Medicine Catalyst*. https://catalyst.nejm.org/doi/full/10.1056/CAT.18.0035.

Goldstein, Joseph L., and Michael S Brown. 2015. "A Century of Cholesterol and Coronaries: From Plaques to Genes to Statins" *Cell*, 161(1): 161–172.

Gottlieb, J. D., A. H. Shapiro, and A. Dunn. 2018. "The Complexity of Billing and Paying for Physician Care" *Health Affairs*, 37(4): 619–626.

Gupta, Atul, Abhinav Gupta, Sabrina T. Howell, and Constantine Yannelis. 2021. "Does Private Equity Investment in Healthcare Benefit Patients? Evidence from Nursing Homes" National Bureau of Economic Research Working Paper Series, No. 28474.

Hall, Robert E., and Charles I. Jones. 2007. "The Value of Life and the Rise in Health Spending" *The Quarterly Journal of Economics*, 122(1): 39–72.

Handel, Benjamin R., Igal Hendel, and Michael D. Whinston. 2017. "The Welfare Effects of Long-Term Health Insurance Contracts" National Bureau of Economic Research Working Paper Series, No. 23624.

Harrington, Brooke. 2021. "The Anti-Vaccine Con Job is Becoming Untenable" *The Atlantic*. August 1. https://www.theatlantic.com/ideas/archive/2021/08/vaccine-refusers-dont-want-blue-americas-respect/619627/.

Hart, Oliver, and Luigi Zingales. 2017. "Companies Should Maximize Shareholder Welfare Not Market Value" *Journal of Law, Finance and Accounting*, 2(2): 247–275.

Health Care Cost Institute. https://healthcostinstitute.org/ (accessed June 18, 2021).

Heath, Jermaine, Ellen Meara, and Eric Wadsworth. 2018. "Baystate Health: Navigating a Path between Volume and Value" Dartmouth College. Unpublished teaching case.

Heffler, Stephen K., Todd G. Caldis, Sheila D. Smith, and Gig A. Cuckler. 2020. "The Long-Term Projection Assumptions for Medicare and Aggregate National Health Expenditures" Department of Health and Human Services, Centers for Medicare and Medicaid Services. https://www.cms.gov/files/document/long-term-projection-assumptions-medicare-and-aggregate-national-health-expenditures.pdf.

Herman, Bob. 2019. "Blue Cross Blue Shield Replaces United in Health Data-Sharing Deal" *Axios*. November 12, 2020 https://www.axios.com/2019/11/12/blue-cross-blue-shield-hcci-unitedhealthcare-data-sharing.

Holmes, Thomas J., David K. Levine, and James A. Schmitz. 2012. "Monopoly and the Incentive to Innovate When Adoption Involves Switchover Disruptions" *American Economic Journal: Microeconomics*, 4(3): 1–33.

Holmes, Thomas J., and James A. Schmitz. 2010. "Competition and Productivity: A Review of Evidence" *Annual Review of Economics*, 2(1): 619–642.

Holmgren, A. J., Vaishali Patel, Dustin Charles, and Julia Adler-Milstein. 2016. "US Hospital Engagement in Core Domains of Interoperability" *The American Journal of Managed Care*, 22(12): 1.

Hult, Kristopher J., Sonia Jaffe, and Tomas J. Philipson. 2018. "How does Technological Change Affect Quality-Adjusted Prices in Health Care? Systematic Evidence from Thousands of Innovations" *American Journal of Health Economics*, 4(4): 433–425.

Hussey, Peter S., Eric C. Schneider, Robert S. Rudin, Steven Fox, Julie Lai, and Craig E. Pollack. 2014. "Continuity and the Costs of Care for Chronic Disease" *JAMA Internal Medicine*, 174(5): 742–748.

Institute of Medicine Committee on Quality of Health Care in America. 2001. *Crossing the Quality Chasm: A New Health Care System for the 20th Century*. Washington, DC: National Academy Press.

Institute for Clinical and Economic Review. "Methods and Process" *ICER: Institute for Clinical and Economic Review*. https://icer.org/our-approach/methods-process/ (accessed June 18, 2021).

Javitt, Jonathan C., James B. Rebitzer, and Lonnie Reisman. 2008. "Information Technology and Medical Missteps: Evidence from a Randomized Trial" *Journal of Health Economics*, 27(23): 585–602.

Jha, Ashish K., Catherine M. DesRoches, Eric G. Campbell, Karen Donelan, Sowmya R. Rao, Timothy G. Ferris, Alexandra Shields, Sara Rosenbaum, and David Blumenthal. 2009. "Use of Electronic Health Records in U.S. Hospitals" *The New England Journal of Medicine*, 360(16): 1628–1638.

Kaiser Family Foundation. 2016. "Kaiser Family Foundation: State HMO Penetration Rate" KFF.org. http://kff.org/other/state-indicator/hmo-penetration-rate/?currentTi meframe=0 (accessed February 22, 2017).

Kaiser Permanente's Big EHR Bet Paying Off. 2012. "Kaiser Permanente's Big EHR Bet Paying Off" *Health Data Management*. https://aushealthit.blogspot.com/2012/03/kai ser-permanente-just-seems-to-be.html.

Kaiser Permanente Institute for Health Policy. 2015. "Transforming Care Delivery with Telehealth at Kaiser Permanent" Kaiser Permanente Institute for Health Policy. https:// www.kpihp.org/wp-content/uploads/2018/11/Telehealth_FactSheet_040318_230pm- .pdf (accessed July 28, 2021).

Kaplan, Robert M. 2019. *More than Medicine*. Cambridge: Harvard University Press.

Kelley, A. S., and R. S. Morrison. 2015. "Palliative Care for the Seriously Ill" *The New England Journal of Medicine*, 373(8): 747–755.

Kim, Soomi, Danielle Li, and Leila Agha. 2020. "Insurance Design and Pharmaceutical Innovation" National Bureau of Economic Research Working Paper Series, No. 27563.

Kolstad, Jonathan T. 2013. "Information and Quality when Motivation is Intrinsic: Evidence from Surgeon Report Cards" *The American Economic Review*, 103(7): 2875–2910.

Kowalzyck, Liz. 2018. "Steward Health Care Pressured Doctors to Restrict Referrals outside Chain, Suit Says" *Boston Globe*.

Kremer, Michael. 1998. "Patent Buyouts: A Mechanism for Encouraging Innovation" *The Quarterly Journal of Economics*, 113(4): 1137–1167.

Kremer, Michael, and Rachel Glennerster. 2004. *Strong Medicine*. Princeton; Oxfordshire: Princeton University Press.

Kremer, Michael, Jonathan Levin, and Christopher M. Snyder. 2022. "Designing Advance Market Commitments for New Vaccines" *Management Science*, 68(7): 4786–4814.

Kremer, Michael, Jonathan D. Levin, and Christopher M. Snyder. 2020. "Advance Market Commitments: Insights from Theory and Commitments" National Bureau of Economic Research Working Paper, No. 26775.

Kremer, Michael, and Christopher M. Snyder. 2015. "Preventatives versus Treatments" *Quarterly Journal of Economics*, 130(3): 1167–1239.

Kremer, Michael, and Christopher M. Snyder. 2018. "Preventives versus Treatments Redux: Tighter Bounds on Distortions in Innovation Incentives with an Application to the Global Demand for HIV Pharmaceuticals" National Bureau of Economic Research Working Paper, No. 24206.

Kremer, Michael, and Heidi Williams. 2010. "Incentivizing Innovation: Adding to the Tool Kit" *Innovation Policy and the Economy*, 10(1): 1–17.

Kuziemko, Ilyana, Katherine Meckel, and Maya Rossin-Slater. 2018. "Does Managed Care Widen Infant Health Disparities? Evidence from Texas Medicaid" *American Economic Journal. Economic Policy*, 10(3): 255–283.

Kyle, Margaret, and Heidi Williams. 2017. "Is American Health Care Uniquely Inefficient? Evidence from Prescription Drugs" *American Economic Review*, 107(5): 486–490.

Lacetera, Nicola, Mario Macis, and Robert Slonim. 2013. "Economic Rewards to Motivate Blood Donations" *Science*, 340(6135): 927–928.

Lakdawalla, Darius, Anup Malani, and Julian Reif. 2017. "The Insurance Value of Medical Innovation" *Journal of Public Economics*, 145: 94–102.

Larson, Erik J. 2021. *The Myth of Artificial Intelligence*. Cambridge, MA; London: The Belknap Press of Harvard University Press.

Laugesen, Miriam J., and Sherry A. Glied. 2011. "Higher Fees Paid to US Physicians Drive Higher Spending for Physician Services Compared to Other Countries" *Health Affairs*, 30(9): 1647–1656.

Leonhardt, David. 2009. "If Healthcare is Going to Change His Ideas Will Change It" *New York Times*, November 8, Mag: 1.

Lerner, Josh. 2009. "The Empirical Impact of Intellectual Property Rights on Innovation: Puzzles and Clues" *The American Economic Review*, 99(2): 343–348.

Levitt, Steven D., and Chad Syverson. 2008. "Market Distortions when Agents are Better Informed: The Value of Information in Real Estate Transactions" *The Review of Economics and Statistics*, 90(4): 599–611.

Liao, J. M., L. A. Fleisher, and A. S. Navathe. 2016. "Increasing the Value of Social Comparisons of Physician Performance Using Norms" *JAMA*, 316(11): 1151–1152.

Lin, Jennifer S., Margaret A. Piper, Leslie A. Perdue, Carolyn M. Rutter, Elizabeth M. Webber, Elizabeth O'Connor, Ning Smith, and Evelyn P. Whitlock. 2016. "Screening for Colorectal Cancer: Updated Evidence Report and Systematic Review for the US Preventive Services Task Force" *JAMA*, 315(23): 2576–2594.

Lin, Sunny C., Jordan Everson, and Julia Adler-Milstein. 2018. "Technology, Incentives, Or both? Factors Related to Level of Hospital Health Information Exchange" *Health Services Research*, 53(5): 3285–3308.

Martin, Anne B., Micah Hartman, David Lassman, and Aaron Catlin. 2021. "National Health Care Spending in 2019: Steady Growth for the Fourth Consecutive Year" *Health Affairs Web Exclusive*, 40(1): 14–24.

May, Peter, Charles Normand, J. Brian Cassel, Egidio Del Fabbro, Robert L. Fine, Reagan Menz, Corey A. Morrison, Joan D. Penrod, Chessie Robinson, and R. S. Morrison. 2018. "Economics of Palliative Care for Hospitalized Adults with Serious Illness: A Meta-Analysis" *JAMA Internal Medicine*, 178(6): 820–829.

McCullough, Jeffrey S., Stephen T. Parente, and Robert Town. 2016. "Health Information Technology and Patient Outcomes: The Role of Information and Labor Coordination" *RAND Journal of Economics*, 47(1): 207–236.

McNeil, Donald G., Jr. 2019a. "200,000 Uninsured Americans to Get Free H.I.V.-Prevention Drugs" *New York Times*. https://www.nytimes.com/2019/12/03/health/truvada-prep-hiv-gilead.html#:~:text=McNeil%20Jr.&text=With%20donated%20drugs%20and%20services,The%20announcement%2C%20by%20Alex%20M.

McNeil, Donald G., Jr. 2019b. "Gilead Will Donate Truvada to U.S. for H.I.V. Prevention" *New York Times*. https://www.nytimes.com/2019/05/09/health/gilead-truvada-hiv-aids.html?searchResultPosition=2 (accessed May 10, 2019).

McWilliams, J. M., M. E. Chernew, and B. E. Landon. 2017. "Medicare ACO Program Savings Not Tied to Preventable Hospitalizations or Concentrated among High-Risk Patients." *Health Affairs*, 36(12): 2085–2093.

McWilliams, J. M., L. A. Hatfield, M. E. Chernew, B. E. Landon, and A. L. Schwartz. 2016. "Early Performance of Accountable Care Organizations in Medicare." *The New England Journal of Medicine*, 374(24): 2357–2366.

McWilliams, J. M., Laura A. Hatfield, Bruce E. Landon, Pasha Hamed, and Michael E. Chernew. 2018. "Medicare Spending after 3 Years of the Medicare Shared Savings Program." *The New England Journal of Medicine*, 379(12): 1139–1149.

McWilliams, J. M., Ellen Meara, Alan M. Zaslavsky, and John Z. Ayanian. 2007. "Health of Previously Uninsured Adults after Acquiring Medicare Coverage." *JAMA*, 298(24): 2886–2894.

Medicare Payment Advisory Commission. 2016. "Report to Congress: Medicare and the Health Care Delivery System. Congressional Publications." https://www.medpac.gov/document/http-www-medpac-gov-docs-default-source-reports-june-2016-report-to-the-congress-medicare-and-the-health-care-delivery-system-pdf/.

Medicare Telehealth Frequently Asked Questions (FAQs). https://www.stfm.org/media/2774/medicare-telehealth-faqs-031720.pdf (accessed July 28, 2021).

Mehrotra, Ateev, Christopher B. Forrest, and Caroline Y. Lin. 2011. "Dropping the Baton: Specialty Referrals in the United States." *The Milbank Quarterly*, 89(1): 39–68.

Meier, Diane E. 2009. "Finding My Place." *Journal of Palliative Medicine*, 12(4): 331–335.

Meyer, Gregg S., Akinluwa A. Demehin, Xiu Liu, and Duncan Neuhauser. 2012. "Two Hundred Years of Hospital Costs and Mortality—MGH and Four Eras of Value in Medicine." *The New England Journal of Medicine*, 366(23): 2147–2149.

Milstein, Arnold, and Elizabeth Gilbertson. 2009. "American Medical Home Runs." *Health Affairs*, 28(5): 1317–1326.

Mokyr, Joel. 2016. *A Culture of Growth*. Princeton: Princeton University Press.

Morgenson, Getchen. 2017. "A Costly Drug, Missing a Dose of Disclosure." *New York Times*.

Morrison, Sean R., Diane E. Meir, Maggie Rogers, Allison Silvers, Stacie Sinclair, and Rachael Heitner. 2020. "America's Care of Serious Illness." Center to Advance Palliative Care, 1–39. https://reportcard.capc.org/wp-content/uploads/2020/05/CAPC_State-by-State-Report-Card_051120.pdf.

Mukherjee, Siddhartha. 2019. "New Blood: The Promise and Price of Cellular Therapies." *New Yorker*, 95(20). https://www.newyorker.com/magazine/2019/07/22/the-promise-and-price-of-cellular-therapies.

Mukherjee, Siddhartha. 2010. *The Emperor of All Maladies: A Biography of Cancer*. New York: Scribner.

Murphy, Kevin M., and Robert H. Topel. 2006. "The Value of Health and Longevity." *Journal of Political Economy*, 114(5): 871–904.

National Ambulatory Care Survey: 2010 Summary Tables. http://www.cdc.gov/nchs/data/ahcd/namcs_summary/2010_namcs_web_tables.pdf (accessed February 3, 2020).

Navathe, Amol S., and Ezekiel J. Emanuel. 2016. "Physician Peer Comparisons as a Nonfinancial Strategy to Improve the Value of Care." *JAMA*, 316(17): 1759–1760.

Nelson, A. L., J. T. Cohen, D. Greenberg, and D. M. Kent. 2009. "Much Cheaper, Almost as Good: Decrementally Cost-Effective Medical Innovation." *Annals of Internal Medicine*, 151(9): 662–667.

Neumann, Peter J., Joshua T. Cohen, and Milton C. Weinstein. 2014. "Updating Cost-Effectiveness—the Curious Resilience of the $50,000-Per-QALY Threshold." *The New England Journal of Medicine*, 371(9): 796–797.

Nordhaus, William D. 2002. "Modeling Induced Innovation in Climate-Change Policy." In *Technological Change and the Environment*, ed. A. Grubler, N. Nakicenovic, and W. D. Nordhaus, 182–209. N.p.: Routledge.

Nordhaus, William D. 1996. "Do Real-Output and Real-Wage Measures Capture Reality? The History of Lighting Suggests Not." In *The Economics of New Goods*, ed. Timothy F. Bresnahan and Robert J. Gordon, 27–70. Chicago: University of Chicago Press.

Nyweide, D. J., D. L. Anthony, J. P. Bynum, R. L. Strawderman, W. B. Weeks, L. P. Casalino, and E. S. Fisher. 2013. "Continuity of Care and the Risk of Preventable Hospitalization in Older Adults." *JAMA Internal Medicine*, 173(20): 1879–1885.

Nyweide, David J., William B. Weeks, Daniel J. Gottlieb, Lawrence P. Casalino, and Elliott S. Fisher. 2009. "Relationship of Primary Care Physicians' Patient Caseload with Measurement of Quality and Cost Performance." *JAMA*, 302(22): 2444–2450.

Ollove, Michael. 2019. "Drug-Price Debate Targets Pharmacy Benefit Managers." *Stateline.org* (accessed February 8, 2020).

Outterson, Kevin, Unni Gopinathan, Charles Clift, Anthony D. So, Chantal M. Morel, and John-Arne Røttingen. 2016. "Delinking Investment in Antibiotic Research and Development from Sales Revenues: The Challenges of Transforming a Promising Idea into Reality." *PLOS Medicine*, 13(6): e1002043.

Outterson, Kevin, and Anthony McDonnell. 2016. "Funding Antibiotic Innovation with Vouchers: Recommendations on How to Strengthen a Flawed Incentive Policy." *Health Affairs*, 35(5): 784–790.

Outterson, Kevin, John H. Powers, Gregory W. Daniel, and Mark B. McClellan. 2015. "Repairing the Broken Market for Antibiotic Innovation." *Health Affairs*, 34(2): 277–285.

Overview of the SEER Program. https://seer.cancer.gov/about/overview.html (accessed June 18, 2021).

Papanicolas, I., L. R. Woskie, and A. K. Jha. 2018. "Health Care Spending in the United States and Other High-Income Countries." *JAMA*, 319(10): 1024–1039.

Pearl, Robert. 2021. *Uncaring: How the Culture of Medicine Kills Doctors and Patients*: New York: PublicAffairs.

Pearl, Robert M. 2017. "Engaging Physicians in Telehealth." *New England Journal of Medicine Catalyst*. https://catalyst.nejm.org/doi/full/10.1056/CAT.17.0458.

Plackett, Benjamin. 2020. "Why Big Pharma Has Abandoned Antibiotics." *Nature*, 586(7830): S50.

Popp, D. 2002. "Induced Innovation and Energy Prices." *The American Economic Review*, 92(1): 160–180.

Popper, Karl R. 2020. *The Open Society and its Enemies*. Princeton: Princeton University Press.

Powell, Michael. 2016. "Comparative Effectiveness Testing." Unpublished working paper.

Prasad, Vinay, and Stephan Lindner. 2018. "Why is Research in Early-Stage Cancer Research So Low?" *Journal of Cancer Policy*, 17: 4–8.

Price, Gary, and Tim Norbeck. 2018. "U.S. Health Outcomes Compared to Other Countries are Misleading." *Forbes*. April 9, https://www.forbes.com/sites/physiciansfoundation/2018/04/09/u-s-health-outcomes-compared-to-other-countries-are-misleading/?sh=2b251cda1232.

Pryor, Katherine, and Kevin Volpp. 2018. "Deployment of Preventive Interventions—Time for a Paradigm Shift." *The New England Journal of Medicine*, 378(19): 1761–1763.

Rebitzer, James B., and Lowell J. Taylor. 2011. "Extrinsic Rewards and Intrinsic Motives: Standard and Behavioral Approaches to Agency in Labor Markets." In *Handbook of Labor Economics*, ed. Orley Ashenfelter and David Card, 701–772. Vol. 4. Amsterdam: North-Holland.

Rebitzer, James B., and Mark E. Votruba. 2011. "Organizational Economics and Physician Practices." National Bureau of Economic Research Working Paper, No. 17535.

Reinhardt, Uwe E. 1997. "Wanted: A Clearly Articulated Social Ethic for American Health Care." *JAMA*, 278(17): 1446–1447.

Richards, Kevin T., Kevin J. Hickey, and Erin H. Ward. 2020. "Drug Pricing and Pharmaceutical Patenting Practices." Congressional Research Service.

Roberts, John. 2004. *The Modern Firm: Organizational Design for Performance and Growth*. Oxford: Oxford University Press.

Robertson, Kathy. 1999. "Reversal for Kaiser: Keep Morse Ave. Hospital." *Sacramento Business Journal*, 15(50): 1.

Robinson, James C. 2020. "Slouching towards Disruptive Innovation." *Health Affairs Blog*. https://www.healthaffairs.org/do/10.1377/forefront.20200227.395178/full/ (accessed February 28, 2020).

Robinson, James C. 2015. *Purchasing Medical Innovation: The Right Technology, for the Right Patient, at the Right Price*. Oakland: University of California Press.

Robinson, James C. 1999. *The Corporate Practice of Medicine: Competition and Innovation in Health Care*. Berkeley: University of California Press.

Roman, Benjamin R. 2014. "Avastin for Metastatic Breast Cancer." In *Redirecting Innovation in U.S. Health Care: Options to Decrease Spending and Increase Value*, ed. Steven Garber, Susan M. Gates, Emmett B. Keeler, Mary E. Vaiana, Andrew W. Mulcahy, Christopher Lau, and Arthur L. Kellerman, 1–12. Santa Monica, CA: Rand Corporation.

Romano, M. J., J. B. Segal, and C. E. Pollack. 2015. "The Association between Continuity of Care and the Overuse of Medical Procedures." *JAMA Internal Medicine*, 175(7): 1148–1154.

Roth, Alvin E. 2007. "Repugnance as a Constraint on Markets." *The Journal of Economic Perspectives*, 21(3): 37–58.

Sampat, Bhaven, and Heidi L. Williams. 2019. "How do Patents Affect Follow-on Innovation? Evidence from the Human Genome." *The American Economic Review*, 109(1): 203–236.

Sample Size Calculator. https://clincalc.com/stats/samplesize.aspx (accessed July 30, 2021).

Satz, Debra. 2010. *Why Some Things Should Not be for Sale*. New York: Oxford University Press.

Savage, Lucia, Martin Gaynor, and Julia Adler-Milstein. 2019. "Digital Health Data and Information Sharing: A New Frontier for Health Care Competition?" *Antitrust Law Journal*, 82(2): 593–621.

Schmitz, James A., Jr. 2005. "What Determines Productivity? Lessons from the Dramatic Recovery of the U.S. and Canadian Iron Ore Industries Following their Early 1980s Crisis." *Journal of Political Economy*, 113(3): 582–625.

Schneider, Monika, Gregory W. Daniel, Nicholas R. Harrison, and Mark B. McClellan. 2020. "Delinking US Antibiotic Payments through a Subscription Model in Medicare"

Margolis Center for Health Policy, Duke University. https://healthpolicy.duke.edu/sites/default/files/2020-02/margolis_subscription_model_14jan2020.pdf.

Scott, Dylan. 2018. "The Trump Administration is about to Delete an Important Medical Resource." *www.vox.com*. https://www.vox.com/policy-and-politics/2018/7/16/17578548/voxcare-national-guideline-clearinghouse (accessed July 16, 2018).

Seeley, Elizabeth, and Aaron S. Kesselheim. 2019. "Pharmacy Benefit Managers: Practices, Controversies, and what Lies Ahead" Commonwealth Fund Issue Brief. PMID: 30990594.

Shapiro, Carl. 2012. "Competition and Innovation: Did Arrow Hit the Bull's Eye?" In *The Rate and Direction of Innovative Activity Revisited*, ed. Josh Lerner and Scott Stern, 361–404. Chicago: University of Chicago Press.

Shiller, Robert J. 2020. *Narrative Economics*. Princeton; Oxford: Princeton University Press.

Shortell, Stephen M., Carrie H. Colla, Valerie A. Lewis, Elliott Fisher, Eric Kessell, and Patricia Ramsay. 2015. "Accountable Care Organizations: The National Landscape" *Journal of Health Politics, Policy and Law*, 40(4): 647–668.

Shrank, William H., Teresa L. Rogstad, and Natasha Parekh. 2019. "Waste in the US Health Care System: Estimated Costs and Potential for Savings" *JAMA*, 322(15): 1501.

Simon, M., N. K. Choudhry, J. Frankfort, D. Margolius, J. Murphy, L. Paita, T. Wang, and A. Milstein. 2017. "Exploring Attributes of High-Value Primary Care" *Annals of Family Medicine*, 15(6): 529–534.

Skinner, Jonathan, and Douglas Staiger. 2015. "Technology Diffusion and Productivity Growth in Health Care" *The Review of Economics and Statistics*, 97(5): 951–964.

Smith, Sheila, Joseph P. Newhouse, and Mark S. Freeland. 2009. "Income, Insurance, and Technology: Why Does Health Spending Outpace Economic Growth?" *Health Affairs*, 28(5): 1276–1284.

Sobel, Dava. 1995. *Longitude*, Repr. ed. Harmondsworth: Penguin Books.

Solow, Robert S. 1987. "We'd Better Watch Out" *New York Times Book Review*.

Spatz, Erica S. 2014. "Implantable Cardioverter-Defibrillator." In *Redirecting Innovation in U.S. Health Care: Options to Decrease Spending and Increase Value: Case Studies*, ed. Steven Garber, Susan M. Gates, Emmett B. Keeler, Mary E. Vaiana, Andrew W. Mulcahy, Christopher Lau, and Arthur L. Kellermann, 63–82. Santa Monica, CA: Rand Corporation.

Srinivasan, Malathi, Steven Asch, Stacie Vilendrer, Samuel C. Thomas, Rika Bajra, Linda Barman, Lauren M. Edwards, Heather Filipowicz, Lena Giang, Olivia Jee, et al. 2020. "Qualitative Assessment of Rapid System Transformation to Primary Care Video Visits at an Academic Medical Center" *Annals of Internal Medicine*, 173(7): 527–535.

Starr, Paul. 1982. *The Social Transformation of American Medicine*. New York: Basic Books.

Stoner, Isaac. 2020. "Saving Lives Should Be Good Business. Why Doesn't that Apply to Finding New Antibiotics?" *STAT*. https://www.statnews.com/2020/03/18/saving-lives-should-be-good-business-why-doesnt-that-apply-to-finding-new-antibiotics/.

Taylor, Timothy. 2018. "What's the Value of a QALY?" *Conversable Economist*. http://conversableeconomist.blogspot.com/2018/06/whats-value-of-qaly.html?m=1.

Teillant, Aude, Sumanth Gandra, Devra Barter, Daniel J. Morgan, and Ramanan Laxminarayan. 2015. "Potential Burden of Antibiotic Resistance on Surgery and Cancer Chemotherapy Antibiotic Prophylaxis in the USA: A Literature Review and Modelling Study" *The Lancet Infectious Diseases*, 15(12): 1429–1437.

The National Commission on Physician Payment Reform. 2013. "Report of the National Commission on Physician Payment Reform." https://www.rwjf.org/en/library/research/2013/03/report-of-the-national-commission-on-physician-payment-ref orm.html.

The Principles that Guide the Development of NICE Guidance and Standards. https://www.nice.org.uk/about/who-we-are/our-principles (accessed June 18, 2021).

Tikkanen, Roosa, and Melinda K. Abrams. 2020. "U.S. Health Care from a Global Perspective, 2019: Higher Spending, Worse Outcomes?" *Commonwealth Fund*. https://www.commonwealthfund.org/publications/issue-briefs/2020/jan/us-health-care-glo bal-perspective-2019.

Timmins, Nicholas, Michael Rawlins, and John Appleby. 2016. *A Terrible Beauty: A Short History of NICE, the National Institute for Health and Care Excellence*. Bangkok: Amarin Printing and Publishing Public Co., Ltd.

Trump Administration is Shutting Down Practice-Guidelines Clearinghouse for Doctors. 2018. https://www.statnews.com/2018/06/13/ahrq-practice-guidelines-clearingho use-shutting-down/.

Tuller, David. 2018. "HIV Prevention Drug's Slow Uptake Undercuts its Early Promise." *Health Affairs*, 37(2): 178–180.

US Renal Data System. 2019. "Executive Summary." In *Annual Data Report: Epidemiology of Kidney Disease in the United States*. Bethesda, MD: National Institute of Diabetes and Digestive Kidney Diseases.

Van Alstyne, Marshall W., Allesandro Di Fiore, and Simon Schneider. 2017. "4 Mistakes that Kill Crowdsourcing Efforts." *Harvard Business Review Digital Articles*. https://hbr.org/2017/07/4-mistakes-that-kill-crowdsourcing-efforts.

Verma, Seema. 2020. "Early Impact of CMS Expansion of Medicare Telehealth during COVID-19." *Health Affairs Blog*. https://www.healthaffairs.org/do/10.1377/forefr ont.20200715.454789/.

Volk, JoAnn, Dania Palanker, Madeline O'Brien, and Christina L. Goe. 2021. "States' Actions to Expand Telemedicine Access during COVID-19 and Future Policy Considerations." *Commonwealth Fund*. https://www.commonwealthfund.org/publi cations/issue-briefs/2021/jun/states-actions-expand-telemedicine-access-covid-19.

Vollrath, Deitrich. 2015. "Market Power Versus Price-Taking in Economic Growth." *Growth Economics Blog*. https://growthecon.com/blog/market-power-versus-price-taking-in-economic-growth/ (accessed January 7, 2021).

Volpp, Kevin G., Andrea B. Troxel, Mark V. Pauly, Henry A. Glick, Andrea Puig, David A. Asch, Robert Galvin, Jingsan Zhu, Fei Wan, Jill DeGuzman, et al. 2009. "A Randomized, Controlled Trial of Financial Incentives for Smoking Cessation." *The New England Journal of Medicine*, 360(7): 699–709.

Watzinger, Martin, Thomas Fackler, Markus Nagler, and Monika Schnitzer. 2020. "How Antitrust Enforcement Can Spur Innovation: Bell Labs and the 1956 Consent Decree." *American Economic Journal: Economic Policy*, 12(4): 328–359.

Weisbrod, Burton A. 1991. "The Health Care Quadrilemma: An Essay on Technological Change, Insurance, Quality of Care, and Cost Containment." *Journal of Economic Literature*, 29(2): 523–552.

Williams, Heidi L. 2017. "How Do Patents Affect Research Investments?" *Annual Review of Economics*, 9(1): 441–469.

Williams, Heidi L. 2013. "Intellectual Property Rights and Innovation: Evidence from the Human Genome." *Journal of Political Economy*, 121(1): 1–27.

Yin, Wesley. 2008. "Market Incentives and Pharmaceutical Innovation" *Journal of Health Economics*, 27(4): 1060–1077.

Zuvekas, Samuel H., and Joel W. Cohen. 2016. "Fee-for-Service, while Much Maligned, Remains the Dominant Payment Method for Physician Visits" *Health Affairs*, 35(3): 411.

Index

For the benefit of digital users, indexed terms that span two pages (e.g., 52–53) may, on occasion, appear on only one of those pages.